Indian Theological Tendencies

Studien zur interkulturellen Geschichte des Christentums
Études d'Histoire Interculturelle du Christianisme
Studies in the Intercultural History of Christianity

Herausgegeben von/édité par/edited by

Richard Friedli
Université de Fribourg

Walter J. Hollenweger
University of Birmingham

Hans Jochen Margull
Universität Hamburg

Band/Vol. 21

PETER LANG
Berne · Frankfurt am Main · Las Vegas

Antony Mookenthottam M.S.F.S.

Indian Theological Tendencies

Approaches and Problems for Further Research as Seen
in the Works of Some Leading Indian Theologians

PETER LANG
Berne · Frankfurt am Main · Las Vegas

CIP-Kurztitelaufnahme der Deutschen Bibliothek

Mookenthottam, Antony:
Indian theological tendencies: approaches and
problems for further research as seen in the
works of some leading Indian theologians /
Antony Mookenthottam. – Bern, Frankfurt/Main,
Las Vegas: Lang, 1978.
    (Studien zur interkulturellen Geschichte des
    Christentums; Bd. 21)
    ISBN 3-261-04613-9

Published with the support of the Missionswissenschaftliches Institut,
Missio e. V., Aachen, West-Germany

Printed by Lang Druck AG, Berne/Liebefeld

DEDICATED

TO THE HOLY TRINITY

TABLE OF CONTENTS

Volume I

1

2

5

6

8

11

12

13

Part Three

The Possibility of an Approach

19

Introduction

Theological reflection in India has been growing with the growth of the Indian Church. Western theologians who have resided or who are residing in India and native Christian thinkers, have been reflecting on the mysteries of Christian revelation. While some of them give expression to the traditional patterns of thought, others go further and try to integrate Indian culture and religious tradition. It is in this latter direction of thought that our interest is centred. This reflection of Christian revelation which takes into consideration the Indian cultural, social and religious context, we term "Indian Theology".

Indian theology has not developed uniformly. Various approaches to an Indian theology have been suggested and they show evidence of different trends. It is in this context that we propose a complementary approach in our thesis entitled: "A Pluridimensional Approach to an Indian Theology from the Concept of Truth and Reality *(Satya)* in the Hindu, Jaina, Buddhist and Christian Scriptures".

What is published here amounts to a survey of the leading Indian theological tendencies from the beginning of Christianity in India to our own times. This forms the First Part of our thesis. In tracing these trends, it has been possible to select only some among the theologians who seemed to us to represent the principal tendencies.

Here certain methodological remarks are necessary. 1) It is important to bear in mind that what is published here is only a survey of the leading Indian theological tendencies. 2) My concern has been to present, in so far as this is possible, the thought of the theologians in such a way as to allow them to speak for themselves; hence the frequency of quotations. 3) The problems grouped in chapter four are those which arise from particular situations, or which the authors in question have raised or tried to answer, or which the theological positions of the authors concerned give rise to. 4) On the question of uniformity, a distinction is to be made between what we write and the quotations, the theology of the author discussed etc.[1] 5) The same method of transliteration of Sanskrit words have been followed even in quotations so as not to confuse the reader who does not know Sanskrit.

6) Sanskrit words are put in italics, except those which have become quite common. 7) My residence in Europe limited the availability of literature published in India. A semester spent there for the express purpose of coming abreast of recent theological writing was helpful, but insufficient.

Finally, I express my profound gratitude to Prof. R. Friedli, without whose encouragement, corrections and suggestions, this thesis would never have been completed. My deep gratitude is due also to Prof. C. Regamey, who encouraged, corrected and guided the Second Part of the original thesis. My heartfelt thanks are due to Prof. A. Schenker, for encouraging, correcting and helping to complete the Third Part of the original thesis, especially, in all that concerns Sacred Scripture. To all the three, I am much indebted for their great patience, kindness and openness, and for their understanding and human approach. My sincere gratitude is due to Prof. J. Baumgartner who kindly read the text and suggested improvements.

I am deeply grateful to Bro. F. McCann of the Marist Brothers, Second Novitiate, Fribourg, and to Mr. R. Humphrey, M.A., of Gonville and Gaius College, Cambridge, who did the first and second reading of the text and to Miss W. A. Goldsworthy, who did the final typing.

Chapter I

1   Early Indian Theology

1.1 Ancient Times

The synod of Udayamperur[1] and the missionary method and activity of Robert de Nobili are, according to our opinion, the principal events known to us from the history of the early Indian Church which are important from the point of view of an Indian theology.

1.1.1   The Theology of the Early Indian Church

1.1.1.1   Justification of the Inquiry

a) East-West contacts in ancient times

Any attempt towards an Indian theology has to take into consideration the history and life of the Church in India. The negative and positive experiences of the past could provide lessons for today. Consequently it is worth asking whether the early Indian Church had a theology of its own. This question is valid in the case of the existence of an early Indian Church. We may make the following remarks about the history of the early Church in India.[2] The denial of the existence of an early Indian Church is based on the assumption by certain scholars that the term 'India' used by early western writers was a common one applicable to Arabian countries. A.C. Perumalil, in a learned work, has proved that the India of the early Greeks and the Romans from the time of Alexander the Great to the fall of Alexandria in 641 A.D., is India itself and not any other country.[3]

The existence of commercial relations between the West, especially Rome and India even before the birth of Christ and during the first century of the Christian era is an established fact.[4] Therefore it was quite possible for an "apostle" to come to India.

b) The existence of an ancient Christian community

In fact, various testimonies point to the existence of a Christian community in Kerala on the south-west coast of India from the early centuries of the Christian era.[5] This community claimed its origin from the preaching of St. Thomas the Apostle. Those who belong to it even now call themselves St. Thomas Christians. They perpetuate the same tradition and claim. Various traditions and socio-cultural factors remain unsatisfactorily explained, if not unexplained, unless reference is made to the apostolic origin of this Church.[6] The existence of this ancient Church justifies our inquiry into her theology. A detailed study is not envisaged and only some elements connected with our study are taken up.

1.1.1.2 An Implicit Theology

a) Problems of verification

Did the early Indian Church develop a theology of her own? The Persian domination of the early Christian community in India followed by that of the Portuguese in no way favoured indigenous theological thinking. There seem to have been learned doctors among the ancient Christians.[7] It seems that there was a kind of ecclesiastical university in Angamali.[8] Hence it is probable that the ancient Church in India had developed some theology of its own. The decrees of the assembly of Udayampērur restricting the use of Syriac books,[9] encouraging the burning of certain offices from liturgical books,[10] and the actual burning of many books[11] render it extremely difficult to verify any theological contribution from the ancient Christianity in India. But it is not books alone which bear

witness to a theology. The life, experience and tradition of a Christian
community disclose the theology it lives.

b) Socio-cultural life of the community

St. Thomas Christians could be scarcely distinguished from the higher castes
of the Hindu society.[12] A number of their customs were of Brahmin origin. Their
identification with their socio-cultural milieu was so thorough that the assembly
of Udayampērur thought it necessary to interdict men from boring ear-lobes in
order to distinguish them from Hindus.[13] There was no difference too in
architecture. The churches were built on the model of Hindu temples.[14] This
oneness with their socio-cultural milieu implies an implicit incarnational theology
lived, an awareness that Christ in becoming man assumed everything human and
redeemed all social and cultural values. Does this socio-cultural unity mean also
unity in their relations with other communities?

c) Relations with Non-Christians

Another expression of the theology of the early Indian Church may be found
in her relation to non-Christian communities and in the belief which prompted it.
The assembly of Udayampērur forbade the presence of Hindu musicians in the Church
during mass;[15] it interdicted the clergy from going to eat with pagans, Turks or
Jews.[16] These prohibitions indirectly betray the friendly and cordial relations
which existed between the Christian and non-Christian communities.[17]

d) Source of tolerance

The creation of such communal harmony owes much to the tolerance and
magnanimity of Hindu rulers and Hindu brethren.[18] It is possible that the
Christian precept of brotherly love and tolerance, practised in apostolic
communities found a favourable soil in India and contributed its share. Had not
Christ told his disciples that "any one who is not against us is for us"
(Mk 9.40), and insisted on loving even enemies and doing good to them (Lk 6.
27-35)? As a consequence, Christians had greater reason for keeping friendly

relations with their magnanimous Hindu neighbours. To this attitude, Indian culture and tradition lent support. This seems to be evident from the condemnation pronounced by the assembly of Udayampērur on certain errors which had crept into the Christian community on account of its communication with pagans. The third error mentioned in the decree is:

"Each one can be saved in his own law, all laws are right:
This is fully erroneous and a most shameful heresy:
There is no law in which we may be saved except the law of Christ our
Saviour..." and the foot-note says: "This is a perverse dogma of
politicians and those tolerant... Consequently being indifferent they
wander very far away from the truth."[19]

These texts of 1599 deserve a deeper study in the context of the then Hindu and Christian beliefs and the Portuguese knowledge of them to evaluate their full theological implications, a study which we cannot undertake here. Nevertheless the following observations may be made. The assembly expressly mentions that the error originates from contact with pagans; the condemned error is reminiscent of modern Hinduism; Christian theologians have now begun to ascribe a certain salvific value to non-Christian religions. Under the impact of Indian culture and tradition, early Indian Christianity seems to have given its own interpretation of the relation between it and non-Christian religions.

e) Freedom in liturgical interpretation

Some other practices give further insight into the theology which this community lived. The assembly of Udayampērur forbade the use of one's own words to consecrate bread and wine in mass and the addition of any other words to the formula of consecration.[20] It is evident that what was forbidden was followed earlier. Rice cakes and coconut wine seem to have been used for eucharistic celebration.[21] These usages are evidences of the facility with which this ancient Church interpreted sacramental rites taking into consideration local

25

situations,[22] and her consciousness that the power of Christ is not limited to
wheat-bread and grape-wine.[23] The liberal interpretation of liturgical rites
and their adaptation to local situations have a great message for the Church in
the India of our own times still rigid and legalistic in her approach to liturgy.

f) Local hierarchy

One of the postulates of an incarnational theology is a local clergy with a
local hierarchy. There was indeed a local clergy in this ancient Christian
community. An Archdeacon was the head of the community.[24] But the ecclesiastical
colonialism of the Persian Church and the Portuguese Patronage stifled the
development of a local hierarchy till the 19th century.

1.1.1.3 Appreciation

All that we have seen so far points to an incarnational theology lived
though not committed to writing in theological form. A theology lived strikes
deeper roots than the exercise of mere speculation. The harmony which existed
between the Hindu community and the ancient Church in India is an incentive to
foster communal harmony in modern India. The problem of the domination of one
local Church over another needs a permanent solution.

While latinization imposed by the assembly of Udayampērur stifled the
spontaneous and indigenous development of the early Indian Church, foreign
missionaries were not wanting whom the witness of the same Church partly influenced. They adopted a new method of evangelization. Among these missionaries
Robert de Nobili may be singled out on account of the great work he accomplished.

1.1.2 Robert De Nobili (1577-1656)

The Portuguese and the missionaries who followed them took it for granted
that the Christians and the converts to Christianity under their sway were to be
westernized. They mistakenly identified Portuguese social habits and culture wit
Christianity. Beside ignorance of the language, this seems to be the reason
behind the translation of the baptismal question: "Do you wish to become a
Christian?" into *"Prangui culam puguda verumo?"* "Do you wish to join the caste

26

of the Parangi (Portuguese)?"[25] The term Parangi was held in abomination by Indians. The Parangis were thought to be members of the lowest caste.[26] As a consequence, their religion, Christianity, shared the same taboo. This was the situation when Robert de Nobili reached India.

1.1.2.1. Life and Context

Robert de Nobili was born in Rome in 1577, became a Jesuit and came to Goa in 1605. Passing through Cochin, he reached Madurai on 15th November, 1606. A year after his arrival in Madurai he adopted the way of life of an Indian sanyāsi and worked untiringly and successfully for the spread of the Gospel till his death on 16th January, 1656.[27]

He had before him the example of his compatriot and confrère Matteo Ricci (1552-1610) in China. Another Jesuit, Jerome Xavier (1549-1617), a grand nephew of St. Francis Xavier was residing at the Mogul emperor's court in India and working for the conversion of Muslims at the time De Nobili started his apostolate in Tamilnadu; Jerome Xavier held religious disputes with Muslims at the Mogul court and wrote works of controversy to establish the superiority of Christianity over Islam.[27a] De Nobili was in contact with the Indian style of life and habits of St. Thomas Christians. This is clear from the appeal he makes to their customs in support of the usages he allowed his Brahmin converts to follow.[28]

In evaluating De Nobili's work, various aspects such as the theology, the mentality of his times and not our own, and his aim are to be taken into consideration. He was first and foremost a missionary. His principal aim was not to write a theology but to find ways and means to announce the Gospel in a manner intelligible and appealing to Indians and to instruct his converts. He wrote partly to defend his method of evangelization against some of his own confrères and some ecclesiastical authorities who were more intolerant and hostile than the Hindus among whom he worked.[29] In spite of such adverse circumstances, De Nobili did contribute to the cause of an Indian theology.

1.1.2.2 De Nobili's Services to an Indian Theology

De Nobili studied Sanskrit and the Hindu religious literature available to him[30] and used the knowledge of them to defend the compatibility with Christianity

of such Indian customs and practices as the brahmaṇical thread *(yajñopavita)*,
the tuft of hair *(kudumi)*, sandal paste *(candana)* and the use of a tiny
ornamental mark between the eyebrows on the forehead *(tilakam)* etc.[31] In the
teeth of opposition, he got these usages by Christians approved by Rome. The
Bull of Gregory XV, *Romanae Sedis Antistes*, accepts the principle of an
indigenous approach to evangelization.[32] Thus he promoted cultural integration.
Far ahead of his times, he advocated a give and take policy in social matters,[33]
the establishment of a Brahmin seminary and the use of Sanskrit for liturgical
services.[34] Had these initiatives been then accepted and worked out, they would
have provided an ideal ground for Indian theological development. His own
contribution to an Indian theology seems to be his concept of Christ as Guru.[34a]
As a missionary, he followed an apologetic method.

All the same, it is not fair to categorize his approach to religious
Hinduism as entirely negative as does Boyd.[35] It is true that De Nobili writes
to refute, but he does not reject what is valuable in Hinduism. He uses Hindu
scriptures to prove his points;[36] he argues against the outright condemnation
of the sciences of the Brahmins as superstitious;[37] he contends that what is
also compatible with true religion is found in the *Vedas*.[38] Hence his approach
to religious Hinduism does not seem to be entirely negative.[39]

1.1.2.3 Appreciation

De Nobili made a great advance in the direction of an Indian theology by
getting access to the religious literature of the Hindus, by studying them with
an open mind and by getting approved the principle of maintaining Hindu social
customs after baptism. We may not speak of an Indian theology of De Nobili,
but rather of the great services he rendered to the development of an Indian
theology. The opposition he had to withstand from some of his confrères and
churchmen was an obstacle to his missionary activity. It posed the problem of
the Church hindering her own progress in the name of truth.

Sufficient attention was not paid to the message of De Nobili. The Church
preferred her western garb to an Indian one, especially in North and North-east
India. Neither the Catholic nor the Protestant Church made any serious effort
to present the message of the Gospel in a way appealing to the Hindu

intelligensia, as did De Nobili. Confronted with the mystery of Christ, his message and his Church in the western garb on the one hand and urgent social, national and religious problems on the other, few Hindu intellectuals took it upon themselves to interpret Christ and his message in an Indian context. Indian theology originates there and in a certain sense, the first Fathers of it are, strangely enough, Hindus. This leads us to modern times.

1.2 Modern Times: Pioneers in Indian Theology

A real effort to interpret Christ and his message both by few prominent Hindus and Christians was made from the beginning of the Indian renaissance, that is, from the end of the eighteenth century up to the twentieth century.

1.2.1 Raja Rammohan Roy (1772-1833)

Raja Rammohan Roy was born in Bengal in 1772.[40] He became a convinced theist and worked untiringly for the religious, social and educational reform of the Hindu community. To foster theism and reform, he founded a society, Brahma Samaj.[40a] On a visit to England, he died in Bristol in 1833.

What concerns us most are the theological problems raised by him.[41] He had no intention of writing Christian theology. His reform movements inspired by Christian ethics, the necessity of defending his theistic conceptions which led him to controversies with Protestant missionaries[42] then working in Serampore were some occasions which impelled him to write on Christian topics.

1.2.1.1 Theism and Christ

What impressed Rammohan Roy most in Christianity was the monotheism and the moral teachings of Christ. His theism, rationalism and the Hindu conception of the impossibility of God having any connection with matter made him deny the divinity of Christ. Rammohan Roy's vision of Christ is well expressed by M. M. Thomas:

"As for Rammohan Roy, he will go so far as to accept that Jesus was the Messiah, in the same sense of the supreme messenger of God, who 'lived in the divine purpose and decree,' but definitely as a creature, not creator."[43]

29

Naturally, he distinguished between the moral teachings of Christ, the essence of Christianity and the person of Christ and historical events which according to him were of less consequence. The denial of the divinity of Christ led also to the denial of the Holy Trinity, the denial of Christ and the Holy Spirit as persons of the Trinity. This is quite understandable in the context of his continuous fight against polytheism and idolatry in Hindu society. Acceptance of the Trinity seemed to him as equivalent to the acceptance of polytheism.[44] So he interpreted the Holy Spirit as the influence and power of God, and Christ as the messenger of God who explains God's will.[45]

1.2.1.2 Some Theological Positions

The denial of the divinity of Christ, in turn, called for a re-interpretation of the doctrines based on it, such as atonement, sacrifice and so forth. Here Rammohan Roy introduced the idea that the apostles accomodated the message of Christ to Jewish categories of the sacrificial system and that today the true meaning of Jesus Christ is to be recovered.[46] Though he interpreted Christian doctrines according to his own lights, his approach to religion deserves attention. He wrote:

"May God render religion destructive of difference between man and man, and conducive to the peace and union of mankind."[47]

1.2.1.3 Appreciation

The Christ of Rammohan Roy is not the Christ of orthodox Christianity. It is one of the first efforts of the Hindu intelligensia to interpret the meaning of Christ and Christianity in an Indian context. This, on the one hand, led to a purification of Hinduism and on the other to the problem of an Indian theology.

Rammohan Roy's works presented Christ to the members of Brahma Samaj. One of those who was set fire with love of Christ and came to a deeper knowledge of Him was Keshab Chandra Sen.

1.2.2 Keshab Chandra Sen (1838-1884)

Keshab Chandra Sen, born in 1838, never became a Christian.[49] All the same, he may be called a pioneer of Christian theology in India because of the profound influence exercised by his thought on later Christian thinkers. He joined the Brahma Samāj in 1857, became its leader and founded the Church of the New Dispensation.[49a] While coming closer and closer to orthodox Christian thinking, he died at the early age of 46 in 1884.

1.2.2.1 His Vision of Christianity

Some of the trinitarian, christological, and ecclesiological aspects of his thought are interesting from the point of view of an Indian theology. We shall examine briefly some of these.

a) Trinitarian ideas

Keshab says: "The apex is the very God Jehovah, the Supreme Brahma of the *Vedas*. Alone, in His own eternal glory, He dwells. From Him comes down the Son in a direct line, an emanation from Divinity. Thus God descends and touches one end of the base of humanity; then running all along the base permeates the world, and then by the power of the Holy Ghost drags up degenerated humanity to Himself. Divinity coming down to humanity is the Son; Divinity carrying up humanity to heaven is the Holy Ghost."[50]

Keshab then shows a certain correspondence of the Trinity with the conception of God as *satcitānanda*, giving, certain equivalents:

Father	Son	Holy Spirit
The Creator	The Exemplar	The Sanctifier
The still God	The journeying God	The returning God
'I am'	'I love'	'I save'
Force	Wisdom	Holiness
True	Good	Beautiful
sat (Truth)	*cit* (Intelligence)	*ānanda* (Joy).[51]

Here it may be observed that since Sen the term *satcitānanda* has now become current in Indian Catholic theology. Keshab sees a descending and ascending movement within the mystery of the Trinity.

b) Christological ideas

The descending and ascending movements seem to form the basis of his christology. The descending God is the Logos, the Word, God creating. The process of creation is seen as a scientific evolution from the lowest to the

31

highest. The Indian conception of incarnation *(avatāra)* is interpreted as "a crude representation of the ascending scale of divine creation" rising "from the lowest scale of life through fish, the tortoise and the hog up to the perfection of humanity."[52] The culmination and crown of this continued evolution of the Logos is Jesus Christ and terms this summit reached, "The last link in the series of created organism, the last expression of Divinity, Divine humanity."[53] Thus Sen seeks to conciliate the Indian conception of incarnation *(avatāra)* with the Christian conception of Incarnation and scientific evolution. This effort at conciliation does not dispense with the basic conviction that everything created is a manifestation of the divine but underlies it.

In Jesus Christ, the ultimate term of the evolution of the Logos, divine sonship is offered to all humanity.

"The problem of creation", says Keshab, "was not how to produce one Christ, but how to make every man Christ."[54]

Now the divine sonship carrying all mankind heavenward is the Holy Spirit, for it is He who makes all mankind share in the divine life by establishing the Logos within us as the Divine Son subjectified.[55]

c) Christ as fulfilment and the Church of the New Dispensation

Jesus Christ, according to Keshab, is thus the correction and fulfilment of Hinduism[56] as he is the culmination of the evolution of the Logos. He regretted the narrow representation of the universal Christ, and explains his conception of Christ as follows:

"Scattered in all schools of philosophy and in all religious sects, scattered in all men and women of the East and the West, are multitudinous Christ – principles, and fragments of Christ – life, – one vast and identical Sonship diversely manifested.... Thus all reason in man is Christ – reason, all love is Christ – love, all power is Christ – power.... It exists even where it is not professed."[57]

As a consequence, the Church has to be universal and indigenous and contemporary to India. He regretted much the western appearance of the Church in India. The universal and indigenous character of the Church is to find its expression in the christo-centric harmony of all religions, and Christ is the bond of unity

between the East and the West. The belief in the supremacy of Christ as God –
man, the assumption that all religions are equally true and the doctrine of
divine inspiration (ādesh) according to which Keshab was commissioned by the
Holy Spirit to bring about the harmony of all religions by selecting elements
from various religions in the light of Christ made him organize his Church of
the New Dispensation. These same convictions made him write in 1883 to the
Bishops of India, Anglicans and Catholics, to consider the urgent problem of
unity. He wrote to the Bishop of Calcutta, Edward Ralph Johnson:

"Secondly: Unity in the Church of Christ. Sectarianism being a thing
carnal is baneful at all times and in all positions. But here in India
it greatly hinders the acceptance of Christ by the people. When so many
Churches and sects offer themselves and demand allegiance, India confounded
and vexed asks, – Which is the true Church of Christ? Is it not possible,
my Lord, to introduce greater harmony into the Christian community in
India?"[58]

What is evident is his concern for unity.

Theologians like M. M. Thomas and Boyd have pointed out his inconsistencies,
his tendency to modalism in his exposition of the Trinity, his lack of concern for
continuity, apostolic authority and so forth.[59] It is not our intention to
evaluate the theology of Keshab. Nevertheless, a few of his contributions to
theological thinking may be enumerated.

1.2.2.2 His Contributions

The concept of the Trinity as satcitānanda, the exposition of the nature of
Christ's divinity in a form of the kenotic theory,[60] the concept of the
transparency of Christ,[61] that of Christ as the journeying God, setting out from
his Father, the still God (a concept which prefigures Karl Barth[62]), the theory
of Christ who is hidden in Hindu faith, foreshadowing Panikkar's thesis,[64] may
be considered some of his original approaches.

1.2.2.3 Appreciation

Keshab, a very touching figure of Christian theology in India, standing on
the border of Hinduism and Christianity, in a sense belonging to both, yet
repudiating Hinduism and Christianity, as he found it practised around him is
a pioneer of Indian theological thinking. Keshab's appeal to disregard the

western appearance of the Church and to give witness to her universal and indigenous character needs an adequate answer. From the early stages of her history, India craved for unity. This age-long aspiration for unity finds an expression in the eclecticism of Keshab, in his Church of the New Dispensation,[65] in his appeal to the Catholic and Anglican Bishops for unity, years before any strong ecumenical movement developed in Christianity.

Keshab stood on the threshold of Christianity. Some of his followers went a step further and entered it. Among them, Brahmabandhab Upādhyāya, a Bengali convert to Catholicism deserves special attention on account of his efforts to create an Indian theology.

1.2.3 Brahmabandhab Upādhyāya (1861-1907)

1.2.3.1 Life

A zealous Brahmin convert to catholicism, a man of vision and the first Indian Catholic theologian, Brahmabandhab Upādhyāya, deserves special attention. It is to be regretted that the Catholic Church in India has not paid much attention to one of her glorious sons of the last century.[66] A short sketch of his life will help one to understand the socio-cultural and emotional background of his theology.

Bhawani Charan Banerji, better known as Brahmabandhab Upādhyāya, was born in 1861 in Khanyan, a small village about thirty miles north of Calcutta.[67] From his early days, he came under Christian influence through his uncle Kali Charan Banerji, a great Christian nationalist of Bengal. At the early age of sixteen, he was an extreme nationalist; he hoped to overthrow British domination through armed revolution. For this end, he tried to get into the army of Gwalior. Being thwarted, he became a teacher. Vivekananda (1863-1902) was his class-mate. He was a friend of Rama Krishna Paramahamsa (1836-1886) and Keshab Chandra Sen; of the latter he became a follower and joined the Brahma Samaj. Contact with Keshab brought him closer to Christ and Christianity. In February 1891, he was baptized into the Anglican Church. In September of the same year, he entered the Catholic Church and took the name of Brahmabandhab, a Sanskrit rendering of Theophilus. In 1894, he put on saffron robes and became a Catholic sanayāsin. He lived like a sanayāsin till the end of his life. During the first years he travelled from place to place teaching, preaching and begging. He and his

disciples nursed and served the sick. They rendered great service during an
epidemic in Karachi. His co-operation with Rabindranath Tagore is often left
unnoticed.

"He opened a school for boys," writes Kaj Baago, "which later moved
to Śantiniketan, where he and Rabindranath Tagore worked together for a
time. The father of the famous 'Tagore institution' in Śantiniketan is
therefore really Brahmabandhab - a fact which is never mentioned in the
many books about Tagore."[68]

He edited an apologetic journal *Sophia*. When it had to be stopped he
started another periodical *The Twentieth Century* and even this also had to cease
publication for reasons indicated later. Then he turned from religion to politics
and edited a daily paper *Sandhya* in Bengali, regarded by the British as one of the
most dangerous journals. After several warnings Brahmabandhab was arrested in
September 1907 and was released on bail. It is worth noting that he was one of
the first, if not the first, to demand complete independence for India. He was
liable to be sentenced to several years' imprisonment. So he wanted to be
operated on for hernia before going to prison. He was operated on but compli-
cations set in and he passed away suddenly in 1907. He was forty-six years old.

Baago writes: "Brahmabandhab was a national hero in the eyes of many
and the news of his death spread through special editions of news-papers.
When a catholic priest reached the place of cremation wanting to bury
Brahmabandhab according to Christian rites, the Hindus had already lighted
the pyre."[69]

The westernized character of the Church in India, the Indian renaissance,
the rising nationalism in Bengal, Keshab Chandra Sen, his theology, and Brahma
Samāj, his conflict with his own Church, the Catholic Church, are some of the
factors which influenced his outlook.

1.2.3.2 His Doctrine

a) The path to Christ, the fulfilment of Hinduism

Brahmabandhab shared the original antagonism of the Brahma Samāj to certain
Hindu doctrines like pantheism, transmigration and so forth. Hence it is only
natural that he should envisage the path to Christianity through the eradication
of the same tenets leading to the establishment of theism and finally to
Christianity.[70] Going a step further than Keshab for whom Christ was the

35

fulfilment of Hinduism, Brahmabandhab asserted that Christianity is the fulfilment
of Hinduism. He says:

"Our object is to present to our countrymen the right and full Christianity –
a Christianity which fulfils all the accumulated goodness of our ancient
country; which, when adhered to and acted upon, will conserve and develop
the peculiar virtues and characteristics of the Hindu race; which is
suited, as we firmly believe, to all ages and all climes; which, in short,
is Catholic."[71]

This view of the relation between Christianity and Hinduism needed further
development.

b) The role of Hinduism

Earlier, Brahmabandhab had given a Christian interpretation to some Hindu
sacred texts. He thereby put the *Vedas* on a level with the Old Testament. An
instance of it is found in his interpretation of the first stanza of the hymn
Ka of the *Ṛgveda*. He writes:

"Who is this *hiraṇyagarbha*? *'Hiraṇya'* commonly means 'gold' and 'garbha'
means womb or source. Therefore *'hiraṇyagarbha'* is he who is begotten of
gold. How can the sole lord of creatures, and holder of heaven and earth,
be begotten of gold? *'Hiraṇya'* does not mean here, according to the
famous commentary *'Ṛjvarta'*, 'gold' but 'wisdom'. *Hiraṇyagarbha*, is,
then, begotten of wisdom.
This *sūkta* glorifies the first begotten, begotten of eternal wisdom. 'He
is the giver of his own self *(ātmada)*; he is the giver of strength; him
all the gods obey; his shadow is immortality; death is subject to him;..."[72]

Indirectly he raised the question of the inspiration of Hindu sacred texts but
did not answer it.[73]

In this conection, certain problems arose. The interpretation of vedic
texts alone is not able to provide a sufficient basis for Christian doctrine.
Just as Thomism then profoundly influenced Catholic thought and life, Hindu
philosophical systems deeply influenced the intellectual and spiritual life of
India. Probably these considerations made him attempt a conciliation between
Thomism and Hindu thought since Thomism appeared to him to be the best
expression of Catholic faith. Certain authors saw in it an effort to

36

conciliate Thomism and Advaita.[74] It does not seem so. For Brahmabandhab writes:

> "The universe is not, as the school of _Rāmānuja_ (qualified monism) supposes, a part of God, neither is it a mere transient existence, as the school of _Śankara_ (monism) imagines, neither is it a self-existent, as other _darśanas_ (philosophies) hold. But _Rāmānuja_ was right in asserting it to be _real_ as opposed to transient; _Śankara_ was right in asserting it to have no independent being of its own; and _Kapila_ was right in asserting it to be made up of matter and form _(prakṛti_ and _puruṣa)_."[75]

It manifests his intention to draw out values acceptable to Christianity from every Indian system and to make use of them as a basis for Christian theology.[76] He strove to explain the compatibility of such values with Thomism. Thus Brahmabandhab hoped to effect a conciliation between Thomism and Indian philosophy, which in itself was also a remarkable attempt at East-West comprehension and integration. It demanded also the interpretation of the Christian message in terms intelligible to the Hindus. For this he used Indian categories with considerable success.

c) Use of Indian categories

A good example of the use of Indian categories is his hymn to the Trinity which runs as follows:

> "I bow to Him who is Being, Consciousness and Bliss.
> I bow to Him whom worldly minds loathe, whom pure minds yearn for, the Supreme Abode.
> He is the Supreme, the Ancient of days, the Transcendent,
> Indivisible Plenitude, Immanent yet above all things,
> Three-fold relation, pure, unrelated, knowledge beyond knowledge.
> The Father, Sun, Supreme Lord, unborn,
> The seedless Seed of the tree of becoming,
> The cause of all, Creator, Providence, Lord of the Universe.

37

The infinite and perfect Word,

The Supreme Person begotten,

Sharing in the Father's nature, Conscious by essence,

Giver of true Salvation.

He who proceeds from Being and Consciousness,

Replete with the breath of perfect bliss,

The Purifier, the Swift, the Revealer of the Word, the Life-giver."77

This hymn, unquestionable in its Christian orthodoxy, keeps even in its English
translation an upaniṣadic and Indian touch. Boyd writes:

"Where terminology is derived from Hinduism" *sat, cit*,
ānanda, 'the seedless Seed of the tree of Becoming,' 'perfect bliss' –
it is fully as expressive, and indeed more vivid than the Greek or
Latin – derived words which might have been used instead... Indeed it
throws fresh light on the doctrine for those who have been brought up in a
a purely western theological tradition."78

The same may be said about his hymn on the Incarnation.79 He used not only Indian
categories but also Indian psychology to explain the mystery of Incarnation as
the union of the Divinity in the person of the Logos with humanity.80 But he
never used the term *avatāra* for which he gave a different meaning.81

d) *Avatāra*

The Hindus are convinced of the plurality of avatāras. The Incarnation of
Christ is unique and Brahmabandhab firmly upheld it. Nevertheless, he seems to
have felt the need to integrate and interpret the Hindu concept of *avatāra*.
He did it by assigning them a creaturely historical status as moral leaders.82
It is in this sense that he accepted Kṛṣṇa as an *avatāra* on account of the moral
teachings of the *Bhagavadgītā*. He rejected at the same time purāṇic stories
about his immorality. While Christ is God Himself beyond *māyā*, the avataras
belong to the realm of *māyā*, contingent being.83

38

e) *Māyā*

The Hindu and Christian concept of creation seemed irreconcilable. Yet
Brahmabandhab tried to harmonize them by giving an original and new interpretation of *māyā*.[84] Quoting from Śankara and Chāndogya Upaniṣad, he argued
that *māyā* is not mere illusion, is the result of choice and not of necessity.
Then he writes:

"*Māyā* is what St. Thomas calls '*creatio passiva*' - passive creation.
It is a quality of all that is not *brahman* and is defined by the
Angelic Doctor as 'the habitude of having being from another, and
resulting from the operation' of God (see *Summa Theologica* 1, XLIV.3).
The word *māyā*, in its significance of 'abundance' (see *Vedanta Sūtra*,
adh. 1, *pada* 1. 13, 14, and *Śankara* on the same) is beautifully
appropriate and significant, for creation is, as it were, the overflow
of the divine Being, knowledge and bliss, and results from the desire
of *brahman* to manifest and impart His own perfections (St. Thomas,
Summa Contra Gentiles, Bk. II, Chapter XIV)."[85]

Vedantists affirm all that is not *brahman* to be *māyā* in the sense of illusion
and according to St. Thomas, creatures apart from *brahman* are falsity, darkness,
nothingness.[85a] Then he continues:

"*Brahman* is Being Itself. He alone is identical with his own Being
while creatures have no right of being but have a merely participated
and dependent existence. They exist by *māyā*, i.e., by the habit of
participating in the Divine Being and springing from the Divine Act.
Māyā is a mysterious divine operation; it is neither real nor unreal....
It cannot be real in the sense of its being essential to the Divine
Nature because *brahman* is self-sufficient and cannot be said to be
under the necessity of being related to the finite. Nor is it unreal,
for by *māyā* comes to exist the finite which possesses being, though
not essentially - the essence of the finite not being identical with
its existence. From an unreality nothing can proceed. *Māyā* is
neither real or necessary, nor unreal but contingent," and creatures

are contingent *(vyavahārika)* and not necessary *(paramarthika)*.[86]
"*Māyā*, then," says Brahmabandhab, "is the fecund Divine Power *(śakti)* which gives birth to multiplicity."[87] This interpretation of *māyā* was given as an illustration of how "all religious truth found elsewhere in scattered, fragmentary and distorted *form* are united into one perfect sphere of universal truth,"[88] in Catholicity, the universal religion. Our thesis is in a special way concerned with the problem of truth.

f) Truth

Brahmabandhab presents Christ as the Universal Teacher of truth and explains his idea of truth.[89] He rejects eclecticism (perhaps he had Keshab in mind) and Hindu syncretism; the whole truth is the full revelation made by Christ to which no addition and from which no subtraction can be made; truth is self-evolving; it unfolds itself gradually and widens the vision of man.[90] Through explanation and harmonization of various systems, reconciliation and synthesis with universal truth are to be effected.[91] This harmonization is achieved by discovering resemblance, similarity, convergence and identity; in several passages, he tries to point out the same.[92] Now, to discover the concordance of views, importance is to be attached to the principle underlying the narration and not to the narrat: itself. After narrating the Hindu story of the origin of man he remarks:

"Though this account of the creation and descent of man differs from that of the Bible, yet it maintains the principle that all men are descended from one progenitor. We also find in it the substantial unity of man and woman."[93]

All these betray his concern for the universal character of truth, its harmonizat and synthesis.

What we have seen so far bears witness to Brahmabandhab's eagerness for a Church universal, Catholic yet Indian in outlook. For him, it was not a speculative concern but a practical one. This brought him into conflict with the Catholic Church.[94]

1.2.3.3 Conflict with the Ecclesiastical Authorities[94]

Difficulties arose first when Brahmabandhab decided to become a Catholic sannyāsin, put on saffron clothes and went to church. He was denied admission into the church by his parish priest. He appealed to the Bishop and the Bishop was ignorant about the question. Brahmabandhab had to remind the Bishop about the permission formerly granted to De Nobili.[95] So he was granted permission to wear saffron clothes. He continued to insist on the Catholic Church in India assuming an Indian socio-cultural outlook. In his *Conversion of India - An Appeal*, he wrote:

> "Protestantism has created a deep-rooted impression amongst the people
> that Christianity is synonymous with denationalization. People have
> a strong aversion against Christian preachers because they are considered
> to be the destroyers of everything national. Therefore, the itinerant
> missionaries should be thoroughly Hindu in their mode of living. They
> should, if necessary, be strict vegetarians and teetotallers and put on
> the yellow *sannyāsi* garb."[96]

In 1897, after mentioning the differences of opinion in Hinduism, he writes:

> "Yet, we have drunk of the spirit of Hinduism. We think with the
> Vedantists that there is an eternal Essence from which proceed all things.
> We believe with the Vaiṣṇavas in the necessity of incarnation and in the
> doctrine that man cannot be saved without grace. We agree in spirit with
> Hindu lawgivers in regard to their teaching that sacramental rites
> *(saṃskāras)* are vehicles of sanctification. With wondering reverence do
> we look upon their idea of establishing a sacred hierarchy vested with
> the highest authority in religious and social matters. In short, we are
> Hindus as far as our physical and mental constitution is concerned, but
> in regard to our immortal souls we are Catholics. We are Hindu - Catholics."[97]

In the language of Brahamabandhab, Hindu seems to be identical with Indian.

Brahmabandhab's concern for the spread of the faith coupled with his passion for something Indian and Catholic made him plan to establish a sannyāsi order with two types of monks, one, yogi type, dedicated to contemplation who by their

41

experience and thinking would contribute to an Indian theology and the other, wandering ones, engaged in preaching and social work. The Bishop of Nagpur, Charles Felix Pelvat (1845-1900) gave him permission to start it in his diocese (1899). Th site chosen was near the narrow gorge of the Marble Rocks on the river Narmada at Jabalpur. There he and two young Brahmins began a very severe ascetical life. Hard had it came into existence, when the Bishop withdrew permission owing to the intervention of Mgr. Ladislao Zaleski,[98] Apostolic Delegate of India (1892-1916).This reverse made him think of going to Rome to see the Pope and present the matter to him. He did go to Rome but all the doors were closed to him.[99]

Matters did not end there.[100] In a series of articles, Brahmabandhab attacked the westernization of the Indian Church. The Apostolic Delegate intervened again and in a letter warned Catholics against *Sophia* and its theological articles in which difficult theological questions were dealt with 'by unqualified persons.' Brahmabandhab offered to publish the magazine under Church censorship. But no answer was given. So he stopped *Sophia* and began a new periodical *The Twentieth Century* which was to deal with political and social matters only. Even this was immediately put on the Index. From then on, he turned more and more to politics. Thus the lack of understanding and consideration of higher ecclesiastical authorities pushed to the margin one of Church's devoted and loyal converts. Here the criticism of Heiler does not seem to be undeserved. He remarks:

"The Roman hierarchy shattered his life's work, paralysed his missionary force and shut his evangelical mouth."[101]

The real issue in this case is not the granting of a permission, the closing of a work or a conflict, but the principles involved, the western apparel of the Church, the purity of doctrine, truth and their relation to ecclesiastical authority.

1.2.3.4 Distinction between Culture and Religion

The conflict just evoked seems to have been the reason for Brahmabandhab's making an important distinction. Writing in *Sandhya* his own Bangali daily, towards the end of his life he distinguishes:

"Our *dharma* has two branches: *samāj dharma* and *sadhan dharma*.... We are Hindus. Our Hinduism is preserved by the strength of *samāj dharma*. While the *sadhan dharma* is of the individual, its object is *sadhan* and *muktee* (Salvation). It is a hidden thing and one to be meditated upon. It has no connection whatever with society. It is a matter known to the *guru* and *śiṣya* only. A Hindu, so far as *sadhan* goes, can belong to any religion."[102]

This distinction is put in a rather radical form but it is to be understood in the context of his struggles both religious and national. The distinction itself has validity in so far as it opens up the possibility of accepting cultural Hinduism without accepting Hinduism as religious truth.[103]

1.2.3.5 Appreciation

Brahmabandhab Upādhyāya rendered distinguished services to the Indian nation and the Church. On the national level he was one of the first to stand for the complete independence of India and suffer for it. As an educator, he was the father of the famous "Tagore institution." As a journalist, he edited *Sophia*, then *The Twentieth Century* and finally *Sandhya*, a Bengali daily. In religion, he was a devoted Catholic, a sannyāsin, a pioneer who tried to establish an Indian monastery, who worked for an Indian theology and for the socio-cultural integration of the Church in India so much so that it may not be too much to call him the Father of Indian Catholic theology.[104] Ever since his death, what he symbolized and stood for has acquired greater breadth and new dimensions. The relation of Hinduism to Christianity and the Christian interpretation of Hindu sacred texts were problems which he tried to solve. They remain theological concerns of our own day.

While Brahmabandhab strove to interpret Hindu thought and systems in a positive manner there were others who adopted a rather negative approach. One among them is Nehemiah Goreh whose theological position we shall examine briefly.

43

1.2.4 Nehemiah Goreh (1825-1895)

Nilakanṭha Śastri Goreh, a Maharaṣtrian, was born in Jhansi in 1925.[105]
He grew up in Benares where his grandfather had settled down. There he
received an orthodox Hindu training. In spite of serious opposition from
relatives and Hindus, he received baptism into the Church Missionary Society
in 1848 and took the name of Nehemiah. Thenceforward he worked hard to make
Christ known and wrote books and tracts to refute Hinduism. His principal
work is *Saddarśana Darpaṇa* in Hindi in 1860. Its translation into English
entitled *A Rational Refutation of Hindu Philosophical Systems* was published in
1862. Later in life, he became an Anglo-catholic, was ordained priest and
became novice in the Society of St. John the Evangelist and remained so till
his death in 1895.

Goreh is to be read in the background of the strictly orthodox training
of his early days, his risking everything to become a Christian, his concern
for the spread of Christianity and his controversies with the theistic Brahma
and Prārthana Samājists.

1.2.4.1 His Approach

Goreh's approach was apologetical;[106] he wrote to refute Hindu tenets.
The doctrine of orthodox Hindu systems, especially the Vedanta was exposed by
him and the inconsistencies, incongruities and absurdities therein pointed
out.[107] Beside factors like the progress of science and technology, Goreh's
criticisms may have been instrumental in progressive Vedantists abandoning
the theory of pure illusion in favour of the degrees of reality.[108] His
principal objection against theistic samājists was their rejection of revelation
as one whole and acceptance of it only in parts according to their preferences.[10]
Goreh's refutations especially his pointing out incoherence and inconsistencies
betray the conviction that truth demands coherence and consistency.[110]

Though he wrote to refute, his attitude to Hinduism was not entirely
negative. He saw in it a preparation for the Gospel. For he writes:

"But a genuine Hindu is rather prepared to receive the teaching of
Christianity... Providence has certainly prepared us, the Hindus,
to receive Christianity, in a way in which, it seems to me, no other
nation - excepting the Jews, of course - has been prepared."[111]

1.2.4.2 Appreciation

Goreh's approach was relevant in his own days. Today its relevance is debatable. All the same, the coherence and consistency of systems of thought need a rational test.

Till now we have examined the efforts made by some of the leading personages of the nineteenth century, both Hindu and Christian, to interpret Christ and Christianity to India. The twentieth century brought further advance and raised more issues. These we shall present in the next chapter.

Chapter II

2   Twentieth Century Approaches to Indian Theology

The work begun by pioneers in the last century was carried on by various
scholars, both Catholic and Protestant, in this century. It is possible to
mention only representatives of certain approaches who fall within our limited
scope. The historical situation of this century is common to all and no one
escapes from its influence.

Two world wars,[1] the rise of international communism, the movements for
national independence, the progressive elimination of colonialism, the
emergence of new nations and the rising nationalism have profoundly changed and
are changing and shaping the structure of society and of nations. The progress
of the instruments of mass communication has brought the people of the world
closer to one another than at any other time in history, with a consequent
tendency towards interpenetration of thought and culture.

In India, the beginning of this century saw the growth and intensification
of the struggle for national independence. This revolution, which achieved
national independence in 1947, owes much to the confidence of Gandhi in non-
violence, in the force of the spirit, and to the English sense of decency.
What marred this event was the Hindu-Muslim communal riot , an outcome of the
division of the country into India and Pakistan.

The post-independence era is marked by the efforts at national integration
and reconstruction, war against poverty, population explosion, experiment in
democracy and of numerous other political and social problems. The western attit
to India has been mostly negative, pessimistic, unsympathetic, critical and
lacking in comprehension in the socio-political sphere.

46

On the religious level too, many changes took place. Rammohan Roy and Keshab Chandra Sen accepted the supremacy of the moral teachings of Christ. From Vivekananda to Radhakrishnan, there is the affirmation of the superiority of Hinduism over all other religions. Hindu philosophers become more and more influenced by western philosophy. In spite of the renaissance of Hinduism, materialism began to make inroads into Hinduism. This challenge from material-ism, technical progress, scientific discoveries, efforts by various religions to enter into dialogue with Hinduism, and similar factors, are beginning to impress on Hindu philosophers the need for a new interpretation of age-old Hindu tenets.

While these changes were taking place in India and in Hinduism, the Catholic Church in the country did not remain unaffected. In the pre-independence period, the Catholic hierarchy was predominantly western. Priestly formation was regimented. Candidates to priesthood were trained to conform themselves to traditions. This type of formation suffocated initiative and original thinking. The authors studied were occidental. The natural outcome was an unlimited admiration for the West and what is western and a disregard for one's own culture. Little was done to impart a genuine Indian cultural formation. This situation is gradually changing now.

In the post-independence era, the Catholic hierarchy in India became Indian. The need for the integration of Christianity and Indian culture began to be more and more keenly felt, though opposition to it is not wanting. The initiatives of Brahmabandhab had been assumed and developed by far-sighted foreign missionaries like G. Dandoy and P. Johanns in the pre-independence period. Soon Indians too took up the challenge. As a providential sanction came the decree *Ad Gentes* of the Second Vatican Council. The Council itself brought profound changes in the religious outlook of the times, with its insistence on dialogue, cultural integration and religious liberty. An important step towards dialogue was the creation of the Secretariate for non-Christian Religions.

In the Protestant Church too, profound changes were taking place. The

47

aspiration for unity resulted in the organization of the World Council of
Churches and on a national level, the Church of South India. A number of Indians
and foreign missionaries contributed powerfully to the development of an Indian
theology. The 1971 Addis Ababa statement, *The World Council of Churches and
Dialogue with People of Living Faiths and Ideologies, An Interim Policy
Statement and Guide-Lines*, gave official sanction to an indigenous
theology.[2]

It is in this historical context, in this interaction of various currents
political, social, cultural, and above all religious, and partly in response
to it that the men whose theological approach we are going to discuss developed
their thought.

2.1 Catholic Approaches to an Indian Theology

Various scholars were inspired by the witness of Brahmabandhab and by their
contributions gave impetus to the movement to develop an Indian theology.[3]

2.1.1 Pierre Johanns (1882-1955)

Pierre Johanns was born in Luxembourg in 1882.[3a] He became a Jesuit, studie
Sanskrit in Brussels and at Oxford. He came to India in 1921. Ill-health made
him return to Belgium in 1939 where he died in 1955.

Johanns is to be seen in the context of the work of Brahmabandhab and that o
his disciples and followers.

2.1.1.1 A Christian Approach to Vedanta

Johanns' method[4] may be well expressed in the words of Olivier Lacombe, who
writes:

"He addresses the Hindus, making himself similar to one of them. He
speaks to them from the interior of their culture with the sureness
and freedom of movement of a Pandit, but a Christian Pandit to discover,

48

liberate and give full value to points of contact and understanding between Christianity and Indian philosophy."[5]

Inspired by the teaching and method of Brahmabandhab, and following closely the early Fathers and Christian teachers, Johanns proposed to gather valuable elements in Vedanta systems and build an Indian philosophical system akin to Thomism.[6] This he did in his work *To Christ through the Vedanta*.[7] Though he paid more attention to the doctrinal aspects of Hinduism, he did not neglect Hindu religious experience.[8]

2.1.1.2 Appreciation

Following Brahmabandhab, Johanns seems to be one of those who marks the transition from a negative to a more positive approach to Hinduism. Johanns did great service in continuing the work of Brahmabandhab. He thus became a link between him and the new generation. Today the validity of a doctrinal approach is questioned.

Johanns deserves high praise for his work. Some of those who came after him gave a different orientation. Among them, Jules Monchanin may be singled out on account of the profound influence he exercised both in India and abroad.

2.1.2 Jules Monchanin (1895-1957)

Jules Monchanin was born on 10th April, 1895 at Fleurie, a village near Lyons.[9] He was ordained priest in 1922. Because of his intellectual qualities, he was destined for higher studies; he did a licentiate at the theological faculty of Lyons but declined the invitation to do a doctorate, preferring to serve the people in parishes and schools. Monchanin longed to dedicate his life to India. So he joined the Society of the Auxiliaries of Mission. Monchanin came to India to Tiruchirapalli in 1939. From then till 1949, he worked as assistant priest and parish priest in countryside mission stations. In 1950, in collaboration with Henri Le Saux, a French Benedictine monk, he founded the Satcitānanda Ashram in Kulitalai, a village on the bank of the Cavery river not far from Tiruchirapalli. He became very sick in 1957 and had to be taken to Paris for treatment. There he passed away peacefully on 10th October in the same year.

Monchanin is to be seen in the light of his vast culture, his interest in every subject especially philosophy, his thorough acquaintance with western culture, his contacts with Teilhard de Chardin,[10] his predilection for India, his desire that Christ assume every value that is Indian, the immobility of the Church in India, his missionary ideal and the apparent failure of his efforts. He had a contemplative temperament and the contemplative tradition of India appealed to him. He had a great sympathy for Brahmabandhab whom he calls "a little of my guru."[11]

2.1.2.1 Monchanin's Approach

a) Recent study

Various aspects of Monchanin's thought such as India's quest for the Absolute which is to find fulfilment in the Trinity, *satcitānanda*, the special role and appeal of monasticism, apophatic mysticism, contemplation, the Holy Spirit as the Person whom India awaits with special eagerness, the centrality of Christ, the assimilation, purification and transformation by Christ of the whole Indian culture and civilization and other similar aspects have been well summarized by Mattam[12] in his recent study. We may stress the following points.

b) Apparent failure

The life of Monchanin ended in apparent failure. He suffered much; he was depressed;[13] sorrow, joy and peace overwhelmed him.[14] His Ashram was a failure.[15] Through all these vissicitudes he was sure of achieving his purpose. For he writes:

50

"I say (...) the Magnificat every evening; we are chosen to prepare
the advent of this Christ adorned with the glory of India as a Cakravartin
(emperor) having assumed every value of India and finally purified, unified
and transformed into Him through our obscure life and *solitary* death."[16]
Monchanin thus emphasizes the value of self effacement, kenosis, for the
assimilation, purification and transformation of a culture. It is evident that
here his approach is spiritual to the core.

c) Truth and spirituality in Indian thought

His deeply spiritual attitude made him perceive the relation between truth
and spirituality in the Indian outlook. He writes:

"Indian thought has always been permeated with metaphysics. It goes
with ease (or at first) to the problems of being and becoming, of the
world and of God. But it does not conceive the search for truth as really
distinct from the search for perfection. Indian thought therefore
should appear in its liaison with spiritual life."[17]

He returns to the same topic again:

"Indian thought identifies truth and spirituality: *sat* /Being, Truth,
real/. It is hostile to exclusive choice and inclines to syncretism. It has
doubts about reality *(māya)*.

Every truth is in the *sat* of sanctity which alone can go beyond syncretism,
for it is the direct proof of the Christian mystery which excludes only,
but without pity, exclusion itself and receives all truths, all beings in
one unity, which is that of the pleroma."[18]

d) Need of rethinking

Truth in the usual sense finds expression in concepts and categories.
Monchanin had a preference for Greek categories and a horror for confused thought.[19]
He seemed to see in the Christian and Hindu mysticism an appeal to reshape certain
concepts. For he wrote:

"Christian mysticism is, in its essence, then the sharing of God, that is,

the sharing of the trinitarian relationship. It is an intuition above
image and concept, a direct experience - not a man-made one, but a God-
given one - an existential contact with what God is in Himself and for
Himself.

Therefore we are facing two main problems when we try to compare by
analogies and contrast Christian mysticism with Hindu mysticism. Is the
Vedantic vision of Being, *sat*, a challenge to our traditional post-
aristotelian ontology? In a parallel way, is not the mystical experience
of the triune divine Being an appeal to reconsider our idea of *esse*.
The divine existence is a personal one, but not a monopersonal one. God
is not *it*, is not *he*, is not *I*, but rather He is *I* and *I* and *I*. His very
essence is identical with his tri-personal relationship. Therefore, is
not every *esse* a *coesse*, every *sat* a *samsat*, every *being* a *being-together?*

Perhaps the notion of person also has to be reshaped..."[20]
In the same way certain changes were necessary in Hinduism; he suggested that
Hinduism renounce the equation *ātman-brahman*.[21]

e) His attitude towards Hinduism

This appeal for rethinking in Hinduism was not due to any lack of kind
consideration for Hindu thought or customs. In fact, it is rarely that a
foreigner showed such magnanimous comprehension and understanding for Hinduism as
he did. This is evident from his attitude to the problem of castes in India.[22]

f) Intellectual level and alienation

Christian rethinking in India demands great intellectual qualities and a
deep penetration into the Indian culture. Monchanin complained about the low
intellectual level of the Indian clergy, their alienation and that of their
Christians from their own culture.[23] The relevance of these complaints needs to
be examined today.

2.1.2.4 Appreciation

Monchanin was the man destined to awaken among the Catholics of India a
consciousness of their cultural heritage and their responsibility to assimilate,
purify and transform it in Christ. He roused this consciousness through self-
effacement, his writings, and his life, an apparent failure; he did not see

52

the results of his efforts. He desired every Indian value to pass through the paschal mystery of death and resurrection and be assumed into the fullness of Christ.

Monchanin sought to enter deeply into Hindu spirituality. He came too early[24] and had to break down barriers of prejudice, traditional and ecclesiastical. He did it. But he did not live long enough to enter deeply into Hindu spirituality. It was Henri Le Saux who succeeded in this.

2.1.3 Swami Abhishiktānanda (1910-1973)

Henri le Saux, who took the name of Abhishiktānanda on his arrival in India was born in Brittany, France, in 1910.[25] He joined the Benedictine Order, made his religious profession in 1931 and came to India in 1948. He had been in contact with Monchanin and collaborated with him in the establishment of the Satcitānanda Ashram in Kulitalai in 1950. After the death of Monchanin in 1957, he went to North India and lived as a hermit. He worked for the renewal in an Indian context of the Church in India. But his life's work appears to be his search for a conciliation between Christian and advaitic (non-dual) mystical experience. Perhaps it may be better to term it an attempt at the realization of a Christian advaitic spirituality. He passed away in Indore in 1973.

The western monastic tradition of the pre-Vatican period, his contacts with Monchanin, the complete freedom of Hindu hermits and sages in India who are bound neither by religion nor by society, his contact with the Hindu sage and mystic Ramaṇa Maharshi of Arunachalam, South India, his intimate relations with Gnānānanda, another Hindu sage and mystic of the same region whom he considers his guru, the traditionalist, legalist tendency of the Catholic Church in India and above all his interior conflicts arising from his personal advaitic experience and his Christian faith are some of the factors which form a background to his thought.

2.1.3.1 Theological Approach

a) Compatibility of advaitic and Christian experience

Abhishiktānanda felt that advaitic experience is not incompatible with the Christian. For he writes:

"In reality the Advaita lies at the root of the Christian experience.
It is simply the mystery that God and the world are not two. It is

53

this mystery of unity, *ekatvam*, that characterizes the Spirit in God and in the whole work of God."[26]

Consequently,

"Instead of speaking of synthesis and transcendence it would seem much more accurate to speak of the Advaitic dimension of revelation and of Christianity. It is even a dimension inherent in the act of faith which leads to salvation - one should perhaps say a dimension of depth, of which contact with the Upaniṣadic experience gives a more complete awareness."[27] Advaitic experience, therefore is not only compatible with Christianity but also a dimension of it.

b) The advaitic dimension of the Trinity

This advaitic dimension of Christianity finds an excellent expression in the revelation of the Trinity, *satcitānanda*:

"Apart from the Trinitarian revelation there is no possible alternative to the advaita of the *Upaniṣads* "[28]

While the vedic sage feels that every distinction is transcended through his ultimate experience, the Christian *jñāni* (sage) through faith

"knows in truth that in the mystery of God, at the very heart of Being, the Son and the Spirit proceed from the Father, alike in the non-duality (advaita) of nature and in the threefold communion (koinōnia) of Persons."[29]

The advaitic experience of self-awareness is deepened by a clearer perception of this communion through faith. Abhishiktānanda exposes this theme as follows:

"At the very source of Being, the *one without a second* of the Chandogya *Upaniṣad* (6,2), there is *koinōnia*, *co-esse*, 'being with,' 'being together,' community of being, mutual love and communication of life, an eternal call to each other. In its most impenetrable core of non-duality Being is threefold movement within Itself towards Itself, the triple achievement of Itself in Itself."[30]

Hence it seems to us that Christian advaitic experience may be understood in term

of non-duality of Being and trinitarian communion. To put it thus may reduce
the force of Abhishiktānanda's thought unless reference is made to advaitic
experience itself as described by him.

c) Advaitic experience itself

The Vedāntin claims his experience to be transcendent; it is beyond any
conceptual definition. As an experience, it can be understood only on its own
terms.[31] Abhishiktānanda interprets this experience:

"Deep in his heart, the Indian seer heard with rapture the same 'I Am'
that Moses heard on Mount Horeb. (Exodus 3: 14); it was enough for
his contemplation, his peace and joy forever."[32]

This ineffable name 'I Am' can be understood only in the innermost depth of man's
heart and his own experience is a participation of it:

"In this most secret centre of man's being the only means of illumination
is the purest awareness of the self; and this self-awareness is in fact
nothing else than the reflection, the mirror of the unique 'I Am', the
very Name of Yahweh."[33]

When the Christian participates in this awareness through an ever increasing
consciousness of divine presence, his 'I' consciousness is swallowed up

"submerged in the one I Am that fills eternity... the thunder of Sinai,
the immensity of waters mentioned in the Psalms," and the human 'I'
vanishes so to say and only pure unalloyed consciousness remain. [34]

In such an experience,

"In the dazzling splendour of Being, the man Jesus could still distinguish
between himself and his Father, but only he could have done so. Man
cannot attain to his Source without disappearing in it; when he reaches
the sphere of Being itself, there is nolonger either God or himself,
only the blinding glory of He-who-is."[35]

Only faith makes a Christian aware of his personal identity and faith is difficult
for him. [36] Abhishiktānanda from his own experience bore witness to this

tremendous tension between advaitic experience and Christian faith.[37]

d) Interiority and depth

The advaitic experience which causes such tension in the Christian is one of interiority and depth. Abhishiktānanda laid enormous stress on the interiority and depth of India's religious experience which he considered a special gift of God to India.[38] He affirms that India's deep religious experience leads within, without a return where all distinctions and change are transcended.[39] He expresses his conviction that,

"... it is in the inmermost core of the self that man's spirit will increasingly find its true home. In increasing numbers men will discover in their own depths and in the depth of everything that is, the true centre of themselves and of the universe, the very mystery of the Godhead itself."[40]

e) Presence

The experience of interiority and depth is also one of divine presence, a presence inherent in each being.[41] Abhishiktānanda's awareness of this presence is seen in his works.[42] He describes its effect on the mystic as follows:

"When the Christian mystic 'returns' from his own experience, he perceives everywhere in the world the signs of the presence of the trinitarian mystery. In every rustling leaf, in every gentle breeze, in every moment and every event either in nature or history, he hears the *Thou* in which Being awakes to itself, he recognizes the *Abba Father* which the Spirit whispers in the hearts of God's elect."[43]

The advaitic experience, the experience of interiority, depth and presence may be termed contemplation.

f) Contemplation

Contemplation should have primacy in the Church. For Abhishiktānanda says:

"The time must come when the Christian, instead of simply keeping
step with man's slow advance towards self-realization, will attend to
the gentle summons of the Spirit mediated to him by the ancient sages
of the East and will allow the Spirit to carry him away within to the
abyss of the self. Then God will be able to work on him in those
depths of his being which effectively control him, instead of merely
at the level of sense and of those other faculties which man, always too
grudgingly, makes available to his action. Contemplation will then once
more be given its place of primacy in the Church, not merely by the
religious Orders and by those who are dedicated to the acosmic life,
but in the heart of everyone who seeks to make progress in the ways of
the Spirit."[44]

It is through contemplation that the transfiguration of the human society and the
unity of the Church will be realized.[45] Those who lead the acosmic life
(sannyāsa) are the ones totally given up to contemplation.

g) Sannyāsa

"Originally, as was also the case with the first Christian monks," writes
Abhishiktānanda, "to take Sannyāsa simply meant leaving one's own home and
village and departing to the forest or taking to the roads *(parivrajya)*."[46]

In the course of time certain forms evolved, but in his opinion, according to the
Indian view,

"Sannyāsa should not be regarded as a fourth *āśrama*, or state of life.
It belongs to no category whatever, and cannot be undertaken along with
anything else. It is truly transcendent, as God himself transcends all,
being apart from all, beyond all, and yet immanent in all without any
duality."[47]

Sannyāsa transcends all dharmas (religions), all dharmas being a sign of the
Beyond; it is not bound by any tie whatever of family, religion, society or
cult (in Christian terms, sacraments).[48] The sanyāsi is one who has renounced

renunciation and non-renunciation;[49] his renunciation includes the renouncer
himself.[50] He is totally free and his only obligation is to the unique Spirit,
to remain fixed in the vision of the inner mystery, the non-dual *brahman*.[51]
This is to be a sign. In the words Abhishiktānanda,

"Whoever he may be - and God alone knows the secrets of a man's heart -
the sādhu is set among men to be simply the sign of divine Presence,
a witness to the mystery which is beyond all signs, a reminder to
every man of the inner mystery of his own true self."[52]

It is a symbol rather than a sign; it penetrates to the very source of being
and bears within itself the reality it signifies.[53] In brief sannyāsa is a
mystery. It is in this mystery, in the call to sannyāsa that all religions
meet:

"In the end, it is in that call arising from the depths of the human
heart that all the great dharmas really meet each other and discover
their innermost truth in that attraction beyond themselves which they
all share. This fundamental urge towards the Infinite is altogether
beyond the reach of either sense or intellect."

"... Despite all differences in observance, language and cultural
background, they perceive in each other's eyes that depth which the
One Spirit has opened in their own hearts. They sense the bliss, the
light, the ineffable peace which emanate from it; and when they
embrace each other, as they so often spontaneously do, it is a sign that
they have felt and recognized their innate 'non-duality', for in truth
in the sphere of the *ajāta*, the unborn, there is no 'otherness'."[54]

This meeting of religions on the ground of sannyāsa poses the problem of
relations between them.

h) Relation between Hinduism and Christianity

Abhishiktānanda mentions some of the theories advanced and their
limitations.[55] He sees in Hinduism one of the loftiest expressions of the
cosmic covenant, a term which refers to the religious experiences of mankind

apart from biblical revelation.[56] It converges upon Christ and finds its
fulfilment in him. All that is said in the *Upaniṣads* is said of Christ.[57]
The Bible is the crown of the *Upaniṣads*.[58] Hinduism receives from the Church.
The Church also has to receive from the nations.[59] The reading of the *Upaniṣads*
gives a new light to understand the Gospel.[60] Some approaches to mysteries are
complementary. The West contemplates the mystery of inaccessibility of God under
the symbol of higher and higher, while India contemplates the same under the
symbol of deeper and deeper centres of the heart.[61] From these, it is clear
that he did not stick to any particular theory as such. One reason may be that
he did not have much faith in an intellectual approach.

i) Concepts and Formulas

A meeting of religions on the level of truths is difficult and if possible
very limited in its scope. The awakening to the Real of a mighty personality
which gives origin to religion, enshrined in concepts and formulas, are
necessarily culturally and socially conditioned.[62] Abhishiktānanda writes:

"The real stumbling-block is not the advaitic
experience of India but its formulation, which is often one-sided, inadequate and conditioned, and even more, perhaps, the formulations of
the Christian faith which are only too often marred by dualism."[63]

He felt that dualistic and non-dualistic formulations were the result of
conditioning.[64] These ideas recur in various ways and contexts in his writings.[65]

He felt that concepts and formulas never contain or enclose truth.[66] Instead
truth bursts forth in the heart.[67] Consequently it is not on the level of
conceptualized and formulated truth that religions are to meet. A confrontation
between the data of Christian theology and Hindu philosophy cannot produce a
synthesis. It can be achieved only at a deeper level. In the words of
Abhishiktānanda:

"A valuable result can only emerge from an inner symbiosis within the
human heart between the advaitic experience of self-awareness and the
contemplation of **the** blessed Trinity at the source of the very soul."[68]

It seems to us that the author's thought may be summarized as follows: A meeting between all religions, especially between Hinduism and Christianity, is possible on the level of religious experience beyond thought-forms and concepts in the experiential, existential realization of the Absolute in the cave of the heart, in the innermost centre of man's heart, in the self.

2.1.3.2 Appreciation

Abhishiktānanda's rich thought defies, to an extent, categorization. Like Monchanin, his mission was to awaken in the Catholic Church in India a consciousnes of the spiritual riches of India and of her mission to integrate them. His achievement in this field is very remarkable and it will take years before one can evaluate it. In himself, he seems to have achieved an integration between the advaitic and Christian experience. Much care is needed to interpret his thought in a balanced way. Though he emphasizes much the acosmic life and religious experience, he does not disregard other dimensions of human life.

While Abhishiktānanda's principal concern was religious experience itself, more specifically, the Christian and advaitic, another monk, Bede Griffiths, attempted to go behind cultural and social conditionings to discover the essential Truth.

2.1.4 Bede Griffiths (*1906)

Bede Griffiths was born on 17th December 1906 at Walton on Thames, Surrey, England. In his youth he turned from agnosticism to Christianity. He became a Benedictine monk of the Prinknash Abbey and then Prior of Farnborough Abbey in England. He came to India in 1955 and assisted at the foundation of the Kuriśumala Ashram, a monastery of the Syrian rite, in Kerala. In 1968, he went with two monks to Śantivanam Ashram, Kulitalai founded by Monchanin and Abhishiktānanda. The Ashram seeks to become a centre of prayer for all who seek a contact with the divine.

His early agnosticism, his conversion, the Benedictine monastic tradition, the English tradition which keeps a certain continuity with the past and his contacts with various rites in India are some of the factors which form the background of his theological thinking.

2.1.4.1 Theological Approach

a) Some common features

Griffiths stresses the alien character of the Church in India and in the

Far-East,[69] the tendency of the Church in India to imitate Latin Catholicism and western theology,[70] contemplation as a main point of contact with Hinduism[71] and Christ as fulfilment of Hinduism[72] are points common with some of the authors we have discussed before. His recent work, *Return to the Centre*,[73] gives his latest theological position.

b) Complementarity of revelation

"All scriptures and traditions are historically conditioned; they belong to a particular age and culture and are expressed in a particular language and mode of thought. But behind these historic forms of expression lies the original Mystery, the revealed Truth."[74]

The original Mystery is unveiled through revelation, and each revelation unveils some aspect of truth; semitic religions like Judaism and Islam manifest the transcendent aspect, while oriental religions manifest the immanent; these revealed aspects are mutally inclusive; the inner relationship between various aspects of truth is to be discovered to unite them in oneself.[75] Comparing Buddha, Kṛṣṇa and Christ, the author affirms that each is a unique revelation of the divine mystery, to be understood in its particular historical context and mode of thought.[76] There is no opposition between these revelations. For the unduly one-sided character of the concept of God in religions needs to be corrected. And Griffiths concludes:

"Each revelation is therefore complementary to the other, and indeed in each religion we find a tendency to stress one aspect of the Godhead and then another, always seeking that equilibrium in which the ultimate truth will be found."[77]

c) Critical appraisal of revelations in the light of each other

The complementary character of revelation, the particular historical context and the consequent conditioning necessitate a critical evaluation. About this Griffiths says:

"The revelations of the *Vedas*, the Buddhist *Sūtras* and of the Koran have to be evaluated in the light of biblical revelation and of one another. Each has to be seen as a unique revelation of the eternal Truth, the one Word, manifested under particular historical conditions. In each

religion the limitations of these historical conditions have
to be discerned, and the essential Truth, which is ultimately One,
to be discovered."[78]

d) The essential Truth

When we come to the intuitions of the great prophets and seers which form
the basis of all religion, we touch this one Reality; all scriptures, *Ṛgveda*,
Upaniṣads Gītā Buddhist *Sūtras*, the *Zend Avesta*, the Koran, the Old and
New Testaments all alike reflect one Truth in human terms; they are conditioned
by historical situations, but they derive from one Source and point to the one
Reality.[79]

e) Godhead – the Ultimate

The same Reality is expressed in human terms. These terms, even the term
'God', pose problems because the Buddhists and the Jains do not believe in God.
"But of the Godhead (writes Griffiths) of the ultimate Truth, one
cannot ask whether it exists. It is the Ground of all existence. To
exist is to 'stand out' *(ex-sistere)* from this Ground, but the Ground
itself does not 'exist'. It is that by which all things, including
God the Creator, exist. This is the great Tao, of which it is said, 'The
Tao which can be uttered is not the eternal Tao, the name that can be
named is not the eternal name. Without a name it is the origin of
heaven and earth, with a name it is the mother of all things.' It is
the '*nirguṇa brahman*', the *brahman* 'without attributes' as distinguished
from '*saguṇa brahman*', *brahman* 'with attributes', who is the Creator,
the Lord *(Īśvara)*. It is the '*dharmakāya*' of the Buddha, the 'body of
Reality', the ultimate Being, of which the Buddha himself is a manifestatic
It is the One of Plotinus which is beyond the Mind (the Nous) and can only
be known in ecstasy. In Christian terms it is the abyss of the Godhead,
the 'divine darkness' of Dionysius, which 'exceeds all existence and
cannot be named, of which the Persons of the Godhead are the

manifestations."[80]

And the mystery of Christ is to be seen in the context of the Ultimate.
Griffiths affirms:

> "And this Mystery when known in its ultimate ground is one with the
> mystery of *brahman*, *nirvāṇa*, Tao, Yahweh, Allah. It is the one Truth,
> the one Word, the eternal *satcitānanda*.
>
> "The goal of each religion he continues, "is the same. It is the
> absolute, transcendent state, the one Reality, the eternal Truth,
> which cannot be conceived."[81]

f) Knowing through experience and return to the Centre

This original Mystery surpasses the realm of words and thoughts; it defies
dialectics; it is known through experience.[82] Progress does not reveal it; one
has to return to the Centre and discover the depth, the Bottom of the soul, the
Ground of one's being.[83] In this Ground or Centre or Substance of the soul, in
the silence beyond word and thought, the original message, the Sacred Mystery
reveals itself.[84]

g) The essential Truth of Hinduism and its correspondence with the essential
Truth of Christianity

There is only one original Mystery, one Reality, one essential Truth in
every religion received through revelation and known through experience by a
return to the Centre. This essential Truth is the doctrine of *nirvāṇa* in
Buddhism.[85] In Hinduism, it is the doctrine of *brahman*, the Mystery of Being,
the one Reality.[86] There is a correspondence between the essential Truth of
Hinduism and that of Christianity. Using Indian categories, Griffiths tries
to interpret this correspondence; he does not employ the term *satcitānanda*.
According to him, *nirguṇa brahman* corresponds with the Father, the naked
Godhead, the abyss of Being, *saguṇa brahman* with the Son, the Word, the image
and likeness of the Father through whom the Father receives a name.[87] The
Spirit is *paramātman*, the divine *śakti* overflowing from the Father into the Son

63

and in the whole creation.[88] the soul is *jīvātman*. There are two possibilities open to it. It may identify itself with the body and be enclosed in separate existence or it may open itself to the Spirit, transcend separate individuality and realize its identity with the Spirit.[89] The final release, *mokṣa*, is a transformation of the body and soul into the life of the Spirit.[90] This transformation, if we understand correctly, is achieved through *Yoga* by the power of the indwelling Spirit the *ātman*.[91] The author speaks of the three ways of *Yoga*: *karma* (the way of action), *bhakti* (the way of devotion) and *jñāna* (the way of knowledge); of these, *jñāna* seems to be the highest, as it is the way in whic the mind dies to reason, concepts and every mental activity so that a deeper mind the supreme Self, the *paramātman* emerges and by this everything is known.[92]

"This is the end of the journey" writes Griffiths, "beyond this it is impossible to go. For here the human passes into the divine, the temporal into the eternal, the finite into the infinite. What words can describe this state, what thought penetrate it? It is the ultimate mystery."[93]

h) Identity or unity?

This ultimate state, this passing of the finite into the infinite, raises a problem. Does it mean identity? Does it do away with every distinction? Griffiths answers:

"The soul has passed beyond this present mode of consciousness, beyond its created being. The distinction, as we now understand it, between God and the soul has been transcended. It is not God who remains but the Godhead, not *saguṇa brahman*, God with attributes, related to man, but *nirguṇa brahma* God without attributes, the absolute Transcendence, the Abyss of the Godhea We have returned to the Source, to the Ground of being, to the One 'without a second'. Yet in this Ground, in this Source, everything is contained, everything is there, God and the soul, and the body and the universe, but in a manner beyond our conception, where all differences and distinctions, as we understand them, are transcended. This is the peace that passes und standing, the *nirvāṇa* of *brahman*, the Emptiness, the Nothingness, where thought ceases and all is still. But in that stillness, in that silence, Word is hidden, the Word in which everything exists eternally in the pleni of being. And in that Word the Spirit is present, the Spirit which is in all creation and in the heart of every man, and in our own inmost being. And

that Spirit is Love, a love which penetrates every atom in the universe,
which fills every living thing, which moves the heart of every man, which
gathers all into unity. In that Spirit we are all one in the Word, each
one unique in himself, reflecting the light of the Word, and in that Word
we are one with the Father, the Source of all. 'That they may all be one;
even as thou, Father, art in me, and I in thee, that they also may be in
us'. This is our destiny, to be one with God in a unity which transcends
all distinctions, and yet in which each individual being is found in his
integral wholeness."[94]

2.1.4.2 Appreciation

Griffiths' approach to revelation in non-Christian religions is positive.
He does not discard differences; the emphasis is on the one original Mystery,
the one Reality, the essential Truth experienced at the Centre of one's being;
this Mystery is One in all religions. He employs Indian categories and shows
their correspondence with Christian mysteries and tries to integrate Hindu insights. Remaining within the limits of Catholic orthodoxy, he makes a great
effort to make a good synthesis of all that is valuable. We may suggest that
Griffiths clarifies more in detail his affirmation of the complementarity of
revelations and of a unity which transcends all distinctions.

So far we have seen some of the European authors who followed the line of
Brahmabandhab. There are also Indians who followed his inspiration. Among them
Raymond Panikkar deserves special attention on account of his highly intellectual
and original approach.

2.1.5 Raymond Panikkar (*1918)

Raymond Panikkar, son of a Hindu father and Spanish Catholic mother was born
in Barcelona, Spain, in 1918. He was brought up in a Hindu - Christian environment,
studying Hindu scriptures alongside the Bible. He was educated in Spain, Germany
and Italy. He took his doctorate in philosophy in 1945, in Science in 1958 and
in theology in 1961. He was ordained priest in 1946. He has also worked at
the universities of Mysore and Benares. Panikkar now lectures at the

65

University of California, and is engaged in dialogue with Religions and is highly esteemed in ecumenical circles.

The most important fact which influences his theological approach appears to be his experience of two religions, - Christianity and Hinduism. His intimate contact with Indian and European culture, with various religions, cultural and social milieus are some of the other factors which form the background of his theological approach.

2.1.5.1 Encounter of Religions[95]

a) Typology of religious encounter

Panikkar distinguishes five types of encounter between religions,[96] which correspond to five stages of development.

1 *Isolation and ignorance.* Provincialism marks this stage. Each culture, as far as possible, avoids contacts with neighbours, remains closed in itself with very little openess to others, considers itself to be self-sufficient and able to solve its problems.

2 *Indifference and contempt.* This is the outcome of unavoidable contact. Only a few are able to admire the other. The other poses only the problem of how much to emulate.

3 *Condemnation and conquest.* Frequent or even permanent contacts between civilizations lead to inter-cultural competition and efforts to convert the other to our way. The other culture is seen as a challenge to be met.

4 *Coexistence and communication.* With very few exceptions, conquest and domination do not last long. People realize that enduring benefits can accrue only through peaceful coexistence and sincere communication. The other is intriguing. The problem is to keep a proper balance between fidelity to one's own culture and progressive assimilation by the other.

5 *Convergence and dialogue.* Panikkar explains:
"After a while systems of thought on all levels seem to converge; a mutual fecundation seems both possible and desirable... The *other* begins to become an 'other' pole of ourselves. Confrontation turns

into complementarity. New life - styles emerge, although not without victims, on the side of identity as well as on the side of alterity."[97] The meeting of religious traditions today is inevitable, important, urgent, confusing and purifying.[98] Such an encounter calls for certain renouncements from the side of religions.

b) Christian renouncements

An absolutization of Christianity claiming exclusive monopoly of salvation is to be given up.[99] A Christian has no monopoly of moral qualities, neither on the so-called natural nor on the supernatural level; he has no monopoly of truth or salvation.[100] Nowadays, a distinction between essence and form is vital; Christianity today is only one form among the many possible forms of realizing the Christian faith; Christian faith should not be identified with its sociological form.[101] For Panikkar writes:

"Christian faith must strip itself of the 'Christian religion' as it
actually exists and free itself for a fecundation that will affect
all religions both ancient and modern."[102]

Such renouncements may have to be made by all religions[103] and they form only one of the elements in inter-religious dialogue.

c) Need of a common language

Encounter of religions is not a one-way traffic. Both sides should be able to communicate. Inter-religious dialogue, therefore, needs a common language meaningful to the different partners:

"All religions in the broadest sense of the term recognize something
or somebody of one type or another which or who conveys salvation,
understood again in any number of possible ways: Christ, spirit,
logos, *antaryāmin, guru, tathāgata,* savior, grace, doctrine, prophet,
dharma, book, revelation, *Iśvara*, message, love, service, knowledge,
intuition, *tao,* faith, God, gnosis, humanity, lord, goodness, truth, etc.,
are different names for it, though with different connotations certainly,

for which reason these expressions are by no means interchangeable.
Yet, in different and not irrelevant ways, those concepts are symbols
of a reality (for those who believe) which performs the religious
function par excellence: that of conveying to man his salvation, of
permitting him to realize his destiny, reach his goal..."[104]
This variety of terms indicate the need of appropriate categories for religious
dialogue.

d) A theology of religion

A theology of religion cannot be based on any particular theology of
religions; it has to be based on internal and authentic experience of more than
one religion; or else it will be only a mere phenomenology of religions.[105]
It is necessary to experience them from within, since religions are not purely
objectifiable data but essentially personal and subjective.[106] This experience
renders a universal theology of religion possible. For in the words of Panikkar:

"... one can have an internal and authentic religious experience in
more than one existing religious tradition, without betraying either and,
of course, without confusing authentic experience with artificial
experiment."[107]

A theology of religion arising from the experience of more than one religion and
having a common language makes a further step possible.

e) Ecumenical ecumenism

Panikkar express his idea clearly in the following passage:
"Almost two decades ago, I proposed to call *ecumenical ecumenism* the
genuine and sincere encounter of religions following the example of
Christian ecumenism. Christian ecumenism tries to reach a unity without
harming diversity. It does not tally victors and defeated, but reaches a
new point of agreement in deeper loyalty to a principle transcendent to
the different Christian confessions. Ecumenical ecumenism attempts to
reach a mutual fecundation and to allow a corrective criticism among the

68

religious traditions of the world without diluting the unique contribution of each tradition."[108]

One need not necessarily stop at this.

f) Dialogical dialogue

Panikkar explains this new step:

"... I would like to recall the need for a still further step, to call the different 'beliefs' of modern women and men to the arena of a new *dialogical dialogue*, even if they, for comprehensible reasons, shun the label of 'religion'. If traditional religions would give up any pretense to monopoly of what *religion* stands for, if modern 'religions' would agree to enter a common effort, which is what contemporary representatives of religous traditions are also striving for, if, in other words, the common ground could be considered a 'religious' one, if those 'ways' which pretend to 'better' the present human condition could come together in mutual struggle and without hidden, i.e., 'unconfessed' weapons (intentions), we could perhaps discover one of the fundamental and enduring tasks of all *religion*: the rescue of humanity from the danger of perishing."[109]

These are some of Panikkar's views on the problem of encounter with religions in the broadest sense of the term.

2.1.5.2 Relation between Christianity and Hinduism

a) Difference of cultures western and Indian.[110]

The relation between Christianity and Hinduism is influenced by the differences of cultures, western and Indian. Western culture is based on the principle of contradiction while the Indian, on the principle of identity. As a consequence, duality, multiplicity of finite beings, exclusion of the sphere of infinity, a pyramidal concept of being in which God is at the top, and an either/or attitude in the sphere of thought characterize the western outlook. The identity of the self with the Absolute, multiplicity true, only in thought but not real, "not only but also approach" in the sphere of thinking mark the Indian mentality. These may be considered the principal differences in the ontological sphere.

The genius of the European spirit lies in the sharpness of its thought; scrupulous application of the principle of contradiction, analysis, making distinctions and drawing conclusions characterize it. Western culture has a well-ordered, clear-cut way of life, so much so that one may speak of a panjuridism. The consideration of utility dominates. The greatness of the Indian spirit lies in its power of synthesis, its concern for the whole. While western philosophy searches for "the specific" in creation Indian philosophy searches for "the common bond" that unites the Creator and creation. The highest value is union or unity. Dogmas are restrictions; classifications are curtailments; there is a certain relativity in everything. Panconcordism is the dominant note. These outlooks characterize the anthropological sphere in both civilizations.

The ideal of the West is the fulfilment of all desires and needs, generally understood in a hierarchical and harmonious order. The Hindu ideal is the attainment of true freedom in which every desire is overcome, ultimately, liberation. Consequently it is not fulfilment but effacement. These may be termed sociological differences. It is in the context of these cultural differences that the relation between Christianity and Hinduism is to be seen.

b) The image of the Church

India has seen only a distorted image of the Church in the two thousand years of its existence in this country and it appears as an imported foreign good.[11] This is a consequence of the Church's making use of the mediterranean culture as the vehicle of its message; in the past it could not have been otherwise.[112] Christianity is independent of and transcends every culture but needs a culture as a means of expression[113] to proclaim the message of the Gospel.

c) Christianity as fulfilment of Hinduism

The proclamation of the Gospel is not the preaching of a doctrine or the teaching of a moral law or making propaganda for a Church, but the proclamation of the name of Christ, of salvation, of the divinization of man.[114] For sociologically speaking, Christianity is the ancient heathendom, the complex of Hebrew - Greek - Latin - Celtic - Gothic - modern religion converted to Christ with greater or lesser success; Christianity in India should not be an imported highly developed religion but Hinduism converted to Christ, Hinduism that has passed through the mystery of death and resurrection, in substance the old Hinduism but renewed and transformed like the risen Christ.[115]

> "In one word" says Panikkar, "the Church brings every true and genuine
> religion to its fulfilment through a process of death and resurrection.
> The deep meaning of conversion is this: True Christianity is the
> fulfilment of every religion through conversion."[116]

And the mission of the Church is to be salt, light and leaven.[117] For Christ came not to found a religion, much less a new religion but to fulfil every justice and to bring every religion to fulfilment.[118]

d) Christianity and Hinduism meet in Christ.

The encounter of religions belongs not to the essential but to the existential sphere.[119] There is *brahman* or God or the Godhead which is the Absolute, consequently unrelated, unchangeable, simple; the world on the contrary is changeable, manifold, composite; to admit as well as to deny relation between the two leads to monism.[120] Panikkar writes:

> "Even the advaitic and thomistic answer that this 'link' is only one-
> sided (real from one end and not real from the other) does not fully
> solve the difficulties. It is here in this third point that we find
> the place of *Iśvara,* and it is also here where we find one of the
> functions of Christ, in spite of the very many other differences that
> exist between both."[121]

He gives a christological interpretation[122] of the *Brahmasūtra* text "that from which all things proceed and to which all things return and by which all things are" to mean that the true *Iśvara* is God the Son, the Logos, the Christ.[123]

2.1.5.3 Some Christological Problems[124]

a) The identity of Jesus

The Christian claim that Jesus is the Christ, the unique Saviour, the only name, the single way is a stumbling block to Hinduism. Here the question arises: Who is Jesus? It is not a new problem. Certain solutions have been proposed previously.

b) History - centred solution

The central points of reference in answering the question are spatio-temporal coordinates. An approach based on spatio-temporal and thus logical categories answers the question by means of geographical and historical identification of Jesus as a young Jew, born of Mary, and who lived in Palestine and so forth; it has still historical and sociological significance.

"If Jesus Christ were actually *only* what the tempo-spatial coordinates yield," objects Panikkar, "no Christian could speak of the real presence of Christ in the sacraments, nor accept that whatever we do to these little ones we do it unto 'him', nor that he is 'yesterday today and for ever'..."[125]

c) Principle of individuation

Another solution advanced is the application of the principle of individuation which implies that the question what or who is Jesus is understood as synonymous with what makes Jesus Jesus. In this principle, Panikkar distinguishes a double principle of individuation: "a *principle of singularity* which would rely on external factors in order to distinguish one thing from another and a *principle of individuality* which would be grounded in the internal constitution of such beings capable of self-identity."[126]

The application of this principle to Christ is not without problems. A denial of the individuality of Christ will certainly defend his divinity but

72

imperil his humanity. If his humanity is stressed, it is equivalent to the affirmation of something peculiar in him and leads to the affirmation of uniqueness which eliminates singularity and individuality.[127]

d) Personal identity

Panikkar offers an answer by making a fundamental distinction between individual and person. Man is a person, and properly speaking not an individual. While the individual is a concept limited to the problem of quantification and practical purposes, the person is a centre of a network of relations and is unique. Individuality answers the question what one is but not who one is: "Asking for a 'who' means searching for a thou."[128] What is sought for is not what one is exclusively in oneself but what is communicable:

"What makes me 'me' is not individuality but personality, not the private property of my 'substance' but the sharing of the accusative *me* with the nominative *I* that utters it (me), not singleness but communion, not incommunicability but relation. The search for the I – or for the Him – passes always through a Thou."[129]

Thus relation is ontological and constitutive of the person. Hence personal identity is to be understood in the context of relations. That which refers to the core of the human being present to oneself and to others and makes the person to be his or her own self is personal identity. It is different from personal identification, which refers to the external characteristics of a person

e) Jesus and personal identity

A personal encounter under the guidance of the Holy Spirit enables one to discover Jesus as a person and not as an individual for "no one can say Jesus but in the Holy Spirit" (I Cor. XII.3).

"What makes Jesus 'Jesus'" writes Panikkar, "is his personal identity and this personal identity can only be said to be real and thus true if we enter into personal relationship with him. Only then can we discover the living Christ of faith who lives in the interior of oneself."[130]

Personal relationship discloses Jesus as a pole of our personal being, as one of the many traits that make our person.

f) Who is Jesus?

An answer to this question has to avoid two extremes, one holding an individual as universal Saviour and the other diluting Jesus as a mere abstract or conventional sign. Here Panikkar offers an answer:

"... the Jesus of the Christian believer is in fact the Risen Lord, in whatever way he may care to interpret the Resurrection. In other words, he does not mean exclusively the historical Jesus but the Risen One, a Christ who as person enters in the very structure of his own personal existence.

Who is then Christ? He cannot be pointed out exclusively in the outer world of history, nor in the exclusively inner world of one's own thoughts, feelings or beliefs. Morphologically speaking the figure of Christ is also here ambivalent and, in a way, theandric."[131]

For the Christian, Christ is the Lord and Saviour, the mystery unveiled in and through Jesus, through his act of faith extending far beyond an act of historical memory. Christ is the Mediator. He is not the revelation, but the revealer of the Name.

g) A fundamental christology[132]

The terms Christ, Mediator etc., are distinctively Christian terms. Jesus represents the historical 'Incarnation' of that Mystery which transcends history and indeed Judaism and Christianity and is present through the ages. It is common held that there is no salvation except in the name of Jesus (Ac 4.12). The name st for the reality which it expresses. Since there is no salvation except in this reality, every human being has to find that name. There could be a name in religions which performs what Christ stands for, eg., *Iśvara* within a certain sector of Hinduism. It is possible, therefore, to think of a fundamental theology of religion in which a fundamental christology forms one part.

"Just as the different schools of theology," suggests Panikkar, "after
agreeing on some central points, differ in theological explanations, so
I am tentatively suggesting, there could conceivably be a fundamental
christology which would make room not only for different theologies but
also for different religions. And it is here where the concept and
perhaps the name of Christ may serve."[133]

Christology in Christianity implies a theology of the Trinity. For the
Christian concept of Incarnation is essentially bound to the Trinity.[134]

2.1.5.4 The Trinity

a) All religions meet in the Trinity

Creation is not only on the way to God but is in Him, therefore a deep
contact with God cannot exclude the world; every real contact with Godhead
is always consciously or unconscioucly trinitarian, so much so that a dead
or a monistic Absolute is an illusion.[135] Only a trinitarian concept of the
Absolute can indicate the main lines of a synthesis between three apparently
irreducible concepts of the Absolute as presented by the three forms of spirituality,
karma, bhakti and *jñāna mārga*;[136] for the Trinity is the theoretical, practical,
existential basis of Christian life and the junction where the authentic spiritual
dimensions of every religion meet.[137]

b) The trinitarian Mystery

Panikkar explains:

"The Absolute is One. There is only one God, one Divinity. Between the
Absolute or the One, God or the Divinity, there is no difference or
separation: the identity is complete.

The absolute has no name. All religious traditions have recognized
that is is in truth beyond every name, 'un-namable' *a-nāma an-onymos*."[138]

Terms used such as *tao* or *brahman* are only designations, for *tao* named is no *tao* and
brahman known is no *brahman*. The designation of the Absolute in Christian tradition

is "the Father of our Lord Jesus Christ."[139]

> "The Father is the Absolute (explains Panikkar) the only God, *o theos*.
> The Trinity is not tri-theism. It is very significant that the first
> trinitarian formulae do not speak of the Father, the Son and the Spirit,
> but of God, Christ and the Spirit. Neither the Son nor the Spirit is God,
> but, precisely, the Son of God and the Spirit of God, 'equal' to the One
> God (*o theos*) as God (*theos*)."[140]

Panikkar continues:"... the Absolute, the Father, *is not*. He has no *ek-sistence*,
not even that of Being. In the generation of the Son he has, so to speak
given everything. In the Father the apophatism (the *kenosis* or emptying)
of Being is real and actual. This is what elsewhere I have called
'the Cross in the Trinity', i.e., the integral immolation of God, of which
the Cross of Christ and his immolation are only the images and revelations."[141]

He interprets the mystery further:

> "It is the Son who IS, and so *is* God. It is the Son who acts, who creates.
> Through him everything was made. In him everything exists. He is the
> beginning and the end, the alpha and omega. It is the Son, properly speaking,
> and the Son was manifested in Christ - who is the Divine Person, the Lord.
> According to the most traditional theology the term Person cannot even be
> used of the Father and of the Spirit as a real analogy... Thus, strictly
> speaking, it is not true that God is *three* Persons."[142]

The divine immanence is the Spirit. The Spirit is equally the divine immanence
of the Father and the Son. To quote Panikkar:

> "The Spirit is the communion between the Father and the Son. The Spirit is
> immanent to Father and Son jointly. In some manner the Spirit 'passes' from Father
> to Son and from Son to Father at the same time. Just as the Father holds nothing
> back in his communication of himself to the Son, so the Son does not keep to
> himself anything that the Father has given him. There is nothing that he does not
> return to the Father. Thus the trinitarian cycle is completed and con-
> summated, though in no way is it a 'closed cycle.' The Trinity is, indeed,

the real mystery of Unity, for true unity is trinitarian. For that reason,
properly speaking, there is no *Self* in the reflexive sense. The *Self* of
the Father is the Son, his *in-himself*, is the Spirit. But the Son has no
Self: he is the *thou* of the Father; his *Self* in relation to his Father
is a *thou*. Similarly with the Spirit; the Spirit 'in himself' is a contradiction. There is only the Spirit of God, of the Father and Son."[143]

Finally Panikkar sums up his vision of the Trinity:

Now what we would venture to suggest - with the Gospel in hand and at
heart - is the Father, Source; the Son, Being; and the Spirit, Return of
Being (or Ocean of Being). Paul's trinitarian formulation of God '*above*
all, *through* all and *in* all (Eph.4:6) gives us the clue:
- over all, *super omnes*, the Source of Being, which is not Being, since,
if so, it would be Being and not its source.
- through all, *per omnia*, the Son, Being and the Christ, he through whom and
for whom everything was made, beings being participants in Being.
- within all, *in omnibus*, the Spirit, divine immanence and, in the
dynamism of pure act, the end (the return) of Being. For that reason
Being - and beings - only exists in so far as it proceeds from its Source
and continues to flow in the Spirit."[144]

c) The three spiritualities

Corresponding to the interpretation of Father, Son and Spirit are three
spiritualities.[145] Apophatism may be termed the spirituality of the Father in
so far as it corresponds to his kenosis in begetting the Son, in giving up
everything to him, even the possibility of having a name or any reference except
the one to the generation of the Son.[146] The Buddhist experience of *nirvāṇa*
śunya may be situated in this context.[147] Since only the Son is, properly
speaking, Person, personal relationship is possible only with the Son; personalism
may be termed the spirituality of the Son; this may have to be corrected by the
consciousness that the Father is greater than the Son and that interpersonal
communion is realized only in the Spirit.[148] Divine immanence is the spirituality

of the Spirit, the Purifier; everything creaturely is denied; there is danger
of disincarnation.[149] An equilibrium is needed between these three spiritualities
and a synthesis is needed. This synthesis is termed theandrism.

2.1.5.5 Theandrism

a) Reasons for using the term theandrism

The principal reason which Panikkar gives for his use of the term theandric
is the risk which the use of the expression trinitarian spirituality may run
into, namely, the risk of neglecting the necessity of the dimension of Incarnation,
of humanity.[150] Though his own interpretation of the term theandrism is
trinitarian and Christian, he avoids the word trinitarian because of its exclusively Christian connotations.[151]

b) Advantages of the same term

It indicates with sufficient clarity the human and transhuman element in
every spirituality; it is not a concept introduced by Christian faith but the
end to which the religious consciousness of humanity tends; it gives the most
adequate interpretation of religious experience, it maintains a harmonious
synthesis between the tensions and the polarities of life such as body and soul,
spirit and matter, it avoids anthropomorphism and theologism and seeks to
establish a non-dualist vision of reality.[152]

c) Theandrism explained

Theandrism is a non-dualist intuition of a bi-polar reality; the majority
of the thinkers of all ages grasped it; in setting it forth, they often used
inadequate and diverse terminologies incapable of expressing the tension between
two poles; by way of reaction they stressed one of the poles more than the other.
A balance between the two is essential. Panikkar writes:

"A 'purely transcendent' God is an abstraction of the same
sort as a 'purely independent' man. There are not two realities: God *and*
man (or the world); but neither is there one: God *or* man (or the world),

78

as outright atheists and outright theists are dialectically driven to
maintain. Reality itself is theandric; it is our own way of looking
that causes reality to appear to us sometimes under one aspect and sometimes
under another.

God and man are, so to speak, in close constitutive collaboration for the
building-up of reality, the unfolding of history and the continuation of
creation. It is not a case of man toiling here below and God surveying
him from on high, with a view to giving reward or punishment. There is a
movement, a dynamism, a growth in what Christians call the mystical Body of
Christ and Buddhists call *dharmakāya* - to give just one example. God, man
and the world are engaged in a unique adventure and this engagement constitutes true reality."[154]

The neglect of any one of these dimensions of reality leads to a one-sided
spirituality;[155] theandrism, on the contrary," is a spirituality which combines
in an authentic synthesis three dimensions of our life on earth as well as in
heaven."[156] Panikkar seems to use the term dimension in relation to synthesis,
reality and truth.[157]

2.1.5.6 Truth[158]

Panikkar feels concerned about the misunderstandings and differences among
the several visions of reality; not all contradictions are irreducible; it may
be possible to make a transposition of truths themselves.[159] Not everything comes
under the realm of *alētheia*; *emet,* for example, stands out of the realm of
doctrine; ontological truth is outside the realm of judgement and originates from
the order of essences and stays with the inner core of Being and does not belong
to the level of beings, existences or temporality.[160] The whole truth cannot
pass into an interpretation; every interpretation hides truth; no system can
exhaust truth.[161] This conviction may be the raison d'être of two phenomena.

2.1.5.7 Syncretism and Eclecticism[162]

a) Syncretism

Syncretism, etymologically, suggests a provisional, hence superficial union and has a pejorative sense.[163] From a semantic point of view, syncretism may be considered as "an *a posteriori* approach reflecting upon a given situation and the effort to articulate the actual interactions and effected changes, with the recognition that the formulation of the facts belongs to the facts themselves so that they only became actual facts when properly formulated and discovered as such."[164] It has an existentialistic flavour.[165]

b) Eclecticism

The etymological meaning seems to be the forming of a selective opinion through picking up parts of existing doctrines.[166] Eclecticism may be a philosophical, religious or simply human approach which strives to bring together different cultures, religions or merely doctrines within the respective systems by applying a superior criterion of truth and thus build up a more comprehensive world-view.[167] It is predominantly essentialistic in character.[168]

c) Common elements

Both imply the acceptance of a third product out of elements coming from two or more independent sources and resulting from interaction and mutual fecundatio eclectic and syncretic efforts are found in almost all the religious traditions of the world.[169] This is a sign of growth.

d) The category of growth

The word "growth" tries to convey in a dynamic way what eclecticism and syncretism imply; it encompasses both and makes it possible to evaluate the place and role of eclecticism and syncretism in the actual context of the encounter of religions and cultures; it presupposes the presence of certain sen ideas which renders cross-fertilization and mutual fecundation possible; growth comes from within according to an internal pattern and needs to assimilate exter elements.[170] Panikkar says:

"In growth we have continuity as well as novelty, development as well as r assimilation from something which was outside and now becomes incorporated, made one body."[171]

In this process, the role of an eclectic approach is to avoid one-sided concepts and to deal with theoretical issues involved in the encounter of religions and cultures; the role of syncretic method is to see to the taking place of actual interaction in the existential historical situation.[172]

2.1.5.8 Appreciation

Panikkar's thought is original, rich, complex, very intellectual and yet not dissociated from experience. It is expressed in a highly technical language. He analyzes but his principal concern is to offer a good synthesis. The theandric synthesis of Panikkar, provided it does not become dogmatic, is an excellent one. His suggestion of a fundamental Christology is original but needs further elaboration.

Panikkar's theology has great appeal for the intelligensia. Theology has also to develop from experience, not only of the élite, but also of Christian communities. Evangelization and pastoral work bring Christian communities into being and lead them to the realization of Christian experience. It is to this task D. S. Amalorpavadass directs his attention.

2.1.6 Duraisamy Simon Amalorpavadass (*1932)

D. S. Amalorpavadass was born in Kallery near Pondicherry in Tamilnadu, India, in 1932. He was ordained priest and worked as an assistant priest for six months. He started a movement for catechetical renewal at the Regional Catechetical Centre at Tindivanam and edited a Tamil monthly on Catechetics, Bible and Liturgy called *thozhan*. He took his doctorate in theology from the Catholic university of Paris. From the same university he has a Masters degree in Pastoral Catechetics. At present he is Director of the National Biblical, Catechetical and Liturgical Centre, Bangalore.

His theology is to be seen in the context of his pastoral experience, his contact with numerous bishops, missionaries and lay people almost from all parts of the world, his work on an all-India level and his participation in numerous seminars and congresses on regional, national and international levels.

2.1.6.1. Evangelization Seen in the Context of the Hindu Society and the Church in India

a) Crisis of traditional values

India is passing through a crisis of the system of traditional religious values owing to an evolution in every domain of her life.[173] The English education of a secularist, materialist, positivist and rationalist type, though fruitful, was instrumental in gradually weakening the spiritual equilibrium of the country and her fidelity to ancestral customs.[174] Has this education brought about a radical change in the outlook of the people? Do they reject traditional values and adopt new ones? How does this crisis affect evangelization?[175]

Several answers are given. According to the opinion termed "idealist", the changes in India are only superficial; the country remains faithful to her traditional religious values; consequently monasticism and mystical witness are the best way to lead India to Christ.[176] From the realistic point of view, India is as materialistic as the western countries; religious indifference, indiscipline and criminal tendencies are some evidences of it; in such a situation, a path of action the entrance of the Church into the movement of the nation and heralding the message of the Gospel through promoting national welfare without neglecting at the same time the witness of Christian life appear to be the best.[177] A more balanced view is possible. Nearly eighty per cent of Indians live in villages. An analysis of the actual situation shows that modern thought and social and economic evolution have not profoundly changed or modified Indian mentality, rhythm of life and traditional culture of the rural population, nor affected their religious traditions though there might be exceptions; religious traditions are not the principal obstacles to progress.[178] Three kinds of reactions seem to be prevalent among the educated classes and urban milieu confronted with the present crisis: a conservative reaction of defence, an abrupt break with the past in favour of the material values of western civilization and a search for a balanced synthesis of the spiritual heritage and new values.[179]

This crisis calls for a harmonious synthesis of what is durable and transcendental in the spiritual tradition of India with what is necessary and valuable in world civilization; it is this synthesis which the whole world expects from India.[180]

b) A Saviour in this crisis

Who will achieve this relevant and much needed synthesis? In spite of the renaissance of Hinduism, its power of integration and assimilation, it does not seem to be capable of resisting the onslaught of materialism and communism for

lack of organization, unity of direction, clarity of doctrine concerning modern
problems and many similar factors.[181] Communism presents itself as a saviour;
India has not given herself to communism though the danger is not past.[182] The government of India makes an effort at integration but it is based on a vague religiosity
subordinating spiritual values to the material.[183] According to Amalorpavadass,

> "There is another Saviour for India, - Christ. We know that
> he is not 'an imposter' like others (Mt. 27,62), but the true Redeemer,
> the unique Saviour of the universe, of the whole humanity. His message
> of salvation, the Gospel, his instrument of salvation, the Church can
> give India a perfect remedy for all her ills. The void created in the
> spirit by the destruction of ancient gods, the vanity they discover in
> the new idols make them turn precisely, not to atheistic communism, but
> to Christianity. The struggle of the Indian soul to implant a spirituality
> at the very roots of the secular structures imposed by a technico-material
> civilisation is an evident appeal to a religion which by its very nature
> is an incarnation of the spiritual in the material, an appeal to God
> Incarnate and to the Church his body."[184]

If Christ is India's salvation through his Church, then it is necessary to
examine Indian attitude to Christianity.

c) Tolerance

Indian attitude towards religion is one of tolerance; from the beginnings
of history tolerance reflects India's social and political structure, psychology
and religious conviction.[185] Hinduism has no founder, no dogmas and no infallible,
central, controlling authority. Subjective religious experience has primacy and
it relativizes truth. The Absolute, the unique God, the ultimate Reality without
name and form is contemplated under its different aspects by devotees and called
Iśvara by Hindus, Yahweh by the Jews, heavenly Father by Christians and in
similar ways by other religions. The Absolute manifests itself in different
forms. Revelation is an on-going, unending process and religion man's initiative
at self-realization. Religion, therefore, has to adapt itself to the individual,

society and nation. Since man is at the origin of religion, no religion is adequate, or perfect or true. All are more-or-less identical in their usefulness and inadequacy. Considered as such they are partial revelations of the ultimate Reality. These are some of the principles which govern the Indian attitude to religions and on which is based tolerance. The conclusion drawn from these principles is that "since all religions are equally good and necessary, equally lacking in power and inadequate, all deserve an equal tolerance."[186]

Though as old as India, the theory of tolerance was developed during the last hundred years from the time of Rama Krishna Paramahamsa and with Mahatma Gandh (1869-1948) it becomes an axiom.[187] A number of Hindu reformers, like Vivekananda and Radhakrishnan (1888-1975) while remaining attached to the principle of tolerance, claim universal validity for Hinduism side-by-side with Christianity.[188] Though there is tolerance, there have been cases of intolerance, but these are incidents;[189a] there is every reason to hope that the tradition of tolerance continues.[189] There are these and other elements of Hinduism which are favourable or unfavourable to evangelization.[190]

d) The source of the mission of the Church

The mission of the Church has its origin from the trinitarian life, love and dynamism in its internal and external mission.[191] The Church is Christ continued across time and space; the Church is the body of Christ which has to assemble and integrate every man of every country and time in order to reach full stature. If so the Church in India has to ask herself whether she is capable of fulfilling her mission of evangelization.

e) Positive aspects

Some of the signs favourable to evangelization are an extraordinary vitality and élan of the Church in meeting challenges, renewal according to the spirit of the Second Vatican Council, a correct evaluation of past performance, long-term planning, deep study of religion and culture, promoting inter-religious dialogue, catechetical renewal, progress in indigenization, emphasis on the need of contemplation, slow yet steady growth of an Indian spirituality, guidance of the hierarchy and similar factors.[192]

f) Negative aspects[193]

There are numerous factors unfavourable to evangelization. A false, narrow conception of the Church identifies the Church with the Latin-post-tridentine Church. There are deficiencies in pastoral approach from the point of view of catholicity and apostolicity. In this context, what Amalorpavadass says deserves attention:

"In our fidelity to tradition today we expect everything from Rome.
Even if Rome asks us to make use of our intelligence, of our brain as we should, we prefer to receive everything from Rome even to the least detail.
We have simply identified tradition with an eternal museum of ideas and of rules of which the greatest is in Rome.

...She /the Church in India/ would like to show herself more Roman than Rome, more papist than the Pope, more Italian than Italy. She is so obedient to Rome that she goes so far as to disobey Rome however para-doxical this may be. In other words, the Church in India does not wish to change unless Rome gives a formal order, every detail ready made."[194]

There are various scandals like the disunity of Christians, the materialism and the atheism of the West. Lack of missionary zeal, discouragement, inadequate missiological training, lack of trust between theologians, bishops and missionaries, clerical monopoly and institutionalism are some of the other problems. To these must be added another crisis which the Church has to face.

g) The missionary crisis

The crisis in the Mission World touches profoundly the missionary vocation, motivation and activity of the Church; the crisis is not a superficial passing one; it has deep roots and raises fundamental issues which have serious repercussions on the life and activity of the Church, of each community and person.[195] Amalorpavadass explains the reason for this crisis:

"First of all, it is due to *the new attitude towards non-Christian religions and a better appreciation of them as* formulated by recent theological research and affirmed by the documents of the II Vatican Council. (L.G. 16, A.G. 7, G.S. 22). This partly condemns the earlier attitude towards the world religions, widens the missionary aim as hitherto understood, and deepens the missionary motivation. The motives which formerly inflamed the zeal of a missionary and enabled him to spend himself in the service of the gospel are found overnight as baseless, when one studies the insights and trends in the modern theology of evangelization. Formerly one thought that the followers of non-Christian religions were not saved. A missionary was fired with zeal to rush to their rescue and to save them. Today he is told that Christ is at work by his saving presence and action among the non-Christians and that the latter can be saved in the very socio-religious milieu of their own religion."[196]

This has created confusion among many missionaries. The relation between evangelization and dialogue, between evangelization and development is not quite clear for many and this has also increased the prevailing confusion.[197] All these call for a doctrinal synthesis, a clear theology of evangelization.

2.1.6.2 The Theology of Evangelization

a) Requisites for any theology[198]

Till now theology proceeded from principles abstracted from reality; it runs the risk of falsifying and distorting reality. Theology is interested in reality. It studies "the reality of God and men, in the reality of their relationship, in the reality of God's self-communication to men which takes place in the reality of the world and history, society and life."[199] It follows that theology is not a study of God as He is in Himself nor is it an absolute universal science; it is a partial science and needs to be assisted by other sciences like psychology and anthropology, sociology, economics,

politics and history. With the aid of these and similar sciences theology has to
interpret the reality in which we live in a prophetic way discerning God's
activity in the world and where man has to be to work with God. This is a task
of the Christian community, the function of theologizing.[200]
Amalorpavadass writes on this issue:

"Theologizing is a function of Christian communities of local Churches.
The Indian Church will never start theologizing unless and until she
becomes a genuinely local Church. She must be incardinated in the soil,
identified with the life of the Indian society, and be adult to take up
full responsibility to re-think in an original way her message in the
context of the particular human group and to reformulate her message in
order to make it relevant and meaningful to them."[201]

This function of faith - reflection is done in the light of God's Word in actual
involvement in the life of the society. In the Indian context a theology of
evangelization has to study the problem of the salvation of non-Christians as
the vast majority of the Indian society is formed of non-Christians.

b) Salvation in non-Christian religions[202]

Christ is present and active among all peoples of the world, all religions
and all realities; so religions cannot properly be called "pre-Christian," "post-
Christian" or "non-Christian"; the need for terminological distinction and the
fear of the loss of proper identity prevent the application of the term "Christian"
to these religions; hence they may be termed "world religions," "the great religions
of the world," "the religious traditions of mankind" etc.[203] God's saving
presence and action extend far beyond the limits of the Church before the foundation
of the institutional Church and outside it and include all the religions of the
world and all the realities of the temporal order.[204] The universal active
presence of Christ is termed "semina verbi" "seeds of the word" by the Fathers of
the Church; man can come into contact with this saving presence "and thereby
attain salvation *only through historico-socio-religious phenomena* 'in the context

of their religious traditions'."[205] Consequently

"... the beliefs and practices should have their origin in God. Hence
we logically conclude that the reality of *Revelation* is possible in
their religious and life-situations; their Scripture must be inspired
in some way or other (analogically at least) and their religious practices
(...) may be visible means of *salvation*: Revelation, Inspiration and
Salvation should be granted and recognized in them in some sense or other
if we are open to and logical with the Vatican II statements."[206] To
deal with the question of the inspiration of non-biblical Scriptures
Amalorpavadass organized a Research Seminar in December 1974.[207]

c) Uniqueness of the Church

Against this background, the basis of the originality and the uniqueness of
the Church, and that of missionary motivation, are found in the following facts:
the Church communicates explicit knowledge of Christ, the central event of the
history of salvation and deeper union with Him; the Church is the institution
historically instituted by Christ *"as the fully adequate means of salvation,
as the universal sacrament of salvation,* as the animator and leader of the
spiritual movement launched by Jesus Christ for the renewal and unification of
mankind."[208]

d) Necessity of evangelization

Evangelization is necessary because Christian fellowship, universal and
not bound by any culture is essential for peace and harmony in the world and
because it communicates to others what has been confided to the Church for all
men.[209] The role of "... the Church, though a little flock in the diaspora,
has a world-wide mission: to be the leaven for the whole mass of mankind at
all levels of existence, social, cultural, religious."[210] Moreover, the
renaissance, reform and renewal of Hinduism has been partly due to evangelization a
partly to Hinduism's own inner dynamism; Christianity has saved not only Hindus
but also Hinduism, rendering it more prophetic and salvific.[211]

88

Amalorpavadass writes:

"Hinduism needs a deeper metanoia; it is not simply one of
purification and fulfilment, but also one of rejection and
rupture. There is no possibility of new life without real death. Christ
will then be a sign of contradiction, whether we like it or not: the
scandal of the Cross cannot be avoided in any case. Perhaps Hinduism
needs to be provoked and challenged; this may serve as a better way to
discover Christ as the Fulfilment and Saviour."[212]

Evangelization, therefore, is as necessary today as it was ever before.

e) A new approach to evangelization[213]

There are some misconceptions about evangelization: the conception of
evangelization as territorial expansion of the Church, as communication of
mere abstract truths, proclamation of the Gospel as statements formulated in a
past historical and cultural context are some of them. To these may be added
an implicit pessimism towards the world arising from a presumed opposition
between God, world and the Church.

The new approach to evangelization is conscious of God's love for the world
who sent His only begotten Son into the world. God communicates Himself to man
through Jesus Christ. Evangelization, then, becomes an invitation to share
salvation and the experience of a new interpersonal relationship among men and
with God in Jesus Christ who by his death and resurrection achieved the
liberation of the whole mankind from sin and death and from every form of
alienation. It is the Church, the Christian community in its desire to share
the experience of the risen Lord that announces this good news under the
guidance of the Holy Spirit who abides in it. This proclamation leads men from
total or partial ignorance of Jesus Christ to total surrender and commitment to
him in faith. In the words of Amalorpavadass:

"Jesus Christ is everything in Evangelization. He is the Good News and
the substance of it; he it is that we announce; our experience with him
is what we share; our witness in word and deed is to him and to his active

89

presence in our life and society; faith in him and commitment to him is the goal of our ministry; the fellowship we aim at is possible only by an encounter and relationship with him. Thus he is the source, object and end of our evangelization."[214]

This acceptance of Christ involves a complete conversion, a transformation of the believer's basic attitudes making him aware of the need of mankind's liberation from sin and all its consequences, and of his solidarity with men. Those who commit themselves to Jesus Christ in faith from the community of believers who share his Paschal experience and gather together for the celebration of the eucharist.[215] Such is the process of evangelization, which culminates the founding and actualizing of a Local Church.

f) Local Church[216]

The Local Church is not a mere administrative unit of the Universal Church. To consider her as a centrally controlled administrative unit of a vast empire is to deny her mystery.

"The Local Church (explains Amalorpavadass) is precisely that realization by which the Universal Church, the full mystery of the Church, will be incarnated in each place, will express itself and operate through the social, cultural, religious realities of the place, time and people... is the microcosm of the whole reality of what is meant by the Church...; it is the actualization of the whole mystery of the Church in a place, as the dynamic presence of God incarnate through the Spirit of His Son Jesus Christ in the world and history, gathering his people into a community from among the nations, reconciling them with one another and with Himself and realizing a fellowship of love through a process of sharing and giving."[2]

To actualize the full mystery of the Church in a place, the Local Church has to integrate herself fully in her socio-cultural-religious milieu which is one of the many consequences of the new approach to evangelization.

2.1.6.3 Some Consequences of the New Approach to Evangelization

a) Indigenization and adaptation

The theological basis of indigenization and adaptation is the mystery of creation, the mystery of Christ's redemptive Incarnation and the universal mission of the Church.[218] Everything was made through the Word; consequently everything belongs to Christ and tends towards him to be saved and fulfilled.[210]

"In taking our nature (describes Amalorpavadass) in making himself one of us, in coming to save mankind, Christ has assumed, redeemed and integrated all that is human, not only the individuals but also the whole material reality, every civilisation and culture, every form of thought, all religions, all that go to make up man and all that man makes, all human existence and all human activity, every creation of God, particularly every expectation of and search for God and for salvation. Christ has has restored everything, saved everything, has marked everything with the sign of the Cross, has brought everything to its fulfilment by integrating everything in the march of the redeemed humanity towards the Father, through the Spirit in the current of the trinitarian charity. Thus in the mystery of the Incarnation and of the universal Redemption, we find the foundation of every adaptation, and in Christ we have the perfect model of missionary adaptation."[220]

The Church, the mystical body of Christ, participating intimately in the mystery of Christ, Incarnation and Redemption, is the continuation of Christ himself and his adaptation.[221] The Catholic, universal, supra-national, transcendent nature of the Church makes her capable of incarnating herself in every country and in every epoch without attaching herself to any one in particular. "Adaptation thus understood is nothing but the mission of the Church, the prolongation of Incarnation and Redemption."[222] It follows that adaptation applies to every sphere of human life and activity, past, present and future. Of these various spheres we may restrict ourselves to a few.[223]

b) Liturgical adaptation

Of the various spheres in which the Church has to incarnate herself, Liturgy

occupies an important place. For "Liturgy is a sum-total of the efficacious
signs of salvation of men and worship of God through Christ."[224]   Liturgy has
to take into consideration actual life-situations and concerns; it has to be
a spontaneous expression of the interpersonal relationship of the community
with God and one another.[225]   Liturgy, in India, should tend to unity but not
uniformity; a common Indian Liturgy has to be pluriform; the three rites in
India, the Syro-Malabar, the Syro-Malankara and the Latin, while preserving
their autonomy and individuality, have to tend towards something common.[226]
In spite of strong criticism and serious controversy,[227] various measures have be
suggested and taken to adapt Liturgy to India;[228] a meaningful Indian anaphora
was composed.[229]

c) Intervention of the Congregation for Divine Worship

    Though the Indian anaphora obtained sixty votes out of eighty at the
Ordinary General Meeting of the Catholic Bishops Conference of India held in
Madras from 6th - 14th April 1972, it was not declared passed owing to a dispute
on the majority required.[230]   In 1975, the Congregation for Divine Worship
forbade liturgical experiments and the use of Indian anaphora, thus causing a
severe set back to the process of liturgical adaptation.[231]

d) Dialogue

    Another consequence of the new approach to evangelization, of adaptation
is dialogue. For Christ has saved everything; the Church has to save not only
Hindus, but also Hinduism.[232]   To achieve this, dialogue is necessary.

    Dialogue has to be something existential, practical and concrete; a
knowledge of the partners in dialogue is a requirement; Hinduism is too vague
and too general to have a proper dialogue with it; so it is better to have dialo
with Hindus and Hindu communities.[233]   The claims of Christianity are a
scandal for Hinduism; hence a convergence or an integration between the two
religions is not possible; the only meeting point and point of convergence is

God, the summit on which all the ways meet.[234] Though the attitude of Hinduism
is such, three levels of dialogue may be distinguished. They are sensible,
conceptual and spiritual levels.[235] On the level of the senses come all that
was done in the field of indigenization and adaptation; on the conceptual level
dialogue has to lead to the enrichment of Christian philosophical thinking, to
a becoming aware in a new and deeper way of the riches of God and His revelation
in Jesus Christ, and to the development of an Indian theology.[236]

The depth in which Christianity and Hinduism can meet is the search for the
Absolute and the religious quest for the discovery of the ultimate Reality.[237]
It is in one's own experience of God, in the interior of the soul, that a
dialogue between Christianity and Hinduism is to be begun.[238] Christianity,
which has the experience of immanence and transcendence, has to identify itself
with Hindu immanence, assume it and bring it to the transcendence of a personal
God; Hinduism will arrive at Christian transcendence only if Christianity
shows itself to be capable of the same interiority and immanence as Hinduism,
as deep as it in its experience of God; it follows that the meeting between
Christianity and Hinduism is a meeting in God in the experience of God.[239]
Such a dialogue moves towards the eschatological fulfilment of the common destiny
of man.[240] It does not exclude, but includes, all human problems and life
situations.

e) Liberation and development

Another consequence of the new approach to evangelization is involvement
in the struggle for liberation and development. The poor economic and social
condition of the people of India calls for the Church's engagement in the
movement of liberation and development.[241] The theological basis for such an
engagement is found in the concept of salvation achieved by Christ and that
of 'dabar Yahweh' word of God. Salvation is the salvation of the whole man,
body and soul, from every form of alienation and directed to the eschatological
unity and fulfilment of God's kingdom.[242] The word of God is not mere words,

message or doctrine but word and deed together, dynamic, transforming, productive, making history itself; in Incarnation 'dabar Yahweh', the Word of God becomes a human person and reveals God.[243] The consequences of this are more than one; the Church instead of indulging in words has to engage herself actively in the struggle for liberation and development as the conscience of the world denouncing injustice and unjust structure of society and join forces against all that stifle human existence; development means integral progress, progress of the whole man and whole society in all human dimensions.[244] Development is personal and communitarian and requires the removal of glaring economic and social disparities.[245]

2.1.6.4 Appreciation

The main concern of the theology of Amalorpavadass is the domain of evangelization, indigenization and adaptation. His theology is related to his personal experience and has exercised a profound influence in India because of its pastoral and practical character. He has made enormous efforts to share the fruit of his experience, to make not only an élite, but the whole Church in India conscious of the problems confronting her and of the need of renewal and evangelization. His approach takes various aspects of reality into consideration. The problem of an Indian Liturgy and an Indian Rite will remain as a controversial issue for years to come. In such a context, the Congregation for Divine Worship does not achieve anything through the exercise of authority and compulsion. The Congregation concerned has to take into consideration every aspect of the problem. A rethinking of the manner in which it exercises authority may be useful.

We saw that Amalorpavadass encouraged the use of Hindu and other scriptures in the Liturgy. A young Indian theologian, Ishanand Vempeny, proposed a theological justification for the use of non-biblical Scriptures.

2.1.7 Ishanand Vempeny (*1937)

Ishanand Vempeny was born in Kerala in 1937 and entered the Society of Jesus in 1956.[246]

The problem to which Vempeny directs his attention is the application of the concept of inspiration to non-biblical Scriptures with a pastoral purpose, namely the possibility of their use in liturgy.

94

2.1.7.1. Inspiration in the Non-Biblical Scriptures

a) Approach

Vempeny rejects the a posteriori pluralistic approach[246a] and the a priori dogmatic approach.[247] He accepts the dialogical method which, while remaining faithful to the experiential and commitment dimensions of one's own religion, penetrates into the experiential and commitment dimensions of non-Christian religions through genuine love and sharing of religious experience and insights.[248]

b) The problem

All the great religions of the world have their own sacred books for which they claim an origin beyond the natural causality of men.[249] The scriptures of the world religions contain passages which are inspiring.[250] The Old Testament (OT) texts contain parallel passages[251] and some OT texts betray direct influence of non-Christian texts.[252] If this is so, then who was inspired, the first one who produced the passage or only the one who condensed it?[253] Moreover there are uninspiring passages in the OT; some of them contain truth mixed with error; the reason is that there is a progressive revelation in the Bible, beginning in a seminal way and reaching the final stage and fullness in the person of Jesus Christ; those books of the Bible which contain seminal truths are inspired; how can then one say that the sacred books of religions which contain seminal truths are not inspired?[254] This poses the problem of inspiration in the non-biblical Scriptures.

c) The teaching of the Church on inspiration

The teaching of the Church on the subject of inspiration up to the time of the Second Vatican Council may be sumarized as follows:

"The sacred authors wrote the scriptures 'making use of their powers and abilities' 'by the promptings of the Holy Spirit' in such a way that both God and men would be true literary authors and hence the whole of the Bible is free from error."[255]

This teaching shows a tendency to down grade the role of human authors but the Council has affirmed the true authorship of sacred writers.[256] The contribution of individual authors is to be decided in the context of the elements which go to constitute scriptures.

d) Constitutive relation between scriptures and religion

Scriptures exercise a profound normative influence on society and culture,

95

and society exercises a remarkable influence on the formation of scriptures.

This influence is quite evident in the case of conversions which demand a
conversion to the scriptures of the religion to which one is converted.[258]

Vempeny writes:

"This phenomenon shows that the sacred books of these religions belong to
their very constitutive structure and that these books enter into the
constitutive structures of new societies when the new religion is accepted
by these societies."[259]

Society itself enters into the constitution of scriptures; it shows a dialectical
relation between a sacred book and its respective religion.[260] Now the reason for
the society recognizing the work of an individual author as inspired is the
following:

"Society finds its self-expression, the reflecion of its faith, in certain
books while it does not see it in certain others. And it sees, or rather
discerns this by connaturality, to use Fr. Rahner's expression, by a sort
of instinct."[261]

These considerations may be regarded as background for a better understanding of
Rahner's study.[262]

e) Rahner's thesis

Vempeny states briefly Rahner's thesis:

"In creating through His absolute will the Apostolic Church and her constitutive elements, God wills and creates the scriptures in such a way that He
becomes their inspiring originator, their author. The active, inspiring
authorship of God is an intrinsic element in the Formation of the primitive
Church... The inspiration of scriptures is simply the causality of God in
regard to the Church, in as much as it refers to that constitutive element
of the Apostolic Church, which is the Bible."[263]

Rahner applied this thesis to the New Testament (NT). Vempeny applies it to the
OT in a slightly modified form so that an analogical application of the same to
the scriptures of the world religions may be made.

f) Inspiration in the OT

The facts which bear witness to the inspiration of the OT may be reduced to
the following. The OT is Christ - oriented and the OT religion is oriented towards the NT religion.[264] Another reason for this orientation is that God is t'
author of the OT religion through positive interventions in history, such as th

promise and election.[265] This experience of God's interventions is enshrined in
the OT. The OT is the constitutive element of OT religion, as is the case in
any socio-religious phenomenon, and is essentially connected with the Church and
is oriented towards it; this transposition of Rahner's thesis posits inspiration
in the OT.[266] If these characteristics are verified in the non-Christian religions
then it is possible to draw conclusions as to the inspiration in non-Christian
Scriptures on the principle that all socio-religious phenomena are centred on their
scriptures.[267]

g) Inspiration in non-biblical Scriptures

Vempeny strives to prove that God willed the non-Christian religions on the
basis of the universal salvific will of God and the unique saving design of God.
Though the Bible occasionally manifests a hostile attitude towards the gentiles,[268]
it contains unambiguous affirmations of God's will to save all men.[269] Through
salvific faith, man surrenders himself totally to God; this faith commitment
includes moral commitment;[270] the locus of this encounter is the conscience of
each man, which is intrinsically influenced and formed by one's own religion[271]
and its institutions.[272] For Vempeny writes:

"... if God's saving grace meets man always and everywhere (universal saving
purpose) and this encounter takes place through the existing religious
patterns (incarnational economy), and if man responds to this invading grace,
again, it has to be through the medium of the given religion, both because
of man's complex nature and because of his social nature."[273]

The salvific design of God is unique and universal; the Bible and the fact that
God's election of the patriarchs and Israel is an election in view of others bear
witness to this.[274] Consequently God willed these non-Christian religions as
provisional means through which man may respond to God's invitation.[275] This
saving Will of God is manifested in the interventions of God in history in his
making a covenant with Adam (Si 17.4 ff), with Noah (Gn 9.9 ff), with
Abraham (Gn 17.4 ff) making every religion share in some way in this covenant,
in this historical divine intervention and hence in public revelation.[276]

While this covenant is the exterior revelation, there is an interior historical revelation available to every one which starts from the inner self of man and is a complement to the former.[277] Thus non-Christian religions are the result of God's interventions in history and His positive effective will and self-communication.[278]

The OT was canonized because of its ontological connection with the NT. Now it is possible to show that the concept of inspiration can be analogically applied to non-biblical Scriptures by demonstrating that these religions are oriented towards Christ and the Church, the Sacrament of Christ.[279] The gist of Vempeny's thought is found in one of his conclusions:

"According to biblical theology, the history of the world is a history of salvation, this history of salvation is Christo-centric, the economy of salvation in this Christo-centric history of salvation is 'incarnational' and an 'incarnational' economy of salvation in a Christo-centric history of salvation is ecclesial *(Ecclesia ab Abel)*. And from the point of view of the divine plan no religion is outside this *'Ecclesia ab Abel* economy' of salvati This Christo-centric linear history of salvation will find its fulfilment in the *'Christ - omega'* in the sense of Eph. 1:10 and 1 Cor. 15:28. And all the world religions have been and still are caught up in this Christ - oriented dynamism of salvation history, although the particular members of all the religions, including Christianity, can fail to achieve their salvation - fulfilment. Indeed, all the religions including Judaism and Christianity, have to find their meaning precisely in their inclusion in this Christ - oriented dynamism of salvation history."[280]

In the light of various arguments seen so far, Vempeny concludes that there is analogical inspiration in non-biblical Scriptures.

"Since the non-biblical Scriptures, both in the strict and in the broad senses, are the constituent elements of their respective religions, and since God is the Co-Cause, Co-Author and hence Co-Founder of these religions by His interventions in their history, encountering people both in their inner-selves and in the social tangibility of their existence, and since these religions are oriented towards Christ and His Church, because of His immanent, teleological, divinizing presence in them, we say that these Scriptures are 'Co-Authored' by God in spite of the fact that the message contained in them, as in the case of the OT, is 'in complete', and is waiting to be complemented by the explicit NT message."[281]

2.1.7.2 Appreciation

Vempeny has exposed and tried to find a solution for one of the actual and pressing problem of Indian theology, namely, the inspiration of non-biblical Scriptures. He has done a great service in offering a theological justification for the private and public use of non-biblical Scriptures.

While Vempeny tackled a specific problem in Indian theology, another young Indian theologian Joseph Mattam occupied himself with the question of what an Indian theology should be, drawing inspiration from the approaches to Hinduism of some modern European scholars.

2.1.8 Joseph Mattam (*1935)

Joseph Mattam is a member of the Society of Jesus and is at present Professor at Vidyajyoti College, Delhi.

Mattam studies the approaches to Hinduism of a few modern European scholars who are mentioned below, and following on their insights, gives guide-lines for the formation of an Indian theology, in his book *Land of the Trinity, A study of Modern Christian Approaches to Hinduism.*[282] Among the European authors he studies we have already referred to P. Johanns and Jules Monchanin. So it is unnecessary to come back to them.

2.1.8.1 Evaluation of the Approaches of Some European Scholars[283]
a)   Olivier Lacombe[284]

A major contribution of Lacombe is his own witness. In the words of Mattam: "One of the major contributions of Lacombe's approach to Hinduism is what might be called an object-lesson, namely, his profound study and personal assimilation of Hinduism, resulting in a genuine appreciation of its riches and the values it offers to the Church and for humanity, and at the same time, a deep, personal commitment to the Church and to her teaching in all its transcendence."[285]

For a dialogue, Lacombe demands the acceptance of the 'otherness' of the partner, a thorough knowledge of Hinduism, fidelity to Christian message and rejection of syncretism. A doctrinal approach is useful, but it has to be preceded by a meeting on the level of the élan of Hinduism. In this vital impulse, he distinguishes two currents of spirituality, the *bhakti* and the immanent. *Bhakti* in its higher form is close to Christianity; the aspects of interiority, recollection and silence of the spirituality of immanence are an excellent preparation for a Christian spirituality. This élan may be regarded at the experienced 'unexpressed' level and at the expressed level.[286] At the experienced unexpressed level there is a possibility of an experience of the Absolute, an apophatic experience. The expression of this experience in language may be varied, even objectionable and inadequate but there is value in the experience. Mattam comments:

"The value of Lacombe's approach to Hinduism, lies not in the 'names' he gives to the two types of spirituality in Hinduism, but in appreciating the values of the two existing types, and in his balanced grasp of Hinduism."[287]

b) J. A. Cuttat[288]

According to Cuttat, a spiritual dialogue demands acceptance of the other in the totality of his otherness, effort to enter into his spiritual experience, readiness for an inner assumption of every value which in turn demands conversion from mediocrity, rediscovery of forgotten values of one's own religion and deeper personal commitment to one's own faith, which is also the fruit of dialogue The model of dialogue is that of the Hypostatic Union of the Incarnate Word, totus homo-totus Deus, which demands a real incarnation in Hindu religious culture. Mattam reproaches Cuttat for his neglect of *bhakti* trend and for affirming a distance between man and God.[289] In the evaluation of Mattam:

"... the approach which lays stress on the inner transformation of the Christian and his firm attachment to Christ before, during and after his 'venture' into the non-Christian spiritualities and the establishing of the Incarnate Word as the model of an inter-religious dialogue, are two valuable contributions to the field of dialogue."[290]

c) R. C. Zaehner[291]

Religions, despite their differences, converge on Christ, and the Church has to learn from the religions. While respecting differences, without ever watering them down, what is common should be stressed. A study of Hinduism from within

100

beginning with its sacred scriptures discloses ideas which point to Christ;
religions lead to Christ the fullness of revelation. A very good ground for an
encounter between Christianity and Hinduism is mysticism. The idea of God in
Hinduism develops through various stages from polytheism to that of a personal,
transcendent, immanent God who invites man to communion with Him. Similarly the
idea of salvation develops from the isolation of the eternal spirit in man to
desire for communion with Him. Mattam summarizes Zaehner's thought:

> "The personal transcendent - immanent God towards whom Hinduism tends, finds
> its true realisation in one who is truly God and truly man, Christ, who in
> and through His Body, the Church, incorporates and makes 'enter' into Him
> all the believers, 'bhaktas', who abandon all their self-love and egoism for
> His love."[292]

Though Zaehner insists on differences between Hinduism and Christianity, he finds
that they are much less on the level of the theism of the *Gītā*. He lays stress on
the *bhakti* current of mystical experience. Evaluating Zaehner's contribution
Mattam writes:

> "Just as Cuttat insists on the advaitic trend, Zaehner insists almost one-
> sidedly on the theistic trend but none-the-less his approach is valuable,
> for there is no 'one and only' way of meeting Hinduism and all the aspects
> have to be taken into account."[293]

2.1.8.2 The Formation of an Indian Theology[294]

The authors studied writing in the context of the theology of their times
went beyond it, which is an invitation to go beyond the theology of our own days.
It is not necessary to hold on to the theory of fulfilment since fulfilment in
Christ and in the Kingdom needs not necessarily happen in history but at the end
of time.

A great discrimination and discernment is to be exercised in adopting ideas
and practices from other religions. A thorough study of Hinduism past and present,
a study of Hindu and Christian mystics, an experiential knowledge of the modern
Hindu quest of unselfish action and a thorough awareness of the existential
situation in India are all requisites for an Indian theology. The existiential
situation in India demands that Christ be presented as a liberator. The uniqueness
of Christ and the unique mission of the Church should be upheld. In her encounter
with peoples, the Church which transcends every culture has to foster, purify,

strengthen and elevate what is good in every culture. She has the guidance
of the Spirit to achieve this immense task. Mattam writes:

"Hence it is that holiness of life and genuine Christian charity are
insisted on. It is certainly consoling that the Church in India is
giving great emphasis to contemplation and the life of prayer. In
India more than elsewhere what is needed is a 'contemplative' 'mystical'
theology, a theology of the *ṛṣis* of the seers."[295]

To all that India has received from other Churches, India's contribution will be
primarily in the sphere of prayer and contemplation.

The task of an Indian theologian is to live the kernel of the Christian
message and the élan of Hindu spirituality and to allow himself to be penetrated
by them. The requisites for him are an inner transformation and dedication to
Christ, a thorough knowledge of the tradition of the Church, the development of
dogmas, the history of her spirituality and an experiential knowledge of Hinduism.
The theologian then "looks not to any systems but to Christ, to the Bible and to
the other scriptures and to the man of today in his concrete situation."[296]

2.1.8.3 Appreciation

Mattam did well to make available in a condensed form the thought of some
eminent European Catholic scholars on the problem of an approach to Hinduism.
He has rightly pointed out that there is no 'one and only' approach, and
mentioned certain aspects neglected by some of the scholars.

Mattam has insisted on the possibility of many approaches. But it is
necessary to take a definite approach to build an Indian theology. Some
theologians of the religous congregation of the Carmelites of Mary Immaculate
(CMI) seem to be on the way to take such a definite approach suggesting at
the same time various approaches. As far as our knowledge goes, they have not
written any major work on Indian theology as such.[297] This is not to say that
their contribution is any less on that account.[297a] They have paid special
attention to Indological studies[298] which are one of the requisites for an
Indian theology. Among these theologians we refer only to John B. Chethimattam,
Albert Nambiaparampil and T. M. Manickam.[298a]

2.1.9 John B. Chethimattam(*1922)

John B. Chethimattam was born in India in 1922. He holds a Doctorate in

theology from the Gregorian University Rome (1955) and in philosophy from the
Fordham University, New York (1967). At present he is professor at the Centre
for the Study of World Religions, Bangalore and Associate Professor in
Philosophy at Fordham University.

2.1.9.1 Avenues of Approach

a) Complementarity and convergence

It seems to us that we can reduce the essentials of the approach as
proposed by Chethimattam to the following:

The western approach to reality is characterized by a rational outlook,
a rational analysis of thought while the East approaches reality from
consciousness.[299] The result is radically different attitudes and solutions
to partiuclar problems: all the same both approaches are complementary.[300]
A fusion is undesirable,since it involves the loss of uniqueness or special
value.[301] While this is on the level of metaphysics, there is a certain
convergence on the religious level between Christianity and Hinduism with
regard to the value of the material world, of the understanding of the Word,
of Divine Revelation, on the question of Incarnation, tolerance and religion
as being above nationalistic and sectarian consideration.[302]

b) An ethical approach

Chethimattam rejects the comparative method because it is odious and
sterile.[303] He rejects also certain other methods.[304] Drawing from the
experience of Hindu reformers and Hindu converts to Christianity,[305] he
proposes an ethical approach, in which the concept of Christ as Guru is
central. He refers to Brahmabandhab Upādhyāya:

"One who made the Concept of Guru applied to Christ the corner stone of
his Indian Christian theology was Brahmabandhab."[306]

The concept of Guru became a central category in Hinduism under the influence
of Jainism and Buddhism.[307] For the Jains believe in the Teacher Tirthānkara
and the Buddhists believe that Gautama Buddha became a universal Teacher on
his enlightenment.[308]

c) Christ as Guru

Chethimattam applies the concept of Guru to Christ:

"The most significant aspect of the Guru as applies to Christ is the

103

effective divine presence it implies. Guru is a presence, an intensely
energizing personal presence, or rather a supra-personal presence. For
the *śiṣya* the Guru is identical in function with God, because he opens
up a personal relationship that embraces all persons in a single mystery
of the supra-personal Absolute. Guru is the actual presentation to the
individual of the *Īśvara*, the Cosmic Logos. Christ is the unique Teacher
who through his Spirit reveals to us the Father."[309]

Another aspect of the same approach is expressed as follows:

"In the Guru the *śiṣya* discovers his own authenticity. Christ is the one
saving Guru for all men since in his death and resurrection all can discover
their own final glory and self-fulfilment. Christ is God's decisive,
eschatological and soteriological presence to the individual."[310]

Guru has also an ecclesial aspect that of disciples gathered around the Master.[311]
Thus the concept of Guru opens up one of the avenues for an Indian theology.

d) The possibility of a plurality of approaches

Indian religious tradition offers a variety of concepts and thought forms
which, depending on the shift in emphasis, can convey or express the redemptive
mystery accomplished in Christ.[312] The radical pluralism of the Jains, the
radical negativism of Buddha, the positive concepts of Hinduism such as
consciousness and the personalist *bhakti* current, - all provide various
approaches to an Indian theology.[313]

2.1.9.2 Appreciation

Chethimattam has done well to insist on the concept of Guru as the starting
point of an Indian theology and at the same time insist on the possibility of
various approaches. His rejection of comparison needs qualification. Comparison
in itself is not necessarily odious. But the way in which it is made, may
render it odious.

2.1.10 Albert Nambiaparampil (*1931)

Albert Nambiaparampil was born in India in 1931. He is Secretary to the
Dialogue Commission of the Catholic Bishops Conference India and to Kerala
Philosophical Congress.

2.1.10.1 Linguistic Approach

a) Problems posed by the linguistic approach

Both dialogue and an Indian theology necessitate a linguistic approach since linguistic analysis poses the problem of the meaning of religious language and its verification.[314] In a dialogic context "meeting of persons is a meeting of meanings."[315] As a consequence, the believing philosopher has to give meaning to the words and symbols he used in religion while the non-believing philosopher does not accept anything that transgresses the limits of language set by facts and demands the application of the principle of verification to the meaning of religious language.[316]

b) Justification of religious language

Various suggestions have been made to justify the use of religious language; its meaning must be caught, not from the speakers intellect alone, but from his whole person and this often in situations of communication and communion; its function is seen as to provide symbols or to convey eschatological meaning; above all, the Christian thinker is bound to insist on the analogical character of religious language to give meaning to his words.[317] Even analogy has its ambiguities.[318] In such a context, dialogue plays a significant role. Those engaged in dialogue realize that conflicting statements are pointers to the ineffable 'mysterium'.[319] As proposed by Aquinas and explained by Maritain, truth may be approached objectively through analysis and in a dynamic pre-conscious or unconscious manner through connaturality.[320] Nambiaparampil writes about verification through connatural knowledge:

"The positive side of it - negative for those who stand outside - is that verification here is from within, in the involvement, in the very exercise of the act of religion. Dialogue, seen from this perspective, has an important role to play to lead the partners in dialogue to the depths of the religious act of verification through experience, in the quest of the Beyond, in the exercise of Hope."[321]

c) Experience shared in dialogue, the basis of an Indian theology

If experience is taken as a starting point for theology, an answer drawn from experience can be given to those who object on the ground of linguistics to religion being "a non-rational relationship with the divine, encounter with the numinous."[322] According to Nambiaparampil,

"It is in this experience, and in contact with this experience, in continuous return to this experience that a theologian should realize his horizon, the limit of language - game that goes beyond the verifiable or falsifiable of the logical positivists."[323]

Experience is shared in dialogue. Sharing of religious experience results in the shedding of prejudices and in an experience of love that unites and leads one from the ghettos of isolation to the joy of entering into religious communion.[324] Nambiaparampil writes:

"Enriched by this communion of experience the Indian theologian will take his first steps towards an Indian theology when he turns to analyse, to express in a living language, the new experience that is Christian and at the same time, 'Indian'."[325]

2.1.10.3 Appreciation

The merit of Nambiaparampil's answer to linguistic problems posed by non-believing linguistic philosophers lies in his approach from experience and deserves attention and study. A more systematic treatment of experience is undertaken by T. M. Manickam, another young theologian.

2.1.11 Thomas Marshal Manickyakuzhy (*1937)

T. M. Manickyakuzhy[325a] was born in Kerala, India in 1937. His doctoral the
'Dharma according to Manu and Moses' is in the process of publication.[325b] He is Professor at the Centre for the Study of World Religions, Bangalore.

2.1.11.1 Experience (anubhava) in Indian Tradition

a) Three phases of anubhava

Manickam distinguishes three phases in the experiential content of Hindu religious tradition: prakṛtyanubhava, an experience of nature, śrutyanubhava, a sharing in prakṛtyanubhava through hearing, and bhaktyanubhava, an experience of devotion.[326] Of these three experiences śrutyanubhava, on account of its relation to revelation, deserves further development.

b) *Śrutyanubhava*

For a long time till writing developed, *prakṛtyanubhava*, the experience of nature, expressed in symbols and myths was transmitted to posterity through oral tradition and this oral transmission produced *śrutyanubhava*, experience through hearing; the experience it transmitted, the worship of ancestors and the socio-cultural necessity of hearing and remembering added infallibility and inviolability to *śruti*.[327] The Indian tradition associates inspiration or insight and revelation with this oral transmission.[328]

c) Insight

A suitable substitute for the word inspiration seems to be insight *(darśana)*.[329] It is a free gift of God in the form of additional power given to the mind of the sage to perceive intuitively the dimensions of reality; it is a discovery of the meaning of things in relation to God and is not in the capacity of ordinary people; insight is the human element in or human response to the act of God revealing Himself.[330] Manickam explains it:

"As an act, though initiated by God, man goes on opening the deeper layers of his own consciousness wherein he (r̥ṣi) /sage/ meets not his self but the Self of God as embedded in his consciousness. This is not a rationalising process but an intuitive vision which is a glimpse of the divine. Thus one may observe that 'insight' is very much a part of the *anubhava* of man about God in his consciousness."[331]

Hence insight may be defined as a *"gift of the Divine who manifests himself in the Cit (consciousness) of r̥ṣi as 'Anubhava' (experience)."*[322]

d) Revelation according to Hindu tradition

Revelation may be considered as an extension of insight.[333] In the Hindu tradition, consciousness being the inner reality of God and man exercises a primary role in revelation; even in what is called public revelation the communication is from consciousness to consciousness, i.e., from the consciousness of God to that of the Individual, recipient of God's self-communication, and through him to the consciousness of men.[334] There is a mutual immanence of divine consciousness in the human and of the human in the divine in the act of revelation and man discovers his ultimate self and ground in the divine consciousness.[335] In the context of these

107

considerations revelation of God from the Hindu point of view may be defined
as "that manifestation in which God imparts His communicative content to
the consciousness of man, and man experiences this manifestation of the
Divine consciousness as the centre and substrate of his own consciousness."[336]
Divine manifestation and human discovery form two poles of revelation.[337]

e) Revelation as *anubhava*

Human consciousness, the meeting point of the divine and human in
revelation is the centre of all activity in man.[338]   About this Manickam
writes:

> "The primary activity therein is called *anubhava*, experience of the
> Divine as revealed. The special nature of this act of experience is
> that it is the revelation in action, meaning that it is by experiencing,
> 'revelation' is revealing for man. In this sense *anubhava* itself is
> revelation."[339]

2.1.11.2 *Anubhava* as Criterion of an Indian Christology

a) Deeper meaning of *anubhava*

What we have discussed so far on *anubhava* in Indian tradition clearly
indicates that this term has a much deeper significance than its corresponding
English translation. In the words of Manickam:

> "... *anubhava* implies a cumulative awareness of the Reality in the
> sentient, intellectual and intuitive spheres of man. Among these
> spheres there is real psychological overlapping and osmosis of
> consciousness; they give man a concrete and unique context of *anubhava*
> as he encounters Reality. It is with this fuller and deeper meaning that
> we use the term *anubhava* as denoting person to person experience of
> man with Christ in the Indian context."[340]   Such *anubhava* could be a
> criterion.

b) *Anubhava* as *pramāṇa* (criterion)

The general meaning of *pramāṇa* is source or means of information; it
means also the "'criterion' by which to measure the progress of an action...
it takes on new meanings and new dimensions as the action develops."[341]   The
relation between *pramāṇa* and *anubhava* is explained as follows:

"Action contributes to experience, and one unit of experience serves as the *pramāṇa* for the next unit of action. It is here that we see the inter-relation of *anubhava* and *pramāṇa* contributing and interacting mutually. Through this interaction, *anubhava* is perfected with the characteristic elements it receives from the past and present stages of of action, and is open to its future. Action here is the encounter with Christ of numberless men of every age and culture. This encounter which constitutes *anubhava* becomes, therefore, the source and criterion *(pramāṇa)* of further *anubhava*."[342]

Thus *anubhava* as *pramāṇa* could be a working hypothesis for an Indian christology.[343]

c) Towards an Indian christology.

The function of theology is to interpret and explain the actual transmission of the saving Christ – event, the life, suffering, death and resurrection of Christ as enshrined in Scripture, tradition and in the official declarationsof the Church.[344] An Indian christology has to present the Christ – event and Christ – experience purified from all Graeco – Roman cultural expressions and expressed in Indian thought patterns in such a way as to provoke the original Christ – experience and surrender of one's being to Christ.[345] To achieve this, the content of Christ's own existential *anubhaba* of God as revealed in him and through him to the whole cosmos making him Universal Teacher *(Jagadguru)* capable of initiating any number of disciples into his own *anubhava* of God is to be recaptured in the *śrutyanubhava* of the New Testament which is capable of producing *bhaktyanubhava* proper to the Indian context since the risen Christ is present and active everywhere.[346] The Christ – experience of the apostolic times is to be equally recaptured.[347] Similarly the Christ – experience embodied in the Hindu scriptures and tradition[348] and the totality of the Christ – experience of Indian devotees like Rammohan Roy, Keshab Chandra Sen, Brahmabandhab and others are to be taken into consideration.[349]

"To construct a Christology (writes Manickam) *anubhava* may be described as having a threefold dimension:
1) *Śruti-yojyata* or connaturality with the recorded *anuvhava*, in our case the Sacred Scriptures.

109

2) *Sabhā-yojyata* or complementarity to the community – experience. The
life – witness of the believing and worshipping religious community
would come in here.

3) *Yukti-yojayata* or convenience for intellectual communication, i.e.,
speculative systematisation in relation to the totality of human
experience."[350]

Uncritical and syncretic procedure is to be rejected in constructing an
Indian christology.[351] In the view of Manickam:

"To build an Indian Christology we cannot start by accepting ready-made
cultural formulations. We should start, rather, with the real contents
of *anubhava* withhistorical and present, enjoyed meditatively and directly
shared from a personal encounter with Christ, within our cultural environment and community. So we appeal to Christ himself to re-interpret his
Self to our cultural receptivity. This will be his new epiphany, a
manifestation to us through his devotees. Thus the *anubhava* of Christ
will serve as *pramāṇa* for the *christujñāna* (christology) we visualise."[352]

2.1.11.3 Appreciation

Manickam did well to adopt a more systematic approach to *anubhava*. Since
anubhava is fundamental in Indian religious tradition his approach is very
valuable. He rightly appeals to integrate the totality of the Christ –
experience of Indian religious tradition and of Indian devotees. It is
desirable to study the principal types of Indian religious experience and
their relationship, if any, to one another.

What we have seen so far may be taken as the work done by a number of
Catholic scholars to develop an Indian theology. Not only individual authors,
however, but also theological events gave impetus to the growth of theology
in India.

2.1.12 Theological Events

A number of seminars and conferences marked the life of the Church in
India in the past few years. Short references to three of them are given
below on account of their theological importance and impact at a national level

2.1.12.1 All-India Seminar on the Church in India Today, May 15th - 25th, 1969

We shall list only a few of the great achievements of the Seminar.[353] The Seminar brought about an involvement of all the sections of the people of God in India.[354] The Church in India became more conscious of her limitations and shortcomings.[355] The Seminar insisted on the importance of contemplation and monastic life in the Indian context,[356] on the need to give a more Indian character to Liturgy[357] and on the need for an Indian theology.[358] The Seminar recommended "listening to God's Word in the Bible and prayerful recollection on our religious heritage as found in Indian Scriptures be encouraged in a spirit of freedom, in order that our faith may be deepened, and truly Indian theological thought blossom out of this spiritual inwardness and experience; specifically this would have application to India's contribution to world peace;..."[359] Thus the Seminar gave a new orientation and impetus to the whole Church in India.

2.1.12.2 Nagpur Theological Conference on Evangelization

On the occasion of the nineteenth centenary of the death of St. Thomas, the Apostle of India, an International Theological Conference on Mission Theology and Dialogue was held in Nagpur from 6th - 12th October, 1971. It discussed various problems connected with evangelization, such as a theology of non-Christian relgions, evangelization and dialogue and evangelization in the Indian context.[360] The Conference, without departing from the teachings of the Vatican Council, developed it further, as may be seen from paragraphs fourteen and sixteen of the Declaration of the Conference:

"14 As there is a universal providence leading all men to their ultimate destiny, and since salvation cannot be reached by man's effort alone, but requires divine intervention, the self-communication of God is not confined to the Judaeo-Christian tradition, but extends to the whole of mankind in different ways and degrees within the one divine economy."[361]

"16 Since man is a social being, concrete religious traditions provide the usual context in which he strives for his ultimate goal. Therefore the religious traditions of the world can be regarded as helping him

towards the attainment of his salvation. Since men who are saved attain
their salvation in the context of their religious tradition, the different
sacred scriptures and rites of the religious traditions of the world
can be in various degrees, expressions of a divine manifestation and can
be conducive to salvation. This in no way undermines the uniqueness of
the Christian economy, to which has been entrusted the decisive word
spoken by Christ to the world and the means of salvation instituted by
Him."[362] The insistence of the Conference on the role of the Local
Church[363] and on the urgency and motives of evangelization deserve reflection.[364]
It declared dialogue to be good in itself[365] stressed the imperative need of the
Church to concern herself with the problems of liberation and development[366] and
encouraged contemplative awareness and experience.[367] Thus the Conference
promoted theological reflection in India.

2.1.12.3 Research Seminar on Non-Biblical Scriptures, Bangalore 11th - 17th
December, 1974

This Research Seminar[368] was organized by the National Biblical and
Liturgical Centre in response to requests from the All-India Liturgical Meeting
of 1969, 1971 and 1973.[369] Its principal aim was to study the problem of
revelation and inspiration in non-biblical Scriptures and their use in
liturgical service.[370] The great merit of the Seminar lies in the fact that
it approached boldly and with an open mind the problem of revelation and inspiration in non-biblical Scriptures. The participants agreed on some form
of inspiration in non-biblical Scriptures[371] and considered them to provide
a wider anthropological and cosmic perspective of the mystery proclaimed in
Christ,[372] recognized "in the Sacred books of other religions the dynamic
presence of the Spirit leading our fellow country-men ever deeper into that
ineffable Mystery which is revealed to us in Christ"[373] and justified and
proposed their use in liturgy.[374] Certain tensions were also evident in the
Research Seminar, the principal one being that between christo-centrism and
theo-centrism.[375]

2.1.12.4 Appreciation

The theological events mentioned above gave a great impetus to the Church
in India in the realization of her identity, to prayer, contemplation and
theological thinking. The fundamental problems raised or discussed by these
theological assemblies made the Church in India more conscious of her
religious and social tasks and the need of finding a solution to the various
problems which confront her.

These theological events mark a further step in the direction of an
Indian theology. In this context, what the hierarchy of the Church has to
say on the problem of an Indian theology has its own weight and influence.

2.1.13 Pronouncements of the Hierarchy of the Church

A deep study on the teaching of the hierarchy of the Church is not envisaged
here.[376] We intend only to draw attention to certain trends in the hierarchy
of the Church. It would be vain to search for authoritative statements on an
Indian theology as such but the mind of the teaching authority on the subject
is to be gathered from various pronouncements made on the subject of theology,
pluralism, evangelization and so forth.

2.1.13.1 Pope Paul VI

Concerning the task of theologians Pope Paul wrote:
"The task of the Ecumenical Council is not finished with the promulgation
of its decrees; these are not so much a point of arrival as a starting
point towards new goals; the spirit of the Council - a spirit of
renewal - must penetrate the depths of the life of the Church; the
vital germs planted by the Council in the soil of the Church must reach
full maturity. But this is possible only if first the rich doctrinal
patrimony given by the Council to the whole Church is duly studied,
known and possessed.[377]
Encouraging theologians to follow the way and the method of the Council in
their sacred studies, the Pope says:

113

"In this manner the Council indicates the way and method which henceforth
theologians must follow in their sacred studies, in the light of faith
and reason: while constantly faithful to the Word of God, they must have
an open mind for all opinions, all needs, all authentic values of our
rapidly changing epoch. The Council urges theologians to construct a
theology no less pastoral than scholarly, in close contact with patristic,
liturgical and biblical sources, always holding in high honour the
magisterium of the Church, particularly that of the Vicar of Christ;
a theology related to mankind in its history and its present concrete
reality; a theology that is frankly ecumenical and no less frankly and
sincerely catholic."[378]

The Pope exhorted theologians to unity in all that concerns fidelity to the
teachings of the Council.

Then he spoke about the legitmacy of a certain pluralism:
"In dubiis libertas; Within this necessary unity, there is an immense
area for free research (cf. Gaudium et Spes 62). 'This legitimate freedom
is the basis of progress in theology.' There can be various ways and
methods of reaching a knowledge of things divine - a certain pluralism is
legitimate (cf. decress on Ecumenism 17).[379]

In his address to the symposium of African Bishops at Kampala, Pope Paul, after
insisting on the unchangeable revealed doctrine set in certain conceptual formula
spoke about the legitmacy and the desirability of pluralism and encouraged an
African Christianity:
"The expression, that is, the language and mode of manifesting this one
Faith, may be manifold; hence, it may be original, suited to the tongue,
the style, the character, the genius, and the culture, of the one who
professes this one Faith. From this point of view, a certain pluralism is
not only legitimate, but desirable. An adaptation of the Christian life in
the fields of pastoral, ritual, didactic and spiritual activities is not
only possible, it is even favoured by the Church. The liturgical renewal

is a living example of this. And in this sense you may, and you must, have
an African Christianity. Indeed, you possess human values and characteristic
forms of culture which can rise up to perfection such as to find in
Christianity, and for Christianity, a true superior fulness, and prove to
be capable of a richness of expression all its own, and genuinely African."[380]
But Pope Paul's concluding address to the Synod of Bishops, Rome 1974, seems to be
cautious and reserved:

"... we consider necessary a word on the need of finding a better expression
of faith to correspond to the racial, social and cultural milieux. This
is indeed a necessary requirement of authenticity and effectiveness of
Evangelization; it would, nevertheless, be dangerous to speak of diversified
theologies according to continents and cultures. The content of the faith
is either Catholic or it is not. All of us on the other hand have received
the faith of a constant tradition: Peter and Paul did not transform it to
adapt it to the Jewish, Greek or Roman world; but they watched vigilantly
over its authenticity and over the truth of its single message presented in
a diversity of languages."[381]

2.1.13.2 Synod of Bishops, Rome 1974

D. S. Amalorpavadass who served the Synod as Special Secretary seems to
express well what is to be thought of the Synod:

"Since no official final document was adopted and promulgated by the Synod
no one can authoritatively state what the Synod of Bishops proposed as
pastoral recommendations."[382]

The reason for not adopting an official document seems to be what Amalorpavadass
in highly technical terms gently calls the dialectics of inter-relating the
various parts, aspects and dimensions of any reality in a dialectical tension
at work in the theological debate.[383] He gives examples:

"For example: a) the clamour of some Fathers for autonomy and indigenisation
of the local Churches and their consequent pluriformity provoked cautions of

dangers, and led to a call for the unity and universality of the Church, and for an unquestionable fidelity and loyalty to the See of Peter and for communion with other Churches. b) Likewise the affirmation of cultural and social pluralism resulting in pastoral and theological pluralism caused raise a hue and cry on doctrinal confusion and anarchy, as a source of ambiguity, conflict and controversy. While some saw in it an enrichment for the Church and a realisation of Christ's plenitude, others saw there an in-built danger for the purity and integrity of revealed doctrines and a threat to the unity of faith and its common confession."[384] From these we may draw an outspoken, simple and blunt conclusion: There were inevitable clashes of opinions in the Synod and a failure to see the various aspects of one reality in a coherent way; there was no unanimity of opinion and probably a lot of confusion on important theological issues.[385]

It is evident that the Synod as a unified body has nothing quite significant to offer on the problem of an Indian theology.

2.1.13.3 More Confusion?

The statement of Mgr. Giovanni Benelli, the Papal Under-Secretary of State, in no way helps to solve the problem of indigenous theologies and has probably increased the existing confusion. He states:

"The Christian message has a permanent, unchangeable content which is universal. Seen in this way it is clear that there cannot be an 'African theology,' just in the same way as it would be absurd to talk about an 'African faith or an African Christ.'

It's a matter of presenting to Africa eternal truths in a manner conforming to the mentality, culture and character of its peoples, while making it understood that it is a matter of unchangeable truths.

Now it is your turn, Africans, to enrich with your own research and your experiences what you have received.

...   there cannot be a system of theology which is uniquely and in an

116

independent way the work of one country's culture or of a single geographic region or of a single people."[386]

2.1.13.4 The Hierarchy of India

a) The Catholic Bishops Conference of India (CBCI)

The CBCI encouraged the development of an indigenous and Indian theology:

"The Church will realize her Indian identity by adjusting herself to conditions prevailing in the country and developing an indigenous theology. Such a theology will be one of the primary tasks of the local Church, for it reflects on the implications of, and the response to, the Word of God, within a particular religio-cultural tradition."[387]

And again:

"In order to prepare the Christian communities for a fruitful dialogue, spiritual and doctrinal formation should be dialogue - oriented and based on an indigenous theology related to the different religious traditions and cultures of India."[388]

On the role of contemplative communities, the same communication states:

"In order to be truly indigenous, contemplative communities in India must have sādhana or discipline that is rooted in Indian tradition. The ways in which God is spoken of and experienced must be made part of their lives together. Through all this, contemplative life in India will also contribute to showing the way towards the creation of an Indian theology."[389]

Though the attitude of the CBCI was positive during its sessions in 1974, it is difficult to say anything definite about its session in Hyderabad in January 1976 owing to secret sessions, the concern for secrecy and the tension which prevailed during the sessions.[390] Our personal impression is that the January 1976 sessions of the CBCI at Hyderabad did nothing to solve the problem of an Indian theology, and there was a polarization, if not division, caused by the letter of Cardinal Knox of the Sacred Congregation for Divine Worship forbidding liturgical experiments and the use of the Indian anaphora.[391]

b) CBCI irresponsible?

What Joseph Cardinal Parecattil says about the mutual relationship

117

between the CBCI and its Commissions and Committees seems to be an indirect
reproach addressed to the CBCI for its irresponsible and timid behaviour on
the question of the Indian anaphora.[392]   It is difficult to understand how
the CBCI which voted sixty in favour of and twenty against the Indian
anaphora during its General Meeting held in Madras, 6th - 14th April, 1972
could disclaim all responsibility.[393]

2.1.13.5 Appreciation

The encouragement offered by the hierarchy of the Church is praise-
worthy. All the same, a very striking aspect of the teaching of the hierarchy
of the Church on the problems of indigenous theologies, indigenous Christianity
and pluralism is its hesitation dictated by the concern for orthodoxy and fear
of an uncertain future. The teaching authority of the Church has so far been
unable to find a way to reconcile faith, orthodoxy, unity of doctrine or
truth with pluriformity of expression and variety of cultures.

While the Catholic Church in India was thus struggling to discover her
identity in the Indian context, the Protestant Church in India made similar
attempts.

2.2 Indian Protestant Theological Approaches in the Twentieth Century

Indian Protestant[394] theology has made great progress in this century.
Perhaps a certain freedom from an over-all ecclesiastical control may be one
reason. A number of Protestant authors and scholars have made significant
contributions to Christian theology in India. We propose to make a brief
study of the theology of a few of them.[395]

2.2.1 Sādhu Sundar Singh (1889-1929)

Sundar Singh was born of a Sikh family in the state of Patiala in 1889.[396]
His mother trained him in the *bhakti* - tradition of Hinduism and in the Sikh
religion. As a boy he was very much opposed to Christianity and even burnt
a copy of the Bible. Though he studied the *Upaniṣads*, the *Gītā*, even the
Koran and practised *Yoga* he had no peace of mind. One night, at the age of
fifteen, he decided to commit suicide in the morning by lying down on the
railway line, unless he obtained peace. But, early the next morning, he had

118

a vision of Jesus who commanded him to obedience. He obeyed and obtained the gift of peace. On the 3rd September, 1905, he was baptized in the Anglican Church. Soon he adopted the life of a sādhu, one who has abandoned everything, and went about preaching Christ. The himalayan countries and Tibet had a special attraction for him. In 1920, he visited and preached in England, America and Australia and in 1922 in several European countries. After these travels, he did not enjoy good health, so he took to writing short books. In 1929, in failing health he set out for Tibet from which he never returned. Nothing about his death is known.

The early spiritual crisis of Sundar Singh, his training in *bhakti* - tradition, his journeys in India and abroad, his contact with various people both in the East and in the West, his love of nature, his mystical experiences, visions and constant communion with Christ form the background of his theology. Sundar Singh was not a systematic theologian.[397]

2.2.1.1 The Theological Intuitions of Sundar Singh

a) Reality

The concept of reality as the Ultimate, the identification of reality with truth and the means he proposes to attain it seem to betray a marked influence of Hindu religious tradition. After defining the aim and object of religion, Sundar Singh writes:

"This infinite Source of Life, /God/, who is the first cause of visible and invisible things, is Reality."[398]

The revelation of reality is progressive and is adapted to the capacity, age and state of development of every man and every age but there is no change in the truth or reality even though new aspects of them may be revealed.[399] "Truth has many aspects" and every one according to one's capacity and temperament describes the aspects of reality most appealing to him but it is not possible to have an all-embracing view of reality.[400]

Philosophy which sets out to understand reality fails because intellect is unable to grasp reality.[401] It is intuition which is sensitive to the presence of reality and "the heart has reasons of which the head knows nothing"[402] and "has a conception of Reality which is independent of the

119

intellect and whose aptness cannot be understood by the intellect."[403] It
seems to us that, in the language of Sundar Singh, intuition and heart stand
for mystical or religious experience.[404] Such an experience is communion or
fellowship with reality, God.[405] Fellowship implies no identity but love.[406]

b) Love

"God is love," writes Sundar Singh, "and in every living creature He has
set this faculty of love, but especially in man. It is therefore nothing
but right that the Lover who has given us life and reason and love itself
should receive His due tribute of love."[407]

God's love is manifested in the Incarnation and redemption[408] and the highest
worship man can offer God is love,[409] and love is fellowship with God.[409a]
Love makes Christ live in us and "the indwelling Christ, though unseen, will
be made evident to others from the love which He imparts to us."[410]

c) Christo-centric approach

It is through personal relationship and experience that Christ is
accepted as Saviour.[411] Sundar Singh has no doubts about the divinity and
humanity of Christ.[412] Christ is seen as the centre of the universe:

"God, Who is love, is seen in the Person of Jesus sitting on the throne
in the highest heaven. From Him, Who is the 'Sun of Righteousness' and
the 'Light of the world' healing and life-giving rays and waves of light
and love are seen flowing out to the uttermost extent of His universe,
and flowing through every saint and angel, and bringing to whatever they
touch vitalising and vivifying power."[413]

There is no identity of the believer with Christ or of the universe with Christ.
To illustrate the presence of Christ in the believer, he gives the examples of
charcoal and fire, and sponge and water.[414]

d) Consequences of the christo-centric approach

It is this christo-centrism and the awareness of the abiding presence of
God in the universe which make Sundar Singh accept the value of creation and see
it in the process of attaining perfection.[415] Sin is no part of creation and
has no individuality.[416] In envisaging the punishment of sin and the reward of
the good, Sundar Singh seems to have been influenced by the Hindu doctrine of

karma in so far as it is the wicked who exclude themselves from heaven and the just who enter in there owing to a change in their nature brought about by their respective bad or good deeds.[417] Suffering and disease are the fruits of sin, natural issues of man's disobedience.[418] His attitude to suffering is positive.[419] Not to get tainted by sin, the cause of suffering, man has to lead a life of prayer.[420]

2.2.1.2 Appreciation

The influence of Sundar Singh is to be measured not so much from what he wrote as from his witness of religious experience. His interpretation of reality and truth, of the ultimate destiny of man bear a distinctive Indian character.

Sundar Singh followed the *bhakti* - tradition but did not seek to give it a systematic basis. An attempt to give a more systematic basis to the *bhakti* current was undertaken by A. J. Appasamy.

2.2.2 Aiyadurai Jesudasan Appasamy (*1891)

Aiyadurai Jesudasan Appasamy, son of a Hindu convert to Christianity was born at Palayamkottai, Tamilnadu on September 3rd, 1891.[421] At the age of thirteen, he decided to dedicate his life to Christ and enter priestly ministry. He studied at Madras Christian College, then at the theological seminary at Hartford in the United States, and made a special study of the religions of the world for a year at Harvard. He did a doctorate in philosophy at Oxford in England. He was ordained priest in 1930, consecrated Bishop of Coimbatore in 1950 and retired from that post in 1959. He served his Church as writer, teacher, pastor and bishop.

His father, who was deeply interested in religious experience, his close friendship with Sādhu Sundar Singh, his personal contacts with writers like J. N. Farquhar, Frederich von Hügel, Rudolf Otto, Friedrich Heiler, his active engagement in the affairs of the Church, his long membership and work on the Committee for Church Union in South India are some of the factors which form the context of his theology.

2.2.2.1 Theological Approach

a)   Interpreting Christianity to India

Appasamy says that the most effective method of presenting Christ to the
Hindus is what has proved most effective to him:

"That is, we should not preach Christ to them from the outside; we should
preach Christ to them from the inside, feeling with them their intense
feelings, longing with them their deepest longings, thinking with them
through their most baffling problems, following with them their highest
ideals, doing all these in that measure and to that degree which our
loyalty to Christ permits. There cannot be two Christian theologies for
India, one for Christians and one for Hindus."[422]

India's religious genius has found expression in various sacred books, religious
practices and philosophical systems and a choice of what suits the spirit of Christianity is necessary.[422a] The Advaita system is to be rejected because an advaiti
interpretation of Christianity will be Indian but not Christian.[423] Appasamy
rejects the monistic interpretation of Jn 10.30: 'I and my Father are one' and
believes that there is only a moral oneness of Jesus with God which seems to be
one of fellowship.[424] The *bhakti* type of religious thought is helpful to show
the intimate relation between the inner spirit of Christianity and the inner
spirit of Indian religious thought.[425] In the *bhakti* current itself, Appasamy
has a preference for the system of Rāmānuja (+1137)[425a] because the central
convictions of Rāmānuja are close to Christianity. They are:

"God is an ocean of love and forgives the sins of all those who surrender
themselves to Him. He becomes incarnate in the world to meet the ardent
longing of His devotees for a vision of God. His intimate contact with
the world is not confined to those points in time and space at which His
incarnation takes place. It is a continuous and intimate relationship
of immanence."[426]

b)   Immanence

The doctrine of immanence, in the opinion of Appasamy, is an important

122

element in *bhakti* thought.[427] He tries to prove the immanence of Christ in the
world by interpreting the prologue of John's Gospel.[428] He comments on
Jn 1.9-10:

> "The Fourth Evangelist is not anxious to say that the same Divine Life
> which is in men courses through the material universe. While maintaining
> that God is immanent in the universe, he does not group together all creation,
> animate and inanimate, and say that it is all in equal degree the
> dwelling place of God. He does not indeed draw a marked distinction
> between the immanence of God in man and the immanence of God in nature nor
> does he attempt the difficult task of asserting that God is not immanent
> in Nature in the same sense in which He is immanent in man, but He seems to
> be concerned mainly with the immanence of God in man. It is that which
> stirs him deeply."[429]

Appasamy seems to correct his emphasis on immanence in his book *My Theological
Quest*. For he says that when Christianity comes to its own in India, "there will
be a firm emphasis on the doctrine of the indwelling God" and remarks that "the
doctrine of immanence has often run wild in India."[430] Christianity in India
has to stress the doctrine of immanence, but it has to point out at the same
time the different manner in which God is present in different objects.[431]
Bhakti is man's response to immanent God.[432] If the *bhakti* current is best suited
to the Indian situation, and if it is a response to immanent God, what is *bhakti*
itself?

c) *Bhakti* explained

Generally, *bhakti* is considered as "the deep, unselfish love of the whole
man for God, finding its highest bliss in union with Him."[433] The words of
Jesus, "Abide in me and I in you" (Jn 15.4) express the highest union, which
is essentially communion between God and the human soul,[434] and "Abide in my
love" (Jn 15.9), the highest expression of this relation, which is a mystical
relation.[435] To abide in love the commandments of God are to be kept.[436]

Consequently love of God is not mere emotion.[437] The ecstatic and emotional Hindu way of showing love for God is foreign to John the Evangelist.[438]

d) Relating Christianity to Hinduism

Appasamy points out certain defects and exaggerations in Hinduism.[439]
He is aware that Hindus have difficulty in understanding certain Christian
doctrines and tries to interpret such doctrines from within Hinduism by taking
examples therefrom and thus indirectly substantiating or relating Christian
doctrine to Hindu thought.[440] He relates the Old Testament to ancient India.
Just as the OT points to Christ, not through any saying or action of Moses
but through the spirit developed by its teaching and laws, so too the training
imparted by the sages and devotees of India has prepared the way for Christ.[441]
After mentioning some of the different ways through which this preparation
took place, such as the longing for God, detachment and love for God, Appasamy
says:

"In these and in many other ways the Indian soul has been prepared by
the doctrine of *bhakti* to recognize the truth and supreme grandeur of
the message of Jesus."[442]

The relation between the *bhakti* tradition and Christianity seems to be the
closest when it comes to the revelatory nature of love:

"John and the Hindu *bhaktas* are at one in their conviction that love
is the supreme revealer."[443]

Thus Appasamy makes an attempt to interpret Christian faith to Hinduism.

2.2.2.2 *Pramāṇas* for an Indian Theology

To restate Christian faith in terms of the Indian heritage he gives
four *pramāṇas* or criteria of which three, scripture *(śruti)*, reason *(yukti)*
and experience *(anubhava)* are taken from the Indian tradition, to which
he adds a fourth, the Church *(sabha)*.[444] The highest *pramāṇa* for every
one is the Bible *(śruti)*; a scientific study of religion requires reason
(yukti); from belief in God and prayer come direct experience of God

124

(anubhava).[445]

By the Church *(sabha)*, the fourth *pramāṇa*, Appasamy means the teaching of the Church.[446] The collective, organized and historical nature of religion is the principal reason for accepting the Church as a *pramāṇa*.[447] The deep personal experience of religion finds its fullness only when it is shared by others and thus becomes collective; collective religion demands a certain organization for worship and services.[448] Christian experience is to be handed down and God manifests Himself in history as revelation and Incarnation testify.[449] This historical aspect shows also the importance of the Church as a *pramāṇa*.

2.2.2.3 Appreciation

It is remarkable that Appasamy attempted to interpret Christian faith to India, choosing as his tool the *bhakti* - tradition in the early second quarter of this century, and adopted a positive approach to Hinduism when it was not so common and kept a lively interest in Indian theological development to our own days. The experience and works of Abhishiktānanda, as seen above, show that the advaitic experience cannot be easily rejected. It could be interpreted and integrated.

While Appasamy's theology has certain affinities to the *bhakti* trend in Hinduism and to the philosophy of Rāmānuja, a layman, Vengal Chakkarai, tried to rethink Christianity without any special philosophical affiliations.

2.2.3 Vengal Chakkarai (1880-1958)

Vengal Chakkarai Chetty was born in a well-to-do family in Madras on January 17th, 1880.[450] His father died when he was six years old. He was educated at Madras Christian College where he came under the influence of William Miller (1838-1923), a Protestant missionary. Chakkarai was baptised in 1903. In 1906, he qualified himself as a Lawyer and worked for some time with the Danish mission. Chakkarai took part in the struggle for national independence. He was also an active trade-unionist, was Councillor of the Madras Corporation for twenty-five years, Mayor for one term, and member of the Legislative Council in 1954. He died in 1958. Chakkarai was one of the founders of the group, Christo-Samaj, which worked for the Indianization of the Church. He was critical of the institutional Church.

The influence of his mother, who followed the *Vaiṣṇava bhakti* tradition, that of William Miller and that of Mahatma Gandhi (1869-1948), whom he followed for some time, his part in the independence struggle and his politico-social activities are some of the factors which form the context of his theology.

2.2.3.1 Chakkarai's Theological Insights

a) Christological views

The contribution of Chakkarai to an Indian theology is principally in the field of christology.[451] Since the source of a valid knowledge of God is a personal experience of Christ, christology is the starting point of theology.[452] To know Christ it is necessary to know "the living Lord Jesus of history who lived in Nazareth in great humility, who rose from the dead and ascended to the right hand of the Father."[453] On the divinity of Jesus, Chakkarai writes:

"Out of the infinite nebulousness emerges the face of Jesus. God is the unmanifested and Jesus is the manifested. God is the *sat* or being, and Jesus is the *cit* or intelligence, wisdom and love which indicates the nature of the being of God."[454]

Though Christian experience *(anubhava)* is primary, arguments in favour of Christ's divinity are found in his unique God-consciousness, sinlessness and authority.[455] Chakkarai is emphatic in affirming the humanity of Christ, while rejecting at the same time a clear-cut distinction between the two:

"Jesus was one and indivisible; his humanity and divinity, if we are intending to make a clear-cut separation of the two, were inextricably combined, so that one cannot say where one ends and the other begins. I cannot think of Jesus in the way that orthodox theology conceives - in such and such events in His life He was purely human and in such and such He was divine."[456]

And this Jesus of history, through his death on the cross, becomes totally ego-less, a universal indwelling spirit, immanent in us, capable of being experienced by every *bhakta*.[457] Christ becomes the deepest consciousness or *antaryāmin* to those who have received him, and the Holy Spirit is none other than the indwelling spirit of Jesus.[458]

b) Mystical experience and the cross

Such an experience of the Spirit does not imply a facile mysticism; Christ speaks more about his cross to the *bhaktas* than about rewards; there is an intimate connection between the cross and mysticism.[459] In mysticism, he distinguishes three ways, and finds in the lover - loved relation, devotion to the gracious Lord *(bhagavan)*, the highest.[460] Chakkarai recognizes the existence of advaitic experience which he finds rather strange.[461] All the same his attitude to Hinduism was very considerate.

c) Christianity an additional gift

Chakkarai felt that "the deeper elements of Hinduism and those of Christianity have not come to close grips."[462] There is no common standard for the evaluation of religions, and what matters is the call of God:

"When God calls, if the call is heard by man, what moves him is not that his old country is bad but that he has to obey the heavenly invitation. There is nothing in Christianity that can validate its contents except the call and election by God."[463]

No one actually prefers Christianity till the Lord chooses to call him.[464] He felt that the Gospel is a further gift to an accepted soul.[465] This gift is an addition to the existing Hindu religious background.[466]

d) The background of an Indian Theology

It is on a Hindu religious background that an Indian theology can be built. In the words of Chakkarai:

"Christian teaching can only modify and qualify and add new elements, and cannot displace the old. Such has been and still is the religious experience of all - ..."[467]

He felt the need of theological pluralism in Indian theology.[468] To develop an Indian theology, he made use of Indian categories.[469]

2.2.3.2 Appreciation

His affirmation of the divinity and humanity of Jesus, of the relation between mysticism and the cross, and his effort to use Indian categories are some of the valuable elements in the theology of Chakkarai. His explanation of what leads to change of religion from Hinduism to Christianity offers a line of thought along which further research is necessary.

A contemporary of Chakkarai also grappled with the problem of christology

in an original way, different from that of Chakkarai. He was Pandipeddi
Chenchiah, a lawyer.

2.2.4 Chenchiah Pandipeddi (1886-1959)

Pandipeddi Chenchiah was born at Nellore on the 8th of December, 1886.[470]
In 1901, his family came to stay in Madras. In the same year, he and his
family became Christians. Chenchiah was educated at Madras Christian College.
He studied law and was apprenticed to T. Prakasam (1872-1957) who later became
Chief Minister of the State, well-known for his bold and forthright dealings
with all people. Chenchiah followed his legal profession and became Chief
Justice of a small State, Pudukottah. He was an ardent nationalist and a
leading figure in the Rethinking Group of rather unorthodox Protestant
thinkers.[471] Chenchiah passed away in 1959.

He was considerably influenced by the liberal outlook of William Miller
and the spirit of independence of T. Prakasam. The philosophy of Aurobindo
Ghose (1872-1950) of Pondicherry[472] and that of the Yoga School of Master
CVV[473] exercised considerable influence on him and confirmed him in his views.

2.2.4.1 Chenchiah's Theological Approach

a) Relativization of the Church and dogmas

Chenchiah gave only a relative value to the Church, to doctrines and
ceremonies, for he felt that they obscure the original fact of Christ. For
he writes:

> "... doctrines and dogmas, worship and ritual, mysteries and ceremonies,
> gather round till at last the bright nucleus gets enveloped by a huge
> globe of tradition and testimony."[474]

They become centres of influence.[475] He felt that Christianity still laboured
under the politico-social structures of the ancient Roman empire:

> "When Rome was conquered /by Christianity/ - itself a miracle - the
> debacle came with unexpected suddeness. Conquered Rome conquered
> Christianity"[476]

and he continues the same line of thought:

> "Rome rose out of its ruins as the Church of Rome. The Roman Empire
> was incarnated in the Church."[477]

128

Because of this way of thinking, Chenchiah vigorously criticized the Church
and gave her only a relative value:

"India will regard the Church as a useful human institution for the
threefold purpose of worship, fellowship, and propagation."[478]

But not all of reality was relative for Chenchiah.

b) The only Absolute

"Let it be clearly understood," writes Chenchiah, "that we accept nothing
as obligatory save Christ."[479]

Christ is not the Christ of experience but the Christ of history, Jesus; the
Jesus of the gospels presents a harmonized picture of God man – not merely
hyphenated God-Man.[480] He held that Jesus is less than God[481] and "is not the
'Son' – Son of God or Son of Man – He is the product of God and man, not God-
Man."[482] Christ is unique and Chenchiah explains the uniqueness of Christ:

"In reaching the kernel of the uniqueness of Jesus, we have to change from
one half of Pauline theology which the Western and Eastern Churches have
accepted to the other half of his theology which though existing as a
doctrine does not function as a live force. St. Paul and St. John both
regard Christ as a new creation – the emergence in history of a new
chapter in human destiny. Jesus is not man made perfect, but a new creation –
the manifestation of new cosmic energy."[483]

c) The New Creation

Thangasamy explains Chenchiah's favourite theme of New Creation:

"New Creation is not just a matter of individual men and women being
'born again' in the evangelical sense of the term, but it is a further
stage in the planetary life of mankind brought about by the release of
fresh energy through a new and tremendous creative act of God."[484]

He did not conceive the New Creation in terms of a compartmentalization of life
into religious and non-religious spheres, but in terms of the Kingdom of God
and a renewal of the secular order.[485] This New Creation is to be achieved
through a biological process.[486] There is a certain ambiguity as to whether
this New Creation, the new humanity, is the product of both evolution and
New Creation. Thangasmy writes:

"At times Chenchiah seems to envisage the process of the formation of

the spiritual race of man as a biological mutation of the whole species,
but at times also as the creative transforming activity of the Holy
Spirit in individuals within the existing biological state."[487]

d) The Holy Spirit

The vital energy in the New Creation is the Holy Spirit:

"The Holy Spirit is the energy beyond creation, which in Christ has
flowed into the world... The Holy Spirit is the energy through and by
which Jesus is going to re-create a new heaven and new earth - ..."[488]

According to Chenchiah, the Holy Spirit is the universal Jesus who transcends
time - space limitations and becomes the Universal dweller in the human
heart.[489] The future of Christianity in India depends on the discovery of
the tremendous importance of the Holy Spirit by the Indian Church and her
ability to communicate that spirit.[490] Chenchiah writes:

"The Holy Spirit, the doctrine and personality - if my instincts are
sound, will play a decisive role in Indian theology. They may receive a
new interpretation and become the corner stone of Indian Christian
theology."[491]

e) An Indian Christian theology

The true foundation of an Indian Christian theology is to be the direct
and original experience of Jesus and Holy Spirit.[492] An Indian Christian will
explore the meaning of Christ in the context of the contemporary political and
social struggles.[493] Chenchiah says:

"Indian Christians alone can put the majesty and magnitude of Christian
salvation in an idiom intelligible to the Hindu."[494] Thus the Indian Christian
will build a living bridge between Hinduism and Christianity.[495]

f) Christianity and Hinduism related

It seems to us that Thangasamy expresses well Chenchiah's convictions on
the relation between Christianity and Hinduism. He writes:

"First, that the New Creation in Jesus is the essence of the Gospel;
second, that it is so entirely new, that it is other than all the
religions which represent only the old creation, and is little apprehended
even by the Christian religion and the Church; third, that God has been
at work in all religions so that it is possible to build bridges from
Christ to them; fourth that the spiritual treasures of other religions

130

will bring to light new facets of the Person of Christ and of Christian life and experience; and fifth, that the New Creation in Jesus can be realised by all relgions if they are prepared for radical transformation in their spirit and life through the Holy Spirit."[496] Chenchiah fostered dialogue, the sharing of religious experience with devotees of different religions and cooperation with followers of various religious traditions.[497]

2.2.4.2 Appreciation

Though Chenchiah may have gone to certain extremes in his view against the Church as an institution his theology contains valuable elements. His effort to explore the meaning of Christ in the contemporary politico-social situation, his emphasis of the role of the Holy Spirit in Indian theology are valuable insights. In sharing religious experience and promoting dialogue he seems to have been one of the pioneers.

Chenchiah's approach to Indian theology and his concept of New Creation had certain philosophical affiliations with the thought of Aurobindo. Another Protestant theologian, Paul David Devanandan, has deeply influenced modern Indian Protestant theological approaches by his analysis of existential situations to discern the working of God therein. He gave a more scriptural basis to the concept of New Creation

2.2.5 Paul David Devanandan (1901-1962)

Paul David Devanandan, son of an ordained pastor who was a member of The National Missionary Society, was born in Madras on the 8th July, 1901.[498] He graduated from the university of Madras. K. T. Paul (1876-1931), an outstanding Christian leader of India and a friend of Mahatma Gandhi, took Devanandan as his secretary when he went to the United States (1924-1925). After his work with K. T. Paul, Devanandan studied theology at the Pacific School of Religion in California and then did his doctorate in philosophy at Yale University. On his return to India, he taught at the United Theological College in Bangalore for seventeen years. Then he served for a time in the YMCA. In 1956, he took charge of the newly founded Christian Institute for the Study of Religion and Society (CISRS), Bangalore, as Director. Devanandan took an active part in the theological and evangelistic studies of the World Council of Churches. While going to attend a conference at Dehra Dun in North India, he suffered a heart attack and died.

His mother exercised great influence on him. His association with K. T.
Paul, his education in the United States, the period of transition through
which India was passing, which called for rethinking and adaptation on the side
of Christians, and his collaboration with the World Council of Churches are some
of the important factors which influenced the development of his thought.

2.2.5.1 A New Approach

a) Dravida Kazhagam

A short pamphlet of thirty pages entitled *The Dravida Kazhagam*[500] which
Devanandan published in 1959, though not a major work of his, seems to us to be
very typical of his approach and the method he follows.[501] Devanandan traces
the historical development of Kazhagam, analyses its attitude to religion and its
social and political outlook. Finally he distinguishes what is valuable and is
unacceptable from a Christian point of view and concludes by showing what is the
Christian task or concern in the actual context of the movement. This method
may be reduced to the following: Historical Development, (or Description of
the Movement), Religious Concern, Secular Concern and Christian Concern.

b) Historical development

Devanandan traces the origin of Kazhagam to a Dravidian Association organized
in Madras in 1910 to encourage the study of Dravidian culture by the Dravidians
themselves.[502] The Brahmin domination of the political and civil life led to the
founding of South Indian Liberal Federation to fight for the rights of non-
Brahmins and the consequent closing of the Dravidian Association. After passing
through various vissicitudes, the Liberal Federation became the Dravida Kazhagam.
A split occurred in the Kazhagam in 1949, and a new party, The Dravida Munnetra
Kazhagam (DMK), which entered into active politics, was formed under the leadership
of Canjeevaram Natarajan (C.N) Annadurai (1909-1969). It demanded a separate
Dravidastan, independent of the Indian union.[503]

c) Religious concern

Kazhagam has a religious programme in so far as it tries to rid the people
of their belief in Puranic Hinduism and keep them away from religious practices
which need the service of Brahmins.[504] It insists on the supremacy of reason
but does not necessarily deny the existence of God or gods.[505] It claims that
religion is unnecessary, irrelevant and irrational because religions are

132

concerned with beliefs beyond reason and do not relate themselves to what is
of this world and the present life; it urges people to concern themselves with
present realities.[506] Thus Kazhagam is concerned with a secularistic,
humanistic philosophy of life.[507]

d) Secular concern

Kazhagam is positivist, ulilitarian and relativist in its approach to
problems and makes man the measure of all things and maker of his own destiny.[508]
It has pleaded for a high standard of personal and social ethics and has done much
to emancipate the ignorant masses of Tamils from traditional, irrational
customs sanctioned by religion, from child marriage and from discrimination based
on sex; it has upheld the dignity and equality of all men and women.[509]

e) Christian concern

Devanandan felt that a more positive attitude is required to meet the
challenge of Kazhagam rather than the severely critical Roman Catholic and
Protestant reaction in areas where Kazhagam gained the support of Christians.[510]
Devanandan suggests:

"Also the Church needs seriously to take to heart some of the charges
alleged by the Kazhagam leaders against Brahminism. It may not be
always easy to exonerate the Church of the same charge of exploitation
of the ignorant and the incredulous. The temptation to authoritarianism
is always there."[511]

After mentioning the need of instruction in matter of faith, he continues:

"In particular it would seem that earnest measures should be taken to
explain to Christian folk the biblical basis for the Christian view of
man in society, of the nature of social evil as something with which
God is battling in Christ today, and that he is always at work in the
redemption of individual men and women."[512]

This, in general, seems to be the approach followed by Devanandan, and the
same holds good for his treatment of renaissant Hinduism

2.2.5.2 Renaissance of Hinduism and Christianity

a) The background of renaissance

Christian ignorance of the context and claims of contemporary Hinduism

133

is deplorable.[513]   Various factors such as western liberal education,[514]   Hindu
reaction to Christian missionary activity,[515]   Hindu nationalism,[516]   the
changing circumstances of modern life, the inner vitality of Hinduism and its
capacity to adapt itself to environments[517]   contributed to a resurgence of
Hinduism. The changing modern historical environment makes a great impact on the
world outlook (culture), religious practices (cultus), and doctrinal beliefs
(creed) of any religion and causes change, revaluation of religious faith and
new interpretation.[518]   These lead to Reform, Revival, Renaissance or Revolt
movements.[519]   All these types of movements are present in one form or another
in Hinduism from the beginning of the nineteenth century to this day.[520]

b) Characteristics of Hindu Renaissance

Owing to a Renaissance, the Hindu population has become more conscious of itself
as Hindu; there is a remarkable increase in religious fervour in the great
religious centres.[521]   Urbanization has not diminished the hold of religion
on the masses but has made them more sensitive to injustice.[522]   Today,
Hinduism believes that it has a solution to world problems and therefore a
world message implying the failure of Christianity in this respect.[523]   Hindu
missionary activity is encouraged and a plea for peaceful coexistence without
mention of cooperation is made.[524]   Religious relativism, the belief that all religi
are the same and all lead to the same goal, is proclaimed as a dogma, with a view
to developing a sense of community and national coherence.[525]   One of the
significant traits of these movements is the effort made to relate culture and
creed, and to revive and defend or to restate and reinterpret the Hindu creed.[526]

c) Restatement and reinterpretation

Hindu leaders refuse to admit Christian influence on the reinterpretation[527]
of their beliefs but turn to their own scriptures especially the $G\bar{\imath}t\bar{a}$ for
scriptural authority and sanction.[528]   In interpreting the $G\bar{\imath}t\bar{a}$, Mahatma Gandhi
laid stress on activity.

"In particular," writes Devanandan, emphasis was on the validity of
active striving to realize an immediate end in present life which was

134

regarded as contributing to the welfare of all. In other words, the
struggle for independence, all organized endeavour and deliberate
action on the part of people to achieve the goal of freedom was
religiously justifiable."[529]

Radhakrishnan (1888-1975), a philosopher and a former President of India, denied
the illusory character of *māyā* and restated it as meaning that the world is
relatively real and *karma* as purposeful action to create a better future.[530]
Vivekananda "stressed the importance of *karmayoga*, purposeful action in the
world, as one thing needful for the regeneration of the political, social and
religious life of the Hindus."[531] Since the beginning of this Renaissance, there has
been emphasis on the worth of the human individual.[532] Social concern is justified on the religious grounds that God himself is concerned in battling against
evil.[533] Care for social welfare has developed a Hindu secular outlook.

d) Hindu secularism

Side by side with its religiousness, Hinduism had developed a secular outlook
and a concern for material things, as the existence of a school of thought
described as materialist *(lokāyata)* as early as the times of Buddha (sixth
century B.C.) demonstrates.[534] Devanandan writes about the same secular
concern:

"Although not fully worked out, there is profound insight in the traditional
Hindu understanding of religion as being fourfold, *caturvarga*. These four
ends of man are held to consist of righteous living, *dharma*; utilization
of material wealth for spiritual ends, *artha*: all‑round development of
the human person, *kāma*; and deliverance from the present to the ultimate
state of being, or *mokṣa*. Contemporary trends in the renascence of
religions in our world would seem to indicate that, however much we may
differ as men of faith on our various understanding of deliverance *(mokṣa)*,
we are all endeavouring to realize similar ends in the areas of *dharma,
artha*, and *kāma*."[535]

This is the traditional background of Hindu secularism. Some of the traits of modern Hindu secularism are:

"(i) Active interest in *world-life* in the here and now; in material
goods as contributing to the welfare of man; in directing current trends
in world affairs so that peace, security, and human solidarity may be
realized. (ii) A new understanding of the human person as related to
other persons in a way which ought to be so regulated that not only
individual men and women can find fulfilment, but also in such a manner
that a just order of society can be brought into being. (iii) A
consequent tendency to take a critical attitude towards religions in
general and towards traditional Hinduism in particular."[536]

But Indian secularism is not inimical to religion.[537] The Indian secular ideal
offers equal regard for all religions.[538] It is to this religiously renaissant
world which has developed a decidedly secular outlook that the Gospel is to be
communicated.

e) Evangelization[539]

Devanandan emphasized the fundamental missionary character of the Church,
the need for unity in Christian witness[540] and conceived evangelization as a cosmic
process, a historic reality, a divine undertaking, a people's movement and
community endeavour.[541] He describes the task of the Christian missionary:

"All this /the challenge of secularism/ will point to the fact that one of
the functions of the Christian evangelist in India is not so much to
counter forces of secularism and irreligion, but to help Hindus, in city
and village, at all levels of culture, to redefine the very nature of what
is called religion... It means that the preaching of the Gospel would not
only consist in the formulation of valid religious truths, but in the
endeavour to harness the forces of faith to creative action to fulfil God's
purpose."[542]

It is in this sense that Christianity has to help the Hindu to overcome his
limitations of Hindu understanding of man in society, to help him to reconcile

Hindu classical theology with the new anthropology,[543] work for national solidarity and integrated community,[544] and render disinterested services.[545] To be challenging and relevant, the proclamation of the Word to the Hindu has to be in terms of the new concepts of Secularism, Service, Personality and Community.[546] This should not give the impression that evangelization is reduced to the proclamation of a secular gospel. For Devanandan writes:

"Our task in missionary witness is necessarily of the nature of proclaiming this message of hope in our Lord, the communication of the Good News to be widely broadcast that in Jesus Christ God is reconciling the world to Himself."[547]

It is a witness to the activity of God in the world to transform the whole creation.[548]

f) New Creation

"Christian witness" writes Devanandan, "is to the reality of the New Creation in the Risen Christ, as the one determining factor in world history which gives it significance and meaning, despite the confusion and disorder produced by man's endeavour to divert its destiny towards ends of his own devices."[549]

In various contexts Devanandan developed his concept of New Creation. He writes:

"The Incarnation is the beginning of a new creation. This new life is offered to every man. The new world is already present here and now. The old order gives place to the new as world-life becomes increasingly God-centred and, to that extent,less and less man-centred."[550]

God is involved in the New Creation; He is redemptively at work in and through the very revolutionary context of life, directing the entire creation to the achievement of the new order; despite human perversity, God's will will eventually prevail.[551] The renaissance of religions, the Christian task in a secular world, and God's work in contemporary life call for dialogue.

g) Dialogue

The vital forces shaping the living and thinking of man in Asia and Africa

137

today are the renaissance of religons, secularism, unbelief and various forms
of belief.[552] However varied the beliefs in deliverance *(mokṣa)* may be, they
seem to be similar and converge in the areas of righteous living, ultilization
of material wealth and the full development of the human person.[553] Moreover,
Devanandan affirms that:

> "Christians are called to enter into a dialogue with men of other faiths
> for yet another reason. Only then can they enter with sympathetic under-
> standing into the real significance of the 'newness' in contemporary
> Hinduism, Buddhism and Islam."[554]

If dialogue is necessary with men of other faiths, it is no less needed among
the Christians themselves.

h) The Ecumenical Movement

It is the missionary movement which gave birth to the Ecumenical Movement.[555]
The realization that the confusion created by denominationalism is a serious
hindrance to evangelization led to geographical agreements (comity) among
Protestants.[556] The realization that comity perpetuated denominationalism and
fostered regionalism and the wastage in men and money led to the further step
of cooperation; from cooperation the next step was to unity, an example of
which is the organization of the Church of South India .[557] Ecumenism should
not be given a narrow ecclesiastical meaning of realizing the unity of the
Church, a meaning which restricts the mission of the Church, but that of
realizing a true community.[558] Any ecumenical approach has to take into
consideration cultural, national and religious diversities.[559]

i) An indigenous theology

Indigenization, observes Devanandan:

> "is not only a negative endeavour to rid the church of its foreigness, it
> is also a positive effort to make the church at home in its cultural
> environment. Discarding such foreign associations as music, architecture,
> church furnishing, and personnel do not by themselves make the church
> indigenous. A deliberate effort has to be made to relate the church to
> local culture, to reorient its ways of thought and life, and if need be,
> to repattern the structure of the local church so as to identify it with
> the traditional heritage of the land."[560]

It is not the faith of the Christian centred in the Gospel of Jesus Christ which
is made indigenous "but the people who are committed to the claims of that

138

Gospel and who want to witness to the truth of it in that very environment of which they form part."[561] About communicating the Gospel, Devanandan writes:

"Effective communication of the Gospel to the non-Christian man of faith depends on the effective use made of the religious vocabulary with which he is familiar, and of the cultural pattern of life in which he finds self-expression and community being. In our task of missionary preaching we have yet to take the dominant philosophical and religious concepts of the non-Christian faiths and make them into instruments of interpretation of the Gospel. This is undoubtedly a difficult process involving the denuding of their original connotation and a reclothing of them with the new meaning inherent in the Gospel.[562]

2.2.5.3 Appreciation

Devanandan has made a notable contribution in the domain of Christian witness in the actual context of the world. By analysing the renaissance of religions and social and political movements he tried to discern God's will in the existential situation and to enter into dialogue with religions and movements. He had done much to make progress in the field of evangelization, ecumenism, dialogue and an Indian theology.

Devanandan passed away rather unexpectedly before he could give full expression to his thought. Another Indian theologian, M. M. Thomas worked in the same trend of thought and developed it further.

2.2.6 Mamen Thomas Madathilparampil (*1916)

M. M. Thomas,[563] a member of the Mar Thoma Syrian Church of Malabar, a former Chairman of the Central Committee of the World Council of Churches, and the first layman to hold that post, and a Director 'emeritus' of the Christian Institute for the Study of Religion and Society, Bangalore, was born on 15th May, 1916 in Kerala, India. He had his higher education under the University of Madras and did his graduate study at the Union Semiary, New York.

Thomas began his professional life as a teacher and then organized and ran a Home for Waifs in Trivandrum City. His engagement in Christian youth and student movements brought him world experience. Thomas organized or served as speaker for World Christian Youth Conferences in Oslo (1947), Kottayam (1952) and Lausanne (1960). From 1947 until 1953, he was secretary and then vice-chairman of the World Student Christian Federation. During the 1950's, a series of ecumenical

study conferences on social questions in Asia, the first to be held in the
Asian continent, was organized by him. He presided over the World Conference
on Church and Society in Geneva in 1966. From 1968, Thomas began his work
in the World Council of Churches.

His theology is to be read in the context of his work on the staff of the
World Student's Christian Federation, in the Central Committee of the World
Council of Churches, in the East Asia Christian Conference and his contacts with
people of various faiths and ideologies in different parts of the world. The
principal theological concerns of M. M. Thomas seem to be dialogue with religions,
with the revolutionary ferment in the world and with secularism to evolve a
theology of Secular Humanism and thus make a contribution to the humanization of
the world. He pays special attention to the situation in India, the renaissance
of Hinduism, the search for a spiritual framework for Indian secularism and the
development of an Indian theology.

2.2.6.1 Dialogue with Religions

a) The context

The context of Thomas' theological reflection is the actual social, political
and international situation.[564] The difficult world situation, its creative and
destructive potentialities have brought all religious and secular faiths "into
a community of common concern and responsibility to build societies which
realise the highest quality of human life; and within this context, they are
also brought into meaningful dialogue with each other about the fundamentals of
their respective faiths."[565] Such a dialogue demands a common ground.

b) A common ground

The problems of human existence provide such a ground. Thomas states his
position on the issue:

"Our thesis is that dialogue among faiths at spiritual depth can best take
place in the modern world at the point where they are all grappling with
the spiritual self-understanding of modern man, and the problems of true
self-realisation or fulfilment of true humanity within modern existence."[566]

The depths of spiritual reality or religious experience cannot be a common

ground for an encounter of religions concerning problems of human existence
in the modern world; these problems and God-consciousness or religious
experience are not on the same level.[567] Hence anthropology provides a better
ground for a meeting of various religious traditions.

c) Types of religious traditions

Thomas distinguishes two types of religious consciousness – the messianic
vision of reality and the unitive vision of reality – in the religious traditions
of mankind corresponding to their understanding of the Holy or the Divine Ultimate.[568]
The Judaeo-Christian-Islamic traditions have a messianic vision of reality; they
give importance to history, revelation, the saving deeds of God and hold fast
to monotheism.[569] God acts through his prophets, the Messiah and his people to
achieve the purpose of creation and bring it to fulfilment.[570] In messianism
itself, there are two trends: the first is a national messianism of the
Conquering King; it leads to aggressiveness, intolerance, conflict and wars
among religious traditions and ideologies and tends to end in some form of
inhuman totalitarianism.[571] The second is the messianism of the Suffering
Servant which acts as a corrective to the first; it "is the path of the reinterpretation of the modern revolutionary forces and spirit within the framework of the
messianism of the suffering servant and faith in the cruciform humanity of Christ
as the ultimate destiny of mankind."[572]

The religious traditions of African, Indian and Chinese origin have a unitive
vision of reality and see salvation in the realization of a spiritual unity or
harmony of nature, man, spirits and gods which admits no distinction or differ-
entiation whatever.[573] This vision of reality is thought of as a corrective to
the messianism of conquest and as

"a means to moderate and slow down the movements of human creativity and
historical dynamism which bring anxiety, aggressiveness and self-destructivity
in their train, and bring spiritual tranquility to the restless spirit of

modernised man."[574]

Thomas does not seem to agree with this view. He writes:

"However, our thesis is that the universe of unitive faiths is today
being brought into the 'anthropological' and 'theological' circle
of messianic faiths in a radical way."[575]

These two visions of reality, the problems posed by them and the need for a
synthesis render intra-faith and inter-faith dialogues integral to man's
struggles for a new quality of life.[576]

d) The African dialogue

Africa is giving due thought to the new anthropology; she is striving
hard to develop a new humanism by discovering the distinctive African
characteristics and vision of reality which will be her contribution to the
world community.[577] Thomas comments on this issue:

"Of course, both the traditional anthropology and the new anthropology need
to be interpreted in the light of the centrality of the life, death and
resurrection of the New Man Jesus Christ, if African Christianity is to
become indigenous to the modern Africa oriented to the Future."[578]

Such will be Christianity's contribution to a dialogue with Africa.

e) Dialogue with Buddhism[579]

Resurgent Buddhism, in reaction to the theocratic messianism of
Christianity, has acquired a certain militancy; it had not always been faithful
to its mission of love and service to humanity; in this case Christians have
to acknowledge their responsibility and repent.[579a] In a Buddhist environment,
the message of Jesus Christ may be presented as the historical actualization of
the ideal *bodhisattva*.[580] This involves the danger of minimizing the real differences in the meaning and content of the categories used.[581] But the need
for a common language for inter-faith dialogue on fundamental differences and for
greater appreciation of each other's faith may justify such a step.[582]

f) Dialogue with Islam

Islam, under the impact of modernity, is also facing the problem of relating itself to modern anthropology and is also attempting to make a reinterpretation of some of its tenets.[583] The progress of secularization, modernity and the need for a relativization of all religions including Islam in order to acknowledge a positive relationship between religions and modern secularity could provide a ground for dialogue between Christianity and Islam.[584]

The problems posed by the spirit of modernity and modern revolutionary impulses and the consequent need to provide a spiritual foundation for the struggles of modern man have brought about a renaissance of religions;[585] Hinduism is no exception to this; renaissance movements are at work in Hinduism.

2.2.6.2 Hindu Renaissance and Christ

a) Types of Hindu Renaissance

Thomas studies more systematically and in more detail the Renaissance of Hinduism than did Devanandan.[586] He distinguishes two types of Hindu Renaissance; one tries to understand Christ within the framework of Hindu theism with great concern for the moral regeneration of Indian society; Rammohan Roy and Mahatma Gandhi may be considered two representatives of this group.[587] The other tries to understand Christ, Christianity and its ethics within the metaphysical framework of the advaita; Vivekananda and Sarvepally Radhakrishnan, the Hindu philosopher and a former President of India, are two representatives of this group.[588] The approaches of these two groups to Christianity have raised various christological problems.

b) Indifference to the historical Jesus

Vivekananda and Mahatma Gandhi were indifferent to the historical Jesus. Vivekananda held that Vedanta alone, based as it is on the solid, eternal, impersonal principle, could become a universal religion; religions based on the unstable grounds of the historicity of a person could not be universal.[590]

143

He took the historicity of Jesus and his personality for accidents and not as essential.[591] Radhakrishnan interpreted the birth, passion, death and resurrection of Christ not so much as historical facts but as the processes of spiritual life.[592]

c) The historical fact of Jesus

The indifference to the historical Jesus evident in the works of Hindu author makes Thomas stress the historical fact of Jesus:

"The historical fact of Jesus of Nazareth and his significance as God's saving act for men are held together and cannot be separated in the fundamental core of the Christian *kerygma*."[593]

A very important task of the theology of mission "is to restate the significance of the historicity of the Person of Jesus within the essential core of the Christian message."[594] There is ample reason for doing so:

"It is only if a historical event belongs to the essence of the Christian Gospel that historical human existence can acquire a positive relation to our eternal salvation. And certainly the Christian mission which proclaims a historical person, and not merely a principle, as the bearer of salvation for all mankind, stands or falls with the person it proclaims."[595]

The crucial problem of the theology of mission "is the reality of the resurrection of the crucified Jesus."[596] In this reality, three integrally related components may be distinguished:

"Firstly, the bodily resurrection of Jesus as happening in secular history.. The question whether the ultimate spiritual destiny of man involves a redemption and consummation of his history is ultimately based on the resurrection of Jesus being a bodily one-being a *happenedness* with some deposit in the chronological history, and not only in some primal salvation history known only to God or faith or only in the history of the internal soul of individual believers. And in a sense, therefore, the *happenedness* is subject to historical research and in a way dependent upon it.

144

Secondly, the resurrection of Jesus does not acquire any studpendous

significance for the world and world mission unless it is seen as the

unique act of God for the salvation of man."[597]

The resurrection of Jesus Christ transcends the acceptance or the rejection of

man; it is an independent reality "and it will lose its reality if it is

reduced to a subjective self-understanding of man."[597a]

The resurrection of Jesus is discerned through faith. In the words of

Thomas:

"Thirdly one should add that the faith of men in the work of the Holy

Spirit alone can discern it and appropriate it for themselves and their

societies."[598]

Certain consequences follow from the points just mentioned: God did intervene

in secular history; His intervention was a unique divine act of salvation. By

His saving intervention in history, He gave meaning and value to secular history

and human existence. Human existence is not an illusory, unrelated existence but

an existence directed to salvation. The acceptance of the historical Jesus has

great significance in the Indian context, as shown below.

d) Relevance

In the actual context, this historicity is very relevant:

"Secular historicity, its significance as the divine act of salvation in

history, and the faith-response of a historical community – the combination

of these three in the scheme of salvation which the Church proclaims is

relevant to Hinduism at this stage of its life, when Hinduism is seeking an

idea of salvation which does not negate but comprehends and fulfils human

personality and history."[599]

The affirmation of the historicity of the person of Jesus and its relevance to

the Indian situation pose the question of principle and person which is an

important issue in India.

145

e) Principle and person

Rammohan Roy emphasized the value of the moral teachings of Jesus and
Mahatma Gandhi that of the Sermon on the Mount,[600] but both disregarded the
Person of Jesus thus separating the principle from the person. Thomas remarks
that three things are to be clarified from the principle itself:

"First, that the principle is never self-validated, and negates itself
when considered as standing on its own. Second, that when the principle
is made autonomous and self-sufficient, the spirit of self-righteousness
makes it impossible of fulfilment and introduces contradiction and tragedy
in the very movement towards moral regeneration. Third, that the ultimate
validity and fulfilment of the principle posits a realm of transcendence
within the principle itself, and it is necessary to explore the nature of
the origin and goal of this realm."[601]

The principle has to lead to the person from whom it takes its origin. But
Indian leaders as pointed out above disregard the Person of Jesus and give
greater attention to moral principles. They show great concern for morality and
ethics.

f) Morality and ethics

Indian leaders like Jawaharlal Nehru (1889-1964), the first Prime Minister
of India, and Jayaprakash Narayan, (*1902), a Sarvodaya[602] leader, have been
concerned about morality and ethics. Nehru sought to find a spiritual framework
to make secularism subservient to humanism;[603] Jayaprakash believes that the
root of morality lies in the endeavour of man to realize the unity of existence.[60]
Asok Mehta (*1911), an Indian socialist leader, said that man's deepest responses
are to absolute ethic.[605] In examining the relation between dogmatics and ethics,
Thomas says:

"Ethics deals with willing and doing, with the response of faith to the
moral responsibilities of individual and social existence in the world of
men within the context of historical situations. It is faith expressing

146

itself in love."[606]

He comments on Rammohan Roy's idea of unity between Jesus and God as one of
will and design and asks whether it was possible for him to go beyond it and
answers:

"But if it /going beyond/ ever came, it could come only by digging into the
nature of morality and God and their relation in terms essentially of love.
This would have meant a new vision of the centrality of the Cross of Jesus
Christ, at least as the symbol of God in the midst of mankind, and probably
leading to a fuller faith in Jesus as God's self-disclosure to man.[607]

g) The centrality of Jesus Christ and the Cross

Thomas has insisted very much on the centrality of the Person of Jesus
Christ and the cross. What we have seen so far bears witness to a christo-
centric approach. In this approach the cross occupies a very important place.
Thomas writes:

"The Cross, or the self-emptying redemptive love of God revealed in
Jesus has been the central dynamic of all history."[608]

He finds the reconciliation of religions in the preaching of the Cross and
acknowledges the theological validity of attempts to express the Cross in terms
of indigenous religious traditions other than Christian.[609] Thus it seems to
us that Thomas sees in Jesus Christ and the Cross the solution to the issues
confronting Hindu Renaissance. Contemporaneous with the Hindu Renaissance is the
development of Indian secularism.

2.2.6.3 Indian Secularism[610]

a) Spiritual elements in Indian liberalism

Thomas studies the characteristics of Indian liberalism.[611] Then he traces
some of the spiritual elements in its outlook. The teleological interpretation
of Indian history using the category of Providence by liberal leaders whether
they be atheists, agnostics or theists and the emphasis on the moral

responsibility of the present generation are some such elements.[612]   In this
they were influenced by the Bible:

"In fact, the references by Indian liberals to the choice, the preservance
and the disciplining of the Jews by God for their mission as a parallel
to God's choice of India point clearly to the direct influence of
Biblical thought on the liberal thinkers."[613]

Christianity helped to strengthen and correct Indian liberalism:

"It presented Jesus as the prototype of the new humanity, and on the whole
Indian liberals made the character of Jesus their own human ideal, and
made it part of their scheme of values for a regenerated India."[614]

Liberalism had too optimistic a conception of human nature; such optimism
made them put too much trust in British power; they believed that British
power could be made subservient to the interests of the Indian nation by appealing
through constitutional agitation to British reason and conscience; in this they
did not pay sufficient attention to the evil tendency in human nature which
rejects morality or accomodates it to power and politics as happened in the
case of British power in India. A remedy to this optimism of the Indian liberals
is the Christian sense of sin which lends itself to no facile optimism and the
Christian consciousness of the need for divine forgiveness.[615]   The Cross of
Jesus has a relevance as a corrective to the Indian liberal theists' belief that
deliverance can be achieved by personal effort.[616]   Thomas affirms:

"For Christian orthodoxy, the Cross is the revelation not only of the
Divine Humanity of Jesus, as the goal of history, but also of the
spiritual evil which is present in the best of human institutions of
religion, society and state leading to their rejection of that goal and
revealing the need of their redemption by God's initiative."[617]

In a similar way he examines Socialist Humanism,[618] Marxism – Leninism,[619]
Anti-Brahminism,[620] and the ideologies of three among the Indian leaders,[621]
Subhas Chandra Bose (1897-1945?), M. N. Roy (1887-1954) and M. R. Masani (*1905).

148

By way of conclusion, theological insights for a secular anthropology are
proposed.

b) A thesis

Thomas proposes his basic thesis:

"Every theology has an anthropological content inherent in it or derivable
from it; and every anthropology is based on theological presuppositions
either explicitly or implicitly. By theology I mean the intellectual
articulation of man's faith in God or in a structure of meaning and
sacredness which is seen as his ultime destiny. And by anthropology I
mean, in its broad sense, the understanding of the nature of man and his
relation to nature, social culture and history."[622]

The Bible is emphatic on doing the will of God; God's will is accomplished in the
historical realm; liberation from every form of alienation and the achievement
of a righteous society and unity of mankind are to be realized by man according
to God's will; the resurrection of Jesus is the guarantee of the final victory
of God over evil and the transformation of "the Kingdoms of this world into the
Kingdom of God and His Christ."[623] Every form of dehumanizing Secular Humanism
is rejected by the Bible but :

"a Secular Humanism which affirms humanisation of nature, creativity of man in
purposive history, liberation from social bondage and realisation of love in
human relation as the promise and potentiality of mankind in every historical
situation and which struggles to realise them within the limits and possilities
of the situation is integral to the faith and hope of the Christian gospel."[624]

Thomas suggests some elements of Christian theological understanding of man
which could serve to construct "a realistic Secular ideology of Social Humanism."[625]

The first element is *the reality of man as created in the image of God*"
(Gn. 1. 26, 27) as "finite spiritual freedom," with an awareness of
his ability to transcend himself through the excercise of creativity and
responsibility; it implies that "the reality of man, human society and human
history cannot be interpreted in purely naturalistic or purely spiritual terms."[626]

149

The idea of man as the crown of creation which inspires a sense of mystery about his personhood is at the basis of the modern demand for the recognition of the fundamental rights of man.[627]

The second valuable Christian insight is *"the reality of man as a fallen creature."*[628] Man wants to be absolute like God (Gn 3.5) with the consequence of "total alienation from God, neighbour, nature and oneself."[629]

"In secular language" says Thomas, "one might speak of the fall as the innate tendency of individuals and groups for self-love and self-centredness leading to search for power over others. Since this is doing violence to the reality of self and its relation to God and neighbour, it results in self-alienation in the spirit of man."[630]

Man tries to hide his self-love by self-justification through such means as legal morality and utopias; this desire to conceal his self-love shows that he is aware of his self-alienation; in the Christian understanding, this self-alienation affects the whole of human existence and history.[631] This does not mean any kind of equal predetermination:

"What it points to is the fact that every good of man has the potentiality of self-righteousness in it, that every creativity of man has the spirit of destructivity inherent in it, that while man's reason and conscience reflect the imperative of truth and goodness they are also conditioned by the false purposes of the self which they serve."[632]

The third is *"The reality of the Crucified and Risen Jesus Christ* as the true man and as the source of renewal of human nature and through it of all things."[633] The basis of this Christian understanding is the Incarnation of God in human existence tainted with self-centredness.[634] Thomas draws the consequence of Incarnation:

"Jesus Christ crucified and risen is therefore both the proptotype of true manhood in history and the source of ultimate humanisation of human nature and mankind."[635]

The true nature of man is understood only in the light of Jesus Christ; the Cross of Jesus frees man from the need for self-justification; Divine Forgiveness offers security and frees man from the need for such particularisms as caste, race and ideology to justify himself; all such distinctions are transcended through the consciousness of solidarity with all mankind and participation in the new humanity of Christ; and the nucleus of this communion is the Church of Christ confessing Jesus as the Lord.[636] Thomas argues:

"In secular anthropological terms this faith in human
salvation through God in Christ means the recognition of the ultimacy of
the pattern of Jesus' humanity for existence, that a life of mutual self-
giving love is the criterion and goal of mature manhood and human
community. It is also necessary to recognise that this goal transcends
human organisation and planning, ideology and politics; it is the sphere
of voluntary spiritual responses of faith."[637]

The fourth element is *"the reality of man and society in the light of the
consummation of their Absolute future in the Kingdom of God."*[638] This is
Christian hope based on the power of the Holy Spirit to renew and transform the
whole creation; it is an eschatological hope, a hope in the future of mankind,
in the future of the risen Jesus Christ.[639] Thomas explains its secular
meaning:

"The secular meaning of these eschatological affirmations of theology for
anthropology lies in the affirmation in history of a Reality, a Providence,
a Presence which transcends the resources of nature and the purposes of man,
which ultimately determines their Future, and which is available in every
Present to humanise nature, man and society, even when or precisely when,
objective social conditions and subjective human wills give no hope. It
is a Human Hope which can comprehend within itself and grapple with
tragedy as the outcome of the historical process as a whole, and of every
historical situation."[640]

151

This historical process which tends to eschatological fulfilment is achieved through radical transformation as in the case of the Incarnation or the resurrection.[641] Thomas concludes:

"The meaning of every historical action directed to love and justice in history and every fragmentary realization of truth, goodness and beauty in life, is protected, redeemed and fulfilled in the End. How, we do not know. But our guarantee is the Risen Jesus Christ.[642]

Written within the context of Indian secular ideologies, it may be seen as an Indian theological approach to secularism. Certain orientations which Thomas would like to give to the development of an Indian theology are already evident in his theological approach which we have discussed so far.[643] To have a more detailed view, a few more points may be added.

2.2.6.4 Orientations for an Indian theology

a) Humanism, a ground for dialogue

Thomas believes that a rethinking of Christian theology is necessary in India. He writes:

"Some of the fundamentals of Christian theology are to be thought afresh in the light of their relevance to the issues which contemporary Hindu theology is facing. In so doing, the common Christian and Hindu concern for a spiritual basis for true humanisation is the most fruitful reference which can illumine the theological dialogue at depth between Hinduism and Christianity."[644]

The importance which Abhisktananda and Cuttat attach to an encounter between religions at the level of advaitic vision and mystic experience of the ultimate Reality is rather exaggerated; it would be valid only if Divinism, and not humanism, is the valid ground for a meeting of religions.[645] By this statement Thomas minimizes the importance of mystic experience as a ground for the encounter of religions. There is a danger in the mystic approach:

"The peril inherent in all mystic consciousness is that it tends
increasingly to isolate itself from society, and to revert back into
an experience of undifferentiated consciousness which cannot make
moral distinctions. The dialogue should help make spirituality more
relevantly social and moral.

Nevertheless it is not the ontic Christ or the mystic Christ but the
historical Jesus who has made the deepest impact on Hinduism."[646]

It is evident that Thomas stresses humanism as the valid ground for an encounter
of religions. Humanism and secular realities are subject to change and evolution
when they come into contact with cultures; there is need for something stable and
permanent.

b) The changeless core

The social, secular and human aspects of theology may be spoken of as its
changing or situational aspects. But Thomas is aware of the changeless aspects
of theology.[647] The changeless is "the unchanging core of Christian dogma."[648]
This raises the issue of the contact of the changeless core of Christian dogma with
different cultures:

"The creeds and the historical confessions and the teaching authority of
the Church are safe guards against heresy in the reformulation of Christian
faith. But it sometimes amounts to absolutization of the tradition and
assumes that the Church already knows the full 'substance' of the Gospel,
and that no new theological truth can emerge in the encounter of the
Gospel with new cultures and situations."[649]

In this encounter with new cultures, pre-understanding of terms can play a role.

c) Pre-understanding

The witness or the hearer of the Gospel has an earlier pre-Christian
understanding of terms and categories in his culture which may be used to convey
the message.[650] This pre-understanding has only an ancillary function;

existing concepts familiar to a group are employed, the meaning or pre-understanding of which develops as the interpretation develops.[651] Here Thomas seems to be justifying the use of Indian categories. For he comes out against those who criticize the use of non-biblical ideas in theology.

"Where metaphysics is a matter of existential importance, it cannot be dismissed as an exercise in speculation; and faith must find ways of speaking of Jesus Christ and his salvation in metaphysical fashion."[652]

But there is danger in the use of metaphysical thought patterns as normative and not as ancillary and he proposes a remedy:

"The answer to the danger therefore lies in learning to speak of Christ in terms of pre-understanding, and in that process to transform and develop those patterns themselves, bringing them into dialogue with the Gospel of Jesus Christ along with its biblical background."[653]

Thomas is of the opinion that certain non-biblical categories /no examples are given by Thomas here/ could be "very meaningful vehicles for the Gospel in certai contemporary situations."[654] In the light of various considerations he made, he proposes certain criteria for a living theology.[655]

d) An important criterion

Of the criteria Thomas proposes, the following seems to express his fundamental thought. It runs:

"The content of living theology is the discernment of what God-in-Christ is doing in the situation and the interpretation of the truth and meaning of Jesus Christ in terms of the situation and its self-understanding."[656]

2.2.6.5 Appreciation

The concern of Thomas to offer a theology which is relevant to the times is in itself a contribution. His emphasis on the historical fact of Jesus, on activity, his effort to give a theological basis to secularism, his concern for anthropology, humanization, ethics, morality, religious and secular fellowship are very valuable in the Indian context. The emphasis on activity and an anthropological approach is to be balanced by a concern for religious experience which is also a valuable ground for the meeting of religions.

The main context of the theology of Thomas is Hindu Renaissance and secularism in India. Another theologian, S. J. Samartha, proposed a christological approach in the context of advaita.

154

2.2.7 Stanley J. Samartha (*1920)

Stanley J. Samartha was born on the 7th of October, 1920 in Karkal, India.[657]
He was educated at the University of Madras and at the United Theological College,
Bangalore and then did post-graduate work at Union Theological Seminary, New
York City, Hartford Seminary and at the University of Basel, Switzerland.

Samartha, an ordained minister of the Church of South India, was Principal
of Basel Mission's Theological Seminary, Mangalore from 1952-1960. From 1960-
1965, he was Professor at the United Theological College, Bangalore and then
Principal of Serampore College in West Bengal. From 1968, Samartha has been working with the World Council of Churches and is at present Director of the World
Council of Churches' programme of dialogue with living faiths and ideologies.

Samartha's theology is to be seen in the context of his wide contacts with
people of living faiths and ideologies, and against the background of his
dialogue with them.

2.2.7.1 A Christological Approach

a) A relevant christology

The present age is an age of science; it does not always recognize the
relevance of religious values to helping man solve modern problems.[658] Though
secularization is advancing, it has not overcome religion which continues to
influence the life of millions of people.[659] Men are seeking   answers to modern
problems from a variety of faiths, varying from traditional religions and their
reinterpretations to militant atheistic ideologies.[660] This expectation of a
solution to modern problems from religions shows their relevance. To make the
Gospel challengingly relevant to the times, a restatement is necessary; in this
the primacy of Christ is very important as it has always been fundamental to the
Christian faith.[661] Samartha writes on this issue:

> "The important question now is: what does it mean today to affirm that Jesus
> Christ is Lord and Saviour? Therefore, both the credibility of the Saviour
> and the content of salvation he offers are involved in the question of the
> primacy of Jesus Christ to Christian life and witness."[662]

The answer to this problem, a relevant christology, is the task of the Church in
every country; it is not a mere conceptualization of the faith; the total
human response to Christ is to be taken into consideration.[663]

b) Varieties of response

Samartha distinguishes three kinds of responses to Christ to which he adds

a fourth of a different kind. The first is "response to Christ *without*
commitment to him."[664] This is the general attitude of Hindu thinkers like
Rammohan Roy and Mahatma Gandhi who accept the moral teachings of Christ but
ignore the Church.[665] The second is "response *and* commitment to Christ, and
Christ alone, *within* the context of Hinduism itself, but with either indifference
to or to a total *rejection* of the Church."[666] An example of this type of
commitment is found in Kalagora Subba Rao (*1912) of Andhra Pradesh.[667] The
third is "response and commitment to Christ *and* an open entry into the Church
through *baptism*, but with strong criticism of the Church from *within* its
fellowship."[668] Chakkarai and Chenchiah belong to this category.[669] The
fourth, though it does not go methodologically with the others, cannot be
ignored; it is "the effort to discover the *hidden* Christ within Hinduism itself
and to unveil him, even though there is no conscious, visible response to him."[670]
Panikkar's book *The Unknown Christ of Hinduism* is an example of this.[671] It is
in the context of these Christ-experiences and responses to Christ that
Samartha proposes an advaitic approach to an Indian Christology.

c) Preference for advaita

Various reasons make Samartha to use advaita as a framework for christology.
Advaita is the best known and outstanding Indian philosophical system; a
number of leading men in India are influenced by modern interpretations of advaita;
a great effort is made to reinterpret advaita to suit contemporary India.[672]
Another reason is that "the very approach of Śankara to ultimate questions of
   human destiny is one in which all those who are seriously concerned with
   the problems of life might whole-heartedly agree. Śankara demands from
   his pupils a spirit of detachment which includes spiritual, intellectual
   and physical discipline."[673] After giving these reasons, Samartha explains
what he proposes to do:

"What is attempted here is neither to start from the Hindu categories and
   describe Jesus Christ as the great *advaitin* nor to start from within
   Christianity and, by a devious route, discover him within the Hindu
   scriptures. It is a preliminary attempt to express the meaning of the
   Church's faith in Jesus Christ as Lord and Saviour, making use of the
   classical and modern concepts of one of the most reputed and influential
   systems in Hinduism which belongs to the heritage of the whole of India."[674]

156

In the context of India, especially in an advaitic context, "the historical anchorage of the Christian faith must be strongly emphasised."[675]

d) Importance of the historical

Christology has to do a great service to India; India "is struggling to find the meaning of the historical in the midst of its spirituality."[676] Hence christology has to draw out "the implications of the Christian faith in Jesus Christ to man's historical existence."[677] Samartha affirms:

> "This is true particularly in the context of *advaita* where the ontological and the mystical meet in the self-realisation of the individual without relating this private sphere of spirituality to nature on the one hand and society on the other."[678]

As a consequence:

> "The *historicity* of Jesus Christ and therefore, the *historic* nature of the Christian faith are particularly important for Christology in India."[679]

e) Significance of history

Though historicity is important, the real question is not about the historical figure of Jesus Christ which is recognized as the authentic basis of Christianity.[680] "The real issue," writes Samartha, "concerns the *status* of history itself as the totality of events determind by human decisions."[681]

History itself is given a new significance in God's self-revelation of love, compassion and concern for mankind in the life, death and resurrection of Jesus Christ; history, therefore, cannot be discarded as transient or illus   or relegated to the simple realm of Becoming.[682] Man is historical; he is part of nature but he can rise above it; he takes part in history by involving himself in the flux of things; his deeds and decisions exercised in freedom by a part of nature and a member of society constitute history; consequently, the truly historical has a social dimension.[683] A christology cannot exclude this social dimension and cannot be built on the bare fact of Jesus Christ.[684]

Samartha writes:

> "It is pointed out that at the very core of the early Church there was a
> threefold impression of Jesus Christ: he was a historical person who was
> remembered; he was a person still known as a living reality by the members
> of the group; and he was a person about whom certain theological convictions
> were held... it was in the community of faith that the meaning of the
> Christ – event became significant."[685]

There is an objection to these three impressions: they form a subjective
interpretation of a historical fact. This poses the problem of the objective
reality of Christ.[686]

f) The objective reality

The fact of Christ cannot be reduced to a mere subjective reality; though
there are theological reflections in the NT, it is not possible to ignore
the elements of personal confrontation with Christ and "the original confrontation
has certain power and intensity which should be respected."[687] Subjective
acceptance and participation in the significance of the historical event render
it meaningful.[688] In the context of India's growing sense of history,

> "It is necessary for the Church also to acknowledge and to participate
> in the Christ-event so that the meaning of the incarnation might manifest
> in the Church's life with renewed power. Here subjectivity cannot be
> regarded as a distortion of reality but as an attempt to penetrate that
> aspect of reality which manifests itself in subjective forms."[689]

These efforts cannot exhaust the mystery of Christ and as a consequence it is
necessary to make use of ontological terms in formulating a christology but
"the characteristic shape of Christology has to be historical, not ontological."[690]
Three elements are basic in a christology, the ontological status of Christ, his
relation to mystic consciousness and the historic anchorage of the fact of Christ.

2.2.7.2 Christology in the Context of Advaita

a) A complementary understanding of reality

The *Upaniṣads* search for reality, the ultimate ground of Being where
multiplicity gives way to unity.[692] This search culminates in realization:

"The Ultimate is realized as the intimate and the intimate is
acknowledged as the Ultimate."[693]

This quest for reality which culminates in the doctrine of *brahman-ātman* has
two drawbacks:

"The first is this. The quest for the ground of being culminating in
brahman results in minimising the significance of the world of *history*
Secondly, in its search for the essential nature of man culminating in the
ātman, there is a devaluation of the human *personality*. These two together
in their mutual influence and inter-action have contributed to the shaping
of a particular outlook of classical *advaita* which has a tendency to
ignore the *social* dimension of human life."[694]

The correctives to it are "the insights of the Christian faith in Jesus Christ
as Lord and Saviour /which/ would help in recovering the sense of the
the personal, the historical and social in the structure of Hindu spirituality."[695]
Reciprocally, the advaitic vision of the unity of life will serve as a corrective
to a onesided historical interpretation of God's revelation isolating it from
nature and human consciousness to Protestant emphasis on 'personal ego' leading
to fear of interiority and mystical experience.[696] Thus an ontological understanding of the Ultimate has to be related to historical and social dimensions and
the historical event of God's revelation has to be seen in the unity of the cosmic
process.[697]

b) The nature of the Ultimate

A few statements of the *Upaniṣads* and some expositions of Śankara tend to deny
that personal values are compatible with *brahman*; to term *brahman* as impersonal

is misleading.[698]   For Samartha writes:

> "*Upaniṣads* describe the *brahman* sometimes as *nirguṇa* (without qualities)
> and sometimes as *saguṇa* (with qualities). A careful examination of the
> verses in their particular contexts suggests that they do not refer to
> two separate beings or to two different levels of reality but to one and
> the same Reality *viz.*, the *brahman*. These two descriptions are simply
> 'poises of the same Being,' the one in repose and the other in activity,
> the one understood in itself and the other in relation to the world.
> Śankara's point about *parā* (transcendental) and *aparā* (phenomenal)
> reality should not be understood as higher and lower in the ontological
> sense but merely as different ways of looking at the same Being. The
> very fact that, even while pointing out that *brahman* is 'not this, not
> this', the *Upaniṣads* still venture to describe Him as *sat-cit-ānanda*
> (Truth, Consciousness and Joy), indicates that the *brahman* is not devoid
> of all values."[699]

The discussion on the nature of *brahman* cannot ignore the problem of the world.

c) *Brahman* and the world

The world is described as *māyā* in the advaita system; one interpretation
is that *māyā* stands for pure illusion and express the unreality of the world;
some of Śankara's statements may be interpreted in this way.[700]

> "But it should be remembered (writes Samartha) that such statements occur
> in contexts where the world is compared to the *brahman*, the point being
> that since *brahman* alone is *advitīya*, one without a second, everything
> else must be regarded as *māyā* in the sense of having no absolute reality
> but only a dependent or derived status. The ontological status of the
> world cannot be *sat* (Being), that of the *brahman*; neither can it be *asat*
> (non-being). It is this inbetween character of the world that is being
> described by the term *māyā*,..."[701]

He affirms that "Christology can make a genuine contribution in the context
of *advaita* as it grapples with the meaning of the cosmos that includes

nature and history in the totality of its scheme."[702]

It is important to affirm that "in Christ the world of nature and history is

created, redeemed and sustained and, in God's grace, is being directed

to its final consummation."[703]

On the interpretation of $\bar{maya}$ depends the exposition of the nature of the
Incarnation of Christ.

d) The nature of Christ

A discussion on the theory of two natures in Christ or how his divinity is seen
in and through his humanity may not throw much light. Samartna writes, therefore, that

"It is more important to ask what is the Reality

that one encounters in Jesus of Nazareth as the living and risen Lord, in

the totality of his life, death and resurrection, and how, through him,

a renewal of human life is possible."[704]

It is not possible to apply the doctrine of the identity of $\bar{atman}$ with $brahman$
to Christ; it risks a certain depersonalization of man.[705] So the problem of
the divinity of Christ remains. Though some of the NT texts are liable to an
interpretation of Christ as subordinate to the Father, the same reality is
designated by the term 'God our Father' and by 'Our Lord Jesus Christ.'"[706]
Samartha cautions against a facile equation of Jesus of Nazareth with God
Almighty, of giving the impression of having a comprehensive knowledge of the
inexhaustible depths of God, against eliminating the sense of mystery and depth
in God.[707] Thus the divinity of Christ is to be affirmed in the context of the
inexhaustibility of the mystery of God. The mystery of Christ is to be seen
also in the context of the salvation which he offers.

e) Salvation

The advaita sees salvation as liberation from the law of $karma\text{-}sams\bar{a}ra$;
according to this doctrine, the good or bad actions of a man produce good or
bad results respectively and cause a chain of births and rebirths; salvation
here is return to the original perfection.[708] Samartha points out certain
categories such as the freedom and responsibility of the individual personality
and the social and historical dimensions of the human life which do not receive

sufficient attention in this scheme.[709] He observes:

> "It is in this context that one ventures to suggest that the cross and
> the resurrection of Christ manifest the power to overcome evil and
> tragedy in human life and the hope of reaching a consummation which is
> not a return to the old but a bringing in of the new."[710]

Salvation in Christ should not be given a too individualistic interpretation;
the advaita emphasis on the unity of all life could be a remedy to it.[711]

The NT scheme of salvation culminating in the death and resurrection
of Christ has three emphases, namely, that the suffering and death of Christ
was voluntary, vicarious and victorious.[712] This is relevant today:

> "The cross and resurrection of Christ, taken together, far from being
> irrelevant to human need, today provide the inspiration and power to a
> life of worship and service, of suffering and victory."[713]

The reconciliation and salvation extends to the cosmos itself; in modern Hindu
thought, there is a lot of discussion on the consummation of the cosmic process;
this consummation is not a return to the beginning but an enrichment and
fulfilment in God Himself.[714] In this context Samartha writes:

> "This affirmation of the lordship of the crucified and risen Christ
> over all life does not involve any exclusiveness. On the contrary, it
> is the declaration of the universality of the unbound Christ."[715]

This universality of Christ, his being at home in every culture, is an appeal
to dialogue with faiths and ideologies.

2.2.7.3 Dialogue

a) Certain aspects of dialogue

Dialogue is a major Christian concern; today there is great interest in
inter-religious dialogues.[716] It is not a mere discussion on religious subjects
or theological concepts only:

> "It is a meeting of persons, an encounter between people within the total

life of the community, where words and actions, and the relationship
between people of different religious or ideological persuasions, are
very much influenced by the perspectives of faith, whether or not these
are openly articulated."[717]

In another article, Samartha gives the following view of dialogue:

"Dialogue is part of the living relationship between people of different
faiths and ideologies as they share in the life of the community."[718]

Dialogue as a living relationship, a conversation between people of various faiths
and ideologies, need not necessarily be a religious concern. This raises the
question: Is it a purely human enterprise or has it any scriptural foundation?

b) Theological basis

The word 'dialogue' itself is not found in the Bible; all the same,
God's relationship with the patriarchs, the leaders and people of Israel implies
dialogue; in the NT Christ's dealing with Nicodemus, the Samaritan woman and
his disciples, show that dialogue is not contrary to its spirit.[719] Samartha
gives three theological reasons to justify dialogue as a continuing Christian
concern:

First, God in Jesus Christ has himself entered into relationship with men
of all faiths and all ages, offering the good news of salvation. The
incarnation is God's dialogue with men. To be in dialogue is, therefore,
to be part of God's continuing work among us and our fellowmen. Second,
the offer of a true community inherent in the Gospel, through forgiveness,
reconciliation and a new creation, and of which the Church is a sign and a
symbol, inevitably leads to dialogue. The freedom and love which Christ
offers constrain us to be in fellowship with strangers so that all may
become fellow citizens in the household of God. Third, there is the
promise of Jesus Christ that the Holy Spirit will lead us into all truth.
Since truth, in the Biblical understanding, is not propositional but
relational, and is to be sought, not in the isolation of lonely meditation,

but in the living, personal confrontation between God and man, and men and men, dialogue becomes one of the means of the quest for truth. And, because Christians cannot claim to have a monopoly of truth, we need to meet men of other faiths and ideologies as part of our trust in and obedience to the promise of Christ."[720]

c) The problem of truth

Dialogue cannot ignore the issue of truth. A mere conceptual approach to truth is not helpful; it is not possible to express in clear-cut, logical, self-evident formulas religious truth and its symbolic nature and then compare them with similar propositions of other religions; in the past one dominant culture-conditioned definition and criterion of truth prevailed; the fundamental differences in the conception of the mystery of human existence influenced the understanding or experience of truth.[721] About this issue Samartha writes:

"In the Biblical tradition 'doing' the Truth or 'obeying' the Truth is as important as responding to revealed Truth in history. To some Hindu thinkers, however, to whom inwardness of religion is important, Truth is more a state of being than an experience of cognition. *Brahman* is *sat*, Being, and at the same time *satyam*, Truth. To Christians, their faith in Jesus Christ raises not only the question of 'knowing' him *now* and of the nature of historical knowledge but also the relation of these to the 'truth claims' of people of other faiths."[722]

Without subscribing to any facile syncretism, Christianity and the religious traditions of mankind have to grapple with the problem of truth in the context of dialogue.

d) The problem of syncretism

The fear of syncretism haunts the minds of some people when confronted with dialogue.[723] Samartha says:

"Syncretism is an uncritical mixture of different religions. It leads to spiritual impoverishment, theological confusion and ethical impotence."[724]

164

A remedy to syncretism suggested is "a larger framework in which there is 'differentiated interrelatedness' where responsbilities for living together in community could be accepted without in any way ignoring particularities."[725] Thus dialogue can be a safeguard against syncretism.[726] Like the fear of syncretism, there are various issues confronting dialogue.

e) Hindrances to the progress of dialogue

Experience shows that there is an "element of the sinful and the demonic which is present in all human encounters."[727] Such an element is distrust and fear of loosing one's identity.[728] There are other problems arising from accepted religious patterns and polarities as theistic and non-theistic, the need for a common terminology and differences in the understanding of history and in interpreting contemporary historical situation.[729] There are differences in the understanding of spirituality.[730] To these may be added the problem of mission. Samartha explains this issue:

"It would be wrong... to ignore that Buddhism, Christianity and Islam are all deeply involved in 'mission', which is integral to these faiths. Now Hinduism is also involved in 'mission'. To deny or to ignore this would be to take the oil out of their lamps. But what is of critical importance today is how men, committed to each of these faiths, could practice 'mission' in a multi-religious world without destroying the very peace which they all seek to promote through dialogue. This question of 'mission' - its content and its practice - will be one of the crucial issues in the context of ongoing dialogue."[731]

These are some of the problems which confront those who are engaged in dialogue.

2.2.7.4 Appreciation

A contribution of Samartha is his concern for relevance. His approach has the merit of striving to integrate various christological aspects. Christology, history and social concern are seen interrelated and in a global context; seen in a similar way are the ontological status of Christ, his relation to mystic consciousness and the historical fact of Christ. His preference for advaita does not lead him to adopt it uncritically. Samartha is deeply committed to dialogue. These are some of the positive aspects of his theology.

So far the attempts of various authors, both Catholic and Protestant, have been studied. Now it is useful to examine to what category or categories these theological attempts may be assigned.

Chapter III

3   Types of Indian Theology

Indian theology from ancient times to our own days does not follow a uniform
pattern. The two preceding chapters bear witness to it. What is attempted here
is not a person-wise or group-wise classification of theology. The theology of
a person or a group usually emphasizes certain theological aspects or solutions
to particular problems; but it does not necessarily exclude other trends.[1]
Consequently no effort is made here to offer a strict classification.[2]

Our attempt is limited to a certain broad, approximate classification of
general tendencies in Indian theology.

3.1 Incarnational Theology

What we term here as incarnational theology is that theology which draws its
inspiration and principles from the Incarnation, life, death and resurrection of
Christ as the pattern of the incarnation of the Church in any culture. A
Christian community simply grows in the indigenous culture; the cultural
values become part of the life of the community through a natural process of
growth in which they undergo a certain death and transformation. This process
may be implicit or explicit.

3.1.1 An Implicit Incarnational Theology

A Christian community grows in its cultural environment assimilating,
transforming and integrating cultural values with no special effort or
articulation but simply through a natural process of growth in Christ guided
by the Holy Spirit. It implies that the gospel message received is closer to
its original form. It is this type of unarticulated theology which we can

167

derive from the early Indian Church.[3]

3.1.2 Explicit Incarnational Theology

Theological reflection on the significance of the Incarnation, life, death and resurrection of Christ precedes; principles which would help the growth of the Church in a cultural environment are drawn out and practical application is made to various spheres of human life and activity. It implies that the gospel message was received in a culturally and socially conditioned form. A very consistent type of explicit incarnational theology is found in Amalorpavadass.[4] An incarnational theology presupposes evangelization.

3.2 The Theology of Evangelization

The theology of evangelization studies the possibility of presenting the Gospel in a manner relevant to the present situation; it analyzes missionary problems and offers solutions. The theology of Amalorpavadass[5] and Devanandan[6] bear witness to this concern. The concern for presenting Christ to the world has to take into consideration religion and society all over the world.

3.2.1 The Theology of Society and Secular Humanism

The concern of presenting the Gospel to modern secular man in a relevant way is at the basis of the theology of society and secular humanism. One of its principal purpose is to contribute to the evolution of a humanized world community. The theology of M. M. Thomas,[7] Samartha,[8] Devanandan[9] and Panikkar[10] may be seen in this context

3.2.2 The Theology of Dialogue

The theology of dialogue searches for common grounds of mutual understanding, co-operation and mutual correction between religions and ideologies. The theology of Monchanin,[11] Abhishiktānanda,[12] Griffiths,[13] Amalorpavadass[14] Vempeny,[15] Chethimattam,[16] Nambiaparampil,[17] and Manickam[18] enters into dialogue with Hinduism. The theology of Panikkar,[19] M. M. Thomas[20] and Samartha[21] enter into dialogue with religions and ideologies. Dialogue with

168

religions implies relationship between them. This relationship has been interpreted in different ways.

3.3   The Theology of Fulfilment

The theology of fulfilment sees in Christ the fulfilment of Hinduism.
Keshab Chandra Sen said that Christ is the fulfilment of Hinduism;[22]   Brahmabandhab
spoke about Christianity as the fulfilment of Hinduism;[23]   Farquhar gave a
systematic expression to the theory of fulfilment.[24]   Monchanin saw in the Holy
Trinity, the fulfilment of Hinduism and the solution of its antinomies.[25]   Later
it was felt that the theology of fulfilment was one-sided.

3.3.1 The Theology of Mutual Fulfilment

The relationship is envisaged as the mutual acceptance of the riches of each
other. What is wanting to the plenitude of a religion is brought to fullness
through relationship with other religions. It should be noted, however, that
neither the theology of fulfilment, nor the theology of mutual fulfilment is
followed exclusively by theologians.[26]   In a similar way, attention is paid to the
complementary character of certain aspects of religions.

3.3.2 A Theology of Complementarity

Approaches to reality and revelation itself are seen as complementary.
Griffiths follows this approach.[27]   Some theologians, Chethimattam[28]   and
Abhishiktānanda,[29]   for example, point out certain aspects of complementarity
in the religious outlook or world-view of religions. There is still a more
radical view of the relationship between religions.

3.3.3 The Theology of Cross-fertilization

Religions have to divest themselves of their culture and social conditioned
expressions and prepare themselves for a mutual fecundation so that something new
may emerge. Panikkar has spoken in favour of this view.[30]   Indian theologians

169

have not only dealt with the relationship between religions but have also tried
to interpret Christianity in terms of Hindu thought and experience.

3.4 The Theology of Jñāna Mārga

This is a general term which could be applied to different theological
attempts which give importance to jñāna mārga or the way of knowledge. The Vedanta
systems of philosophy attracted the attention of both European and Indian Christian
thinkers. These systems and the religious experience enshrined in them were made
use of to serve Christian theology.

3.4.1 Christian Vedanta[31]

Christian Vedanta is more a philosophical system than a theological one. It
is included here for the following reasons: too strict a distinction between
philosophy and theology cannot be made in this context; it is one of the initial
Christian attempts. Christian Vedanta is a philosophical system akin to Thomism
built from elements of doctrine acceptable to Christianity taken from Vedanta
systems. Brahmabandhab proposed to do it[32] and Johanns achieved it.[33] This may
be called jñāna mārga in a very broad sense in so far as the emphasis is on doctrine
and knowledge. While this approach strove to take into consideration Vedanta
systems, some theologians felt a preference for one or the other of these systems.

3.4.2 Trinitarian Jñāna Mārga

There is a marked preference for the advaita system of Śankara; the principal
source of theological inspiration and reflection is the Trinity. The Trinity is
seen as the answer to India's quest for the Absolute and the solution to all the
problems raised by her. Brahmabandhab[34] and Monchanin[35] follow this line. In
this same trend we may distinguish certain emphases.

3.4.2.1 Christian Advaita or Experiential Jñāna Mārga

Christian advaita does not claim identity with God like the advaita system

170

of Śankara it claims that God and the world are not two. Christian advaita
is to be understood in terms of the non-duality of Being and trinitarian communion.
The principal emphasis is on experience, renouncement and experiential knowledge.
This is why we have termed it also experiential *jñāna mārga*. Abhishiktānanda
is the principal exponent of this tendency.[36]

3.4.2.2 *Jñāna Mārga* of Interiority

This theological approach has also an advaitic background. It is a theology
of the transcendence of distinction in unity. It tries to penetrate into the
interior and discover the ultimate One behind culture-conditioned expression in
a Unity which transcends all distinctions but preserves the integral wholeness
of individual being. It is trinitarian in its approach. The stress is on
interiority and return to the Centre. Griffiths exposes this trend.[37]

3.4.2.3 Theandric *Jñāna Mārga*

The background of this theology is again advaita. God and man are not two
realities nor are they one; the reality is theandric. The harmonization of all
differences and the solution to all problems are seen in the Trinity. Panikkar
develops this approach.[38] The three *jñāna mārgas* mentioned so far are theocentric
and concerned with the growth of a Christian advaitic spirituality. There is
still a different approach with an advaitic background.

3.4.2.4 Christological *Jñāna Mārga*

An effort is made to construct a christology with an advaita framework. The
defects of Christian christological approaches and those of advaita are pointed
out to serve as mutual correctives. A social and historical concern is
integrated. Samartha exposes this approach.[39] While some theologians prefer
jñāna mārga, as we have seen, there are others who prefer *bhakti-mārga*.

3.5 The Theology of *Bhakti-Mārga*

The distinction between man and God is maintained. The union is one of love, surrender and fellowship. This is the general trend but various emphases are evident.

3.5.1 Experiential *Bhakti Mārga*

The emphasis is on the unknowability of Reality, God, and of experiencing this Reality through love and fellowship. The approach to Reality, God, is christo-centric. This is the approach of Sundar Singh whose source is the Bible and the Indian cultural and *bhakti* background.[40] He does not follow any particular system of philosophy.

The theology of Appasamy follows the same trend but shows a preference for the system of Rāmānuja.[41] As a trained theologian, Appasamy writes in a different style from that of Sundar Singh and does not emphasize the unknowability of Reality.

3.5.2 *Bhakti Mārga* of Experience and Action

Insistence on experiencing Christ, having the highest friend to friend relationship to Christ and commitment to him characterize this theology. There is also stress on action. The theology of Chakkarai[42] and Chenchiah bear witness to this trend.[43] But Chenchiah's theology is well-known for another trend.

3.5.3. The Theology of New Creation

The theology of New Creation emphasizes the beginning of a New Creation of God in Christ conceived in terms of the kingdom of God and the renewal of the secular order. Chenchiah's theology of New Creation bears the influence of Aurobindo's system and strives to integrate a certain biological process into it.[44] Devanandan also exposes a theology of New Creation but is entirely based on Scripture.[45]

These are some of the principal trends in Indian Christian theology. There have been also certain tentative theological approaches which cannot be ignored.

3.6 Tentative Theological Approaches

3.6.1 Theology of Non-Biblical Scriptures

This theological attempt tries to establish inspiration in non-biblical Scriptures and to make use of them as a basis for Christian spiritual experience and theology. This is the approach adopted by Vempeny[46] and the Research Seminar on non-biblical Scriptures.[47]

3.6.2 The Theology of Christ as Guru

This theological approach tries to analyze the concept of Guru in Indian religious tradition and presents Christ as the Universal Teacher of Salvation. De Nobili,[48] Brahmabandhab,[49] Chethimattam[50] are among those who suggest this approach.

3.6.3 The Theology of *Anubhava*

In this theological method experience is taken as the criterion of theology and it remains open to the experience of men belonging to the different religious traditions of India. Manickam proposes this approach.[51]

3.6.4 A Theology of Synthesis

It seeks to evaluate the theological approaches of various scholars, makes a synthesis and then proceeds further. Mattam follows this approach.[52]

3.7 Conclusion

In our opinion, all the various tendencies we have seen so far manifest two basic trends in Indian theology. One is theocentric with a preference for the advaita system of Śankara and an emphasis on experience, contemplation and *jñāna mārga* There is less attention to history. Samartha is an exception to this in so far as he prefers advaita but adopts a christocentric approach. Indian Catholic theology in general, with the exception of Amalorpavadass, shows a predominantly theocentric approach.[53]

The second trend is christocentric with a preference for the *bhakti* tradition in Indian religious tradition. The emphasis is on Christ- experience, history, action and social responsibility. Indian Protestant theology and among Catholics, Amalorpavadass show a predominantly christocentric approach.

There is one common element to all these patterns of thought, though it receives greater or lesser emphasis or is only implied, and is interpreted quite differently. And that is *anubhava* or experience.

Such is a general classification of the patterns of thought and tendencies in Indian theology. A number of problems confront this theology. Hence it is necessary to have a general view of the common problems which confront it.

Chapter IV

4   Fundamental Problems in Indian Theology

The study of the approaches of some European and Indian scholars have placed
before us several important problems which confront an Indian theology. A more
orderly grouping and review is helpful.

4.1   Theocentrism and Christocentrism

India's agelong quest for the Absolute has posed acutely the problem of
theocentrism and christocentrism in Indian theology. To do full justice to the
dominant advaita tendency of the Indian thought, a theologian may feel obliged to
stress the Godhead, the original Mystery, the Absolute and as a means to realize
it sannyāsa, monasticism and contemplation, or a trinitarian theology as a solution
to the antinomies of advaita.[1] While theocentrism has the merit of developing a
Christian advaitic spirituality, it has the disadvantage of overlooking the human,
social and secular dimensions of life which have serious consequences in a
developing country.[2] In an advaitic context, the universality and transcendence
of Christ, the Jesus of history and history itself, tend to disappear in the Ultimate,
the Godhead or in the Trinity.[3]

Probably to avoid these drawbacks, especially to prevent Christ and history
from being swallowed up in the Absolute or being too diluted, some theologians
have adopted a christocentric approach.[4] It has the advantage of being very
relevant to the social and secular context of India[5] and of giving due importance
to Christ, history, and the social, secular and human dimensions of life. This
approach is not without disadvantages. The problem of reconciling the primacy
of the Absolute with christocentrism remains. How is growth in an advaitic

175

spirituality to be interpreted in a christocentric context? Too great an emphasis on the social and secular aspect of man runs the risk of diluting the Gospel to a secular Gospel. Thus there are advantages and disadvantages in both approaches and each approach by itself cannot solve all the problems. Both the theocentric and christocentric approaches cannot ignore ecclesiology and evangelization.

4.2 The Church and Evangelization

As the institution commissioned to bear witness to Christ, present him to the world and guard the deposit of faith, the Church has an essential role. Problems arise on two levels, one on the level of the universal character of the Church and the other on the local level. On the universal level, the validity of her institutions, dogmas, doctrines and their formulations to present Christ to the world relevantly and effectively is questioned.[6] The spirit of domination in the hierarchichal structure of the Church and the lack of understanding of indigenous contexts, and the anxiety to keep the purity of doctrine or truth at the cost of witness to Christ is effectively checking the progress of evangelization and the Church.[7] This quasi-suicidal activity lasting from the times of the early Indian Church to our own days is an urgent problem which needs proper solution; it touches also the relation between sister churches. On the national and local level, the alien character of the Church in India, the socio-cultural integration of the Church in an evolving society and the problem of an Indian rite need solutions[8] which will help the Church to bear effective witness to Christ.

The new theology of the missions provoked a missionary crisis.[9] The almost one-sided explicit salvation motive of former times is substituted by an implicit salvation, explicit liberation and humanist motives, the universal Brotherhood, the dynamism of the Church and so forth,[10] which it is not sure whether the missionaries in the field understand or not. The task of effectivel integrating various aspects of evangelization such as salvation, liberation,

dialogue, development, service, personality, community and secularism is not yet
fully achieved.[11] The use of such terms as indigenization and adaptation gives
the impression that the Church is something alien to the soil which needs to be
made native,while by its nature the Church is native to any soil.[12] The
renaissance of religions and secularism demands a response more than the simple
proclamation of the Word.[13] Buddhism and Islam are by their nature missionary
religions; lately Hinduism too has assumed a missionary character.[14] Is the
missionary activity of religions going to be a competition, a fishing for clients
in the troubled waters of the secular world or something more constructive? How
is it possible to have something more constructive when the competing religions,
each claims to bear a message of universal salvation? This poses the problem of
the relation between religions.

4.3 Christianity and World Religions

Today it is accepted to an extent that men can be saved in their own
religious traditions. Their scriptures are believed to be inspired in some way
and to contain some form of revelation.[15] The nature of the inspiration of non-
biblical Scriptures and the possibility of their use on the same level as the
OT need a solution here. Resurgent Hinduism explicitly proclaims the
equality of all religions and implicitly affirms its superiority over others.[16]
Panikkar denies the superiority of any religion over others.[17] The purpose of
the affirmation of equality and the denial of superiority is to relativize
religions. Is it the best way to relativize religions? In spite of their
diverse claims, religions should be a source of peace and harmony; a give-and-take
attitude is required on the side of religions. This makes a meeting of religions
necessary. For an encounter of religions, Abhishiktānanda would propose sannyāsa,
contemplation and religious experience as the best meeting ground[18] and M. M.
Thomas would suggest anthropology and humanism.[19] Which of them is to be
accepted or what is relevant, humanism or religious experience or both?

177

4.4 Problems of Religious Experience

There are a variety of religious experiences in the Indian religious tradition.[20] Do these experiences provide good soil for the growth of Christian experience? Sundar Singh and Appasamy believe that the *bhakti* tradition of religious experience is best suited to Christianity.[21] Abhishiktānanda and Panikkar seem to claim a certain superiority for the advaitic tradition of religious experience.[22] Which of these claims are true? Abhishiktānanda has shown that advaitic experience is compatible with Christian experience but there was in him a tension between Christian faith and advaitic experience.[23] It follows that a clarification of the relation between Christian faith and advaitic experience is necessary. M. M. Thomas and Samartha hold that the advaitic tendency goes against the social and secular demands of a developing nation.[24] Hence it is evident that a full integration between advaitic outlook and society is not yet achieved. Another problem is the communication of advaitic experience itself. If it is not opposed to Christian experience, it is its social and culture conditioned expression which is opposed.[25] This, on the one hand poses the problem of hermeneutics and on the other, the possibility of communicating experience without concepts and categories. From these, it is evident that the problem of religious experience is a fundamental one in Indian theology and it is not yet fully solved.

4.5 Concepts and Categories

Various authors have spoken about denuding or stripping categories and concepts of their culture and social conditioning to reach the essential core.[26] What then is the criterion to say that such is the essential core and what security is there that it is and that it is not an intellectual abstraction? How is continuity to be assured between the past and the present? Brahmabandhab seems to accomodate Indian categories and concepts to interpret

Christian thought;[27] Griffiths and Manickam, for example, make use of Indian concepts and categories;[28] Monchanin prefers Greek categories[29] and M. M. Thomas speaks of the pre-understanding of indigenous categories.[30] It is evident that the question remains open.

One way to solve the problem of concepts and categories in common use is to rethink and redefine them. Rethinking and redefining presuppose that either they are closed or static or outmoded. Once redefined, do they not become closed again and static again? If rethinking and redefining becomes a continual process, then how is it possible to offer a stable and unchanging core? Are open concepts a solution? If so what will keep them open? Another problem which confronts the use of concepts and categories is that of clarity of thought and expression. A number of Indian concepts have extensive, different and deep significations.[31] Is it necessary to indicate the pre-understanding or original meaning? Thus the use of concepts poses various problems. The function of concepts is to convey ideas and truth.

4.6 The Problem of Truth

The Indian consciousness of the unity of truth is manifested in eclecticism and syncretism.[32] Brahmabandhab desired a harmonization of truth found in each religion and system of philosophy.[33] Goreh tried to propagate what he believed to be truth through rational refutation.[34] Griffiths searches for the essential Truth with an awareness of its aspects and partial truths.[35] Dialogue, syncretism and eclecticism raise the problem of truth in religious encounter.[36] In the encounter of religions, the unique contribution of each religion or system is to be preserved.[37] In India, there is an identification of truth and spirituality which raises the issue of the relation between them.[38] To these must be added the neglect of the aspects of truth leading to a one-sided approach.[39]

Another phenomenon is the succession of theories or theologies to solve one problem or other. The interpretation of the relation between Christianity and the religious traditions of mankind is an example of this question. Once crisis theology dominated; then came the theology of fulfilment only to be supplanted by the theology of mutual fulfilment, eschatological fulfilment and cross-fertilization.[40] If the rejection of theories one after another is due to their falsity, then theology becomes a chain of fallacies. If it is due to truths becoming outdated, then the question arises as to how truths can become outdated. If only the 'up-to-date' is true and the previous ones false, then what security is there that the latest is valid? If the rejection of theologies is due to their expressing only partial truths then why are they rejected instead of being made perfect? Or if they have to be rejected, are partial truths taken into consideration? If each theology is only partially true, is it a solution to problems or partial expressions of truth or reality?

Here we are not advocating in any way a return to dogmatism or doctrinal absolutism. The fact is that any theory which radically relativizes becomes another dogma, another absolute. In fact the Hindu doctrine of the equality of religions and tolerance tends to become an intolerant doctrine and dogma as any other dogma.[41] What we wish to point out is the necessity of an outlook on truth which is able to reconcile an absolute and relative element and is able to take the fullness of truth into consideration as well as its partial expressions or manifestations.

4.7 Conclusion

As seen above, there are various problems which confront an Indian theology. The approaches and theological tendencies delineated above, which try to meet the challenge posed by these questions, differ among themselves. But they all converge towards the creation of an Indian theology which is taking shape, and they contribute to its development. One approach alone may not be able to create an Indian theology and solve all the problems. Indian theologians are rightly conscious of the possibility of a plurality of approaches. This has encouraged us to propose one more way leading to the same goal. The approach we propose, as stated in the Introduction, is from the concept of truth and reality (*satya*).

The scriptures enjoy great authority in every religion which has scriptures. An enquiry into the concept of truth and reality *(satya)* in the Indian and Christian scriptures could contribute to a greater understanding of truth among those who belong to these religious traditions. Such a research could offer at least certain insights for a solution to some of the problems mentioned above and contribute to the development of an Indian theology.*

*We hope to publish as a book in India the approach we propose, which is the result of our recent research at the University of Fribourg, Switzerland, on truth and reality *(satya)* in the Indian scriptures, in the OT and in the Johannine Writings.

Footnotes & References

TRANSLITERATION OF THE SANSKRIT ALPHABET

अ	...	a		ड	...	dh
आ	...	$\bar{a}$		ण	...	$\dot{n}$
इ	...	i		त	...	t
ई	...	$\bar{i}$		थ	...	th
उ	...	u				
ऊ	...	$\bar{u}$		द	...	d
ऋ	...	$\dot{r}$		ध	...	dh
				न	...	n
ए	...	e		प	...	p
ऐ	...	ai		फ	...	ph
ओ	...	o		ब	...	b
औ	...	au		भ	...	bh
क	...	k			...	m
ख	...	kh		य	...	y
	...	g		र	...	r
घ	...	gh		ल	...	i
				व	...	v
ङ	...	$\dot{n}$		श	...	$\acute{s}$
च	...	c		ष	...	$\dot{s}$
छ	...	ch		स	...	s
				ह	...	$\dot{h}$
ज	...	j		॰	...	$\dot{m}$
झ	...	jh		ः	...	$\dot{h}$
ञ	...	$\tilde{n}$				
ट	...	$\dot{t}$				
ठ	...	$\dot{th}$				
ड	...	d				

182

Abbreviations[1]

AAS	Acta Apostolicae Sedis
CBCI	Catholic Bishops' Conference of India
CISRS	Christian Institute for the Study of Religion and Society
CM	The Clergy Monthly (now Vidyajyoti)
CMS	The Clergy Monthly Supplement
DMK	Dravida Munnetra Kazhagam
Ed.	Edited, Editor
Eds.	Editors
HTR	The Harvard Theological Review
IES	Indian Ecclesiastical Studies
IJT	The Indian Journal of Theology
ITS	Indian Theological Studies
JD	Jeevadhara
JES	Journal of Ecumenical Studies
LW	The Living Word
RS	Religion and Society
TER	The Ecumenical Review
Tr.	Translated, Translation etc.,
WW	Word and Worship

[1]The Abbreviations of the Books of the Bible are from the Jerusalem Bible except in quotations from authors.

1. The following are some examples. 1) The terms "world religions" or "the
    religious traditions of mankind" are used by us for religions other than
    Christianity; terms like "non-Christian religions" are left unchanged in
    citations or in the theology of the author discussed out of respect for
    his view. 2) Other examples are "recognize", "civilization" etc., used
    by us and "recognise", "civilisation" etc., in quotations. But the
    printers' mistakes in citations have been corrected. 3) The volume
    number of Books are given in Roman numbers and that of Periodicals in
    ordinary numbers. 4) For periodicals volume numbers are given and if
    they are Weeklies, the number of the issue also is given to facilitate
    reference. In case the issue number is not available as in the case of
    certain quotations from the selections, the date or the month and the
    year is given.

Chapter I

Footnotes & References: Early Indian Theology

1   The so-called Synod of Udayampērur (Diamper) in Kerala was an invalid´synod
     held by Archbishop Alexis de Menezes   (✝1617) of Goa in 1599. Since it
     was not a proper synod we have termed it the assembly of Udayampērur. While
     correcting certain absuses and clarifying Christian doctrine and purifying
     it from errors, this assembly supplanted the Persian domination of the
     Church in India by the Portuguese. It has great historical value as it gives
     an insight into the customs and beliefs of the then Christians on the Malabar
     coast. For a study of this synod mainly from the juridical point of view,
     see Jonas Thaliath, *The Synod of Diamper*, Roma, 1958. This work rightly denies
     the legitimacy of the synod against the work of Antão Gregório Magno, *De Synodi
     Diamperitanae Natura atque Decretis*, Goa, 1952, which upholds it.

2   It is beyond our scope to discuss the origin, the date and the development
     of the Church of India.

3   A. C. Perumalil, *The Apostles of India*, Patna, 1971, pp. 1-51.

4   George Mark Moraes, *A History of Christianity in India, From early times to
     St. Francis Xavier*, A.D. 52-1542, Bombay, 1964, pp. 13-24; 36-37; Perumalil,
     op. cit., pp. 17; 22; 30-31.

5   Edouard R. Hambye,Johannes Madey, *1900 Jahre Thomas – Christen in Indien*
     Freiburg (Schweiz), 1972, pp. 12-30; A. Mathias Mundaden, *Sixteenth
     Century Traditions of St. Thomas Christians,* Bangalore, 1970, pp. 88-117;
     Moraes, op. cit., pp. 25-79.

6   Some of these are: a unanimous, unbroken tradition of apostolic origin,
     the fact that the Persian Church never denied the apostolic origin of the

St. Thomas Christians, the presence of the tomb of the Apostle in
Mylapore, archaelogical evidences favouring the dating of the tomb to the
first century, pilgrimages to the same tomb, Northist - Southist divisions
in the same community and so forth. Moraes, op. cit., pp. 25-45;
Mundaden, op. cit., pp. 88-103. There are those who deny the Indian
apostolate of St. Thomas. For opinions connected with the Indian
apostolate of St. Thomas, see Mundaden, op. cit., pp. 2-6.

7   Mundaden, op. cit., p. 150.

8   Ibid., pp. 145; 150-151.

9   *Sacrorum Conciliorum Nova et Amplissima Collectio*, Vol. 35 B, Paris, 1902,
     Actio III, Decreta, XIV, XV, XVI, in J. D. Mansi, Col. 1194-1208.

10   Decretum XV, Art. LXI, ibid., Col. 1207: "In Eucharistia tantummodo
     Christi virtutem, non autem verum Corpus & Sanguinem contineri. Quos libros
     omnes, & breviaria, licet digna sint quae igni tradantur, cum ultra plurimos
     alios errores contineant;   attamen Synodus emendari praecipit... Itaque
     Synodus praescribit, ut primum errores, et commemorationes de haereticis
     deleantur,   deinde quae habentur integra in ipsorum cultum officia, simul
     cum officiis de adventu & Christi Nativitate, a breviariis revulsa, & in
     frustra discerpta comburantur."

11   Thaliath, op. cit., p. 31: "A decree was published under excommunication
     that all who possessed Syriac books should hand them over to the Archbishop
     /Menezes/ on his visit. Some of these books were corrected by Francis Ros,/(1!
     1624), a Jesuit, later Archbishop of Angamali/, and some were solemnly burned
     the Archbishop dressed in the pontificals. Many books perished in the fire."

12   For various customs of St. Thomas Christians see Placid Podipara, *The
     Malabar Christians*, Aleppey, 1972, pp. 28-34; A. Cherukarakunnel,

Indianization among the St. Thomas Christians, in *Jeevadhāra,* (JD), 1, 1971, pp. 361-373; Hambye-Madey, op. cit., p. 12. Moraes, op. cit., pp. 175-177.

13 Actio IX, Decretum XVII, Art. CCLVII, in Mansi, op. cit., Col. 1350.

14 Moraes, op. cit., p. 200. Mundaden, op. cit., p. 159.

15 Actio V, Decretum XIV, Art. CXXXIII, in Mansi, op. cit., Col. 1257.

16 Actio VII, Decretum XI, Art. CLXIX, ibid., Col. 1284.

17 The same tradition of communal harmony has continued throughout the centuries to our own day.

18 Moraes, op. cit., p. 295: ."The fact stands in bold relief that if Christianity survived at all during 1500 years it is because of the large-heartedness and spirit of tolerance of our Hindu brethren. Apart from the unique service to the community, which the Christians were in a position to render, it is a tribute to the sense of justice, fairness and magnanimity of the Hindus that they appreciated the loyalty and efficiency of the Christians and permitted them to the highest posts in the state."

19 *Actio III, Decretum IV, art. XXXVII, XXXIX,* in Mansi, op cit., Col. 1185-1186. Art. XXXVII, Col. 1185: "Comperit Synodus ob communicationem, quam in hac diocesi habent Christiani cum Infidelibus, aliquos ipsorum animis adhaesisse ineptos errores, eosque ab hebetibus, & rudibus hominibus mordicus teneri, & potissum quidem tres hisce Infidelibus familiares..." Then the errors of transmigration and fatalism, things happening by necessity, fate or fortune, are corrected. Art. XXXIX, Col. 1186: "Tertio:

unumquemque sua (d) in lege salvari posse, legesque omnes esse rectas; quod plane erroneum est, ac haeresis turpissima: nulla enim est lex, in qua salvi fieri valeamus, prater legem Christi Salvatoris nostri;..." Foot note (d): "Politicorum et tolerantium in hoc perversum Dogma, in solo enim Christo Jesus opportet nos salvos fieri: unde indifferentes, quam longissime a via veritatis aberrant."

    Translation author's own .

20 *Actio V, Decretum I, Art. CIX,* ibid., Col. 1243. "Primum cum ex doctrina supra tradita de hoc sacramento consisterit, sacerdotem non propriis ipsius verbis, sed verbis tantum Christi Domini Nostri, authoris, ac institutoris ejusdem sacramenti, consecrare: non licet addere in forma consecretionis verba aliqua quantumvis optima,..."

21 Mundaden, op. cit., pp. 165-166.

22 Prior to the arrival of the Portuguese in the 16th century it was not easy to procure wheat and wine in this rice-producing country.

23 We may insist that no theologian or individual should take it upon himself to go against any liturgical regulation. It is for the Church to decide as to what changes are to be introduced.

24 Hambye-Madey, op. cit., p.23.

25 Robert De Nobili, *Première apologie,* 1610, *Text inédit Latin,* Tr. Pierre Dahmen, Paris, 1931, p. 165.

26 ibid., pp. 158-171. p. 162: "... et confirmatur, quia ut ipsemet Pater Gus Fernandez mihi narravit cum in eodem regio consessu de variis mundi

stirpibus coram Naique /Ruler of Madurai/ ageretur, ventum est ad
Prangorum stirpem, utrum Turcarum stirpe sit inferior, in qua re nullo
respectu habito ad legem, ea omnibus communis fuit sententia reliquis
stirpibus Prangorum gentem esse obscuriorem, eo quod nullam politicum
servaret cultum et quam maxime corporis munditia careret."

27 For a life of Robert de Nobili reference may be made to: Peter R.
    Bachmann, *Roberto Nobili, 1577-1656, Ein missionsgeschichtlicher
    Beitrag zum christlichen Dialog mit dem Hinduismus*, Roma, 1972; Peter Dahmen,
    *Robert de Nobili, Ein Beitrag zur Geschichte der Missionsmethode und der
    Indologie*, Münster in Westfalen, 1924; Vincent Cronin, *A Pearl to India,
    The Life of Roberto de Nobili*, New York, 1959.

27a For details refer Armulf Camps, *Jerome Xavier S.J. and the Muslims of
     the Mogul Empire Controversial Works and Missionary Activity*, Fribourg/
     Switzerland, 1957. The liturgical adaptations such as venerating the
     Holy Bible, of separating men and women in the Church and making more
     severe the fasting of new Christians introduced by Jerome Xavier to
     suit the mentality of Muslim converts to Christianity seem to be around
     the year 1611. De Nobili had by then adopted the way of life of a
     Hindu Sannyāsin (1607).

28   De Nobili, *Première apologie*, p. 60, 84, 137 etc. We may add also that
     the two ecclesiastical authorities who gave strong support to De Nobili's
     method were those who were in contact with St. Thomas Christians.
     Archbishop Francis Roz (Ref.11) was their bishop and Archbishop Alexis Menezes
     (Ref.1) had travelled among them and stayed with them.

29   The statement may seem to be exaggerated. The opposition of the Brahmins
     was sporadic. They showed themselves more willing to appreciate his
     teachings and accept his explanations than some of his confrères and

a few ecclesiastical authorities, though he had ardent supporters among them too. See Vincent Cronin, op. cit., pp. 92-220.

30   Only a thorough study of all the works of De Nobili, the Sanskrit texts quoted by him and their sources can enable one to assess the extent of his knowledge of Sanskrit and Hinduism. The fact that he undertook to study a language to which access was very difficult in his times was in itself a step forward.

31   De Nobili's defences may be seen in De Nobili, *Première apologie*, pp. 51-185 and Robert de Nobili, *Informatio de quibusdam Moribus Nationis Indi* (cited as *Informatio*) *ad Patrem nostrum Generalem* (a work considered to be lost and lately discovered), Ed. & Tr. Rajamanickam, *Roberto De Nobili on Indian Customs*, Palayamkottai, 1972, Part I English version, pp. 83-165 and Part II Latin text, pp. 64-123.

32   See the Papal Bull in De Nobili, *Première apologie*, *Appendices*, I, pp. 186-189 and French version, pp. 190-194.

33   De Nobili, *Informatio*, English version, p. 153, after mentioning Alexander the Great's policy of 'mutual interchange of social habits,' De Nobili writes: "... for just as the overlord of city - states (to ensure his sway) must adopt many of the local institutions, so too must the ecclesiastical leader set over the Christian communities; and as the proper government of nations depends on a policy of give and take, so also the pastoral care of souls in view of heaven must comprise (to use Alexander's words) two things, that is, we must both give them certain advantages and learn certain lessons from them; in other words, we must learn and tolerate their human ways of acting in society so that we in turn may teach and strengthen

in them the ways of God."

34   Pierre Dahmen, in his *Introduction* to De Nobili's *Première apologie*,
p. 17. Vincent Cronin, op. cit., pp. 167-173. The late Abhishiktānanda
(Dom Le Saux) strongly advocated a Sanskrit Liturgy. Abishiktānanda,
Towards the Renewal of the Indian Church, Bangalore, 1970, pp. 46-47.
He suggested also the establishment of a Pilot Seminary, adapted to
the Indian situation. Ibid., p. 68.

34a D. Jeyaraj, *The Contribution of the Catholic Church in Tamilnadu in The
17th - 19th Centuries to an Understanding of Christ*, in *The Indian Journal
of Theology*, (*IJT*), *Special Number, Interpreting Christ to India Today*, 23,
1974, p. 185: "De Nobili's specific contribution to Christology seems to
be his concept of Christ as divine Guru. Here, Guru does not mean a
priest who offers sacrifices but one who teaches the way to reach the
shores of *mokṣa* or heaven."

35   R. H. S. Boyd, *An Introduction to Indian Christian Theology*, Madras, 1975, p. 13:
"We should not imagine, however, that his writings really represent an
experiment in 'indigenous theology' using Hindu terminology for the
exposition of Christian doctrine, for indeed his attitude to religious
Hinduism is entirely negative and he writes to refute."

36   Pierre Dahmen, in his *Introduction* to De Nobili's *Première apologie*, pp.
22-23.

37   De Nobili, *Informatio*, p. 8.

38   De Nobili, *Informatio*, English version, p. 42: "... many texts refer to
the real cause of the world's existence, and to God's oneness, such tenets
in fact as might go to enlarge the doctrine of the Gnani sect, and do give

these a handle for proving the laws to be self-contradictory; such too
as may well and should indeed be acceptable even to Christians," and p. 43:
"Finally, they refer to God as truly rewarding the just in these words:
Brahmavid āponti param: i.e. he who knows this God will secure glory.
But, what is yet more surprising, I discover in these texts even an
adumbration of the recondite mystery of the most Holy Trinity, the
Most Gracious and Most High God vouchsafing doubtless even to these far
distant lands some inkling of the most hidden secret of our faith through
the teaching of some sage living among these people, in much the same way
as by a rather mysterious inspiration He deigned to illuminate the Sybils,
Trimagistus and certain other Masters of human wisdom in our parts of the
globe."

39   The fact that De Nobili was under constant attack for his adoption of
Indian social customs is to be taken into consideration. It was only
natural that he should devote more attention to justify and get his
position accepted rather than to seek what is true in Hinduism. We have
referred to passages where he clearly touches religious Hinduism only in
Ref. 38. There are other passages which may be applicable both to
religious Hinduism and social customs; e.g. See De Nobili, *Informatio*,
English version, pp. 45-46. Edward Hambye, *Robert De Nobili and Hinduism*
in *God's Word Among Men*, Ed. G. Gispert-Sauch, Delhi, 1973, pp. 332-333:
"... his principles on adaptation stopped short when confronted with
religious Hinduism as a living and popular religion. Though he seems to
have admitted that it contains an original revelation akin to Christian
doctrines on some points and that the light of reason inspired Hindu sages
to approach God in the right manner, he wants above all to distinguish
what is secular and therefore acceptable from what is regarded then as
the Hindu religion i.e., the rites and the cults." It is not quite clear
whether Hambye considers De Nobili's approach to religious Hinduism as

negative. He speaks of the limitations of De Nobili's approach: ibid., p. 333: "Perhaps the limitations of De Nobili's approach lay in believing that India could be dealt with like the Graeco - Roman world of old." One may speak of the limitations of De Nobili's approach to religious Hinduism rather than term it entirely negative.

40   For a life of Rammohan Roy, refer Nalin C. Ganguly, *Raja Ram Mohun Roy,* Calcutta, 1934. Iqbal Singh, *Rammohan Roy, A Biographical Inquiry into the Making of Modern India,* Bombay, 1958.

40a   The Brahma Samāj was a movement founded by Rammohan Roy for worship, prayer and religious discussion. Worship included recitation from the *Upaniṣads,* a sermon and hymns. It was also engaged in social reform and education and for these purposes missionaries were trained and journals published.

41   For what follows, we are mainly dependent on the following works. M. M. Thomas, *The Acknowledged Christ of the Indian Renaissance,* (cited as *Acknowledged*) London, 1969, pp. 1-37; R. H. S. Boyd, op. cit., pp. 19-26; J. N. Farquhar, *Modern Religious Movements in India,* London, 1929, pp. 29-39; Ganguly, op. cit. We have made use of also the following doctoral thesis not yet published: Antony Kolencherry, *Universalitätsanspruch des neuzeitlichen Hinduismus, Reformbewegung des Brama Samaj, seine Entwicklung und Stellung zum Christentum,* University, Wien, 1976.

42   M. M. Thomas, *Acknowledged,* pp. 21-29 gives an excellent summary of the controversy.

43   Ibid., p. 25.

44   Ganguly, op. cit., p. 60: "Ram Mohun held that the difference between

Hinduism and Christianity consisted in 'a few multiples of the number three,' and that the Trinity contained nothing more than the idea of *bhyuha* (emanations) of the *Pancharātra* system, which had four Gods contained somehow in one Godhead. He stated in the Tyler controversy that 'the same omnipotence which makes three one and one three can equally reconcile the unity and plurality of three hundred and thirty millions, both being supported by a sublime mystery which far transcends all human comprehension."

45   Boyd, op cit., pp. 24-25.

46   M. M. Thomas, *Acknowledged*, pp. 26-27.

47   Ram Mohan Roy, *First Appeal*, p. 125, as cited by Ganguly, op. cit., p. 58.

48   M. M. Thomas, *Acknowledged* , p. 30. Though the author is making the remark when he comments on Parekh's criticism of Rammohan Roy, it expresses the problem well.

49   For our exposition we are mainly dependent on Keshab Chunder Sen, *That Marvellous Mystery - The Trinity* in *Keshub Chunder Sen's Lectures in India*, Vol. II, London, 1904, pp. 1-48; M. M. Thomas, *Acknowledged*, pp. 56-81; R. H. S. Boyd, op. cit., pp. 26-39; J. N. Farquhar, op cit., pp. 41-69; We have made use also Antony Kolencherry, op cit.

49a The Church of the New Dispensation was an eclectic Church founded by Keshab. Kolencherry, op cit., p. 183: "The New Dispensation, according to Keshab was to be a synthesis of religions..." Translation author's own.

50   Chunder Sen, op. cit., p. 16.

51   Boyd., op. cit., p. 34.

52 Chunder Sen, op. cit., p. 13: "The Purāṇas speak of the different
    manifestations or incarnations of the Deity in different epochs of the
    world's history. Lo! the Hindu Avatar rises from the lowest scale of
    life through the fish, the tortoise, and the hog up to the perfection of
    humanity. Indian Avatarism is, indeed, a crude representation of the
    ascending scale of Divine Creation."

53 ibid., p. 14.

54 ibid., p. 15.

55 ibid., p. 42: "Truly the Holy Ghost has leavened us with Christ-leaven,
    and established the Logos within us as the Divine Son subjectified."

56 M. M. Thomas, *Acknowledged*, p. 70; Boyd, op. cit., p. 37.

57 Chunder Sen, ibid., pp. 33-35.

58 Quoted in *The New Dispensation*, Vol. II, pp. 178-82, as cited by
    M. M. Thomas, *Acknowledged*, p. 74.

59 See M. M. Thomas, *Acknowledged*, pp. 65-80; Boyd, op. cit., pp. 27-39.

60 God's entry into humanity in the obscurity of His Divinity or
    concealing His Divinity is Kenosis. See *Die Religion in Geschichte
    und Gegenwart, Handwörterbuch für Theologie und Religionswissenschaft*,
    Band III, Tübingen, 1959, Col. 1246: "Dass es so steht, dass Gott in die
    Verborgenheit seiner Gottheit unter der Menschlichkeit eingeht, das ist
    die Kenosis." Boyd, op. cit., p. 29: "In a remarkable passage which
    foreshadows some of the theological developments of the next 90 years

he expounds the nature of Christ's divinity in a form of the kenotic
theory, taking as his starting point that *locus classicus* of Indian
Christian theologians, 'I and my Father are one,' a text which he
regards as the corner-stone of Jesus' thought about himself."

61   ibid; For the concept of the transparency of Christ, see J. A. T.
Robinson, *Honest to God*, London, 1963.

62   Boyd, op. cit., p. 31: "In a phrase strangely prophetic of Barth he
speaks of Christ as 'the Journeying God' who according to the divine
plan, sets out from his Father, 'the Still God,' to bring salvation to
men." Boyd does not say to which work of Barth he is referring.

63   Boyd, op. cit., p. 37. For the theory of fulfilment, see J. N.
Farquhar, *The Crown of Hinduism*, Oxford, 1913.

64   Boyd, op. cit., pp. 37-38.

65   M. M. Thomas, *Acknowledged*, pp. 76-77: "Keshub's Church of the New
Dispensation has also raised another theological issue in this whole
debate, namely, the Christian status, *vis-à-vis* the Church, of
individuals and groups who have seen and met God in and through Jesus
Christ, and are even prepared to accept him as their God and Saviour
in some verbal confessional form, but are not convinced that they should
leave the society, culture and religion of Hinduism to join the social,
cultural and religious structure of Christianity in India, which
expresses the Church in the main line of continuity with the historic
Church of Christ. There are three questions here. First, what is the
Christian interpretation of the relation of Christian faith to non-
Western cultures and societies and non-Christian religions? Many issues
arise here. Do we seek the conversion of Hindus or the conversion of

Hinduism? In the conversion of the Hindu to Christ, can Hinduism
play any positive role? Can the Hindu who becomes Christian bring
a new understanding of Christ to the world Church? Second, what is
the Christian interpretation of the renaissance taking place among
Hindus and in Hinduism, as a result of their positive response to
Christianity as ethics, religion and/or spirit. Third, how far can
a Hindu Christianity be considered an embodiment of Christ or at least
a preparation for the conversion of Hindus and Hinduism to Christ and
for the fuller development of a truly Indian Church?

66 In the bibliographies available to us we could not find any major work
on Brahmabandhab by any Indian Catholic theologian. A. Väth, *Im Kampfe
mit der Zauberwelt des Hinduismus,* Berlin 1928, is considered to be the
best work so far published on him. We could not procure a copy of it.

67 Our principal sources on Brahmabandhab are, Kaj Baago, *Pioneers of
Indigenous Christianity,* Bangalore 1969, pp. 26-49; 118-150; R. H. S.
Boyd, op. cit., pp. 58-85; M. M. Thomas, *Acknowledged,* pp. 99-110;
Friedrich Heiler, *Christlicher Glaube und indisches Geistesleben,*
München 1926, pp. 51-79. Our Protestant brethern seemed to have paid
more attention to Brahmabandhab than we Catholics. They have given a
kind and considerate treatment of his teaching, though he himself showed
little sympathy to Protestantism, an attitude quite understandable in
the context of his times. For the life of Brahmabandhab we are dependent
on the above-mentioned authors. The principal reason for devoting more
space to his life than we have done for other authors is the comparatively
scanty attention paid to him by Catholic India.

68 Baago, op. cit., p. 48. The school was later developed into a university

197

which sought to blend what is best in Western and Eastern culture.

69   ibid., p. 49.

70   Brahmabandhab Upādhyāya, *Conversion of India, An Appeal,* in *Sophia,*
      October 1894, Baago, op. cit., *Selections*, pp. 118-119: "The first step
      to be taken, according to our humble opinion, to effect her conversion,
      is to eradicate from the minds of the Indian people certain erroneous and
      mischievous doctrines. They are the following: (I) God is all, all is
      God; (2) God, man and matter, all three are eternal; (3) the doctrine
      of transmigration. These three doctrines are eating into the very vitals
      of the Hindu race. So long as these doctrines are the ruling principles
      of their life, it is well nigh impossible to make them even understand
      rightly what Christian faith is. ... Theism is the preamble of faith and
      it will be unwise to attempt to build up the structure of the supernatural
      religion of Christ before the solid foundation of theism is properly laid."
      All quotations from Brahmabandhab, unless explicitly stated otherwise, are
      taken from Kaj Baago, op. cit., *Selections*, pp. 118-150, and the page
      reference will be given in the same manner as above. Reference No. 70.

71   Brahmabandhab, *An Exposition of the Catholic Belief as Compared with the
      Vedanta,* in *Sophia,* January 1898, ibid., p. 132.

72   Brahmabandhab, *The Hymn Ka,* in *Sophia*, February 1896, ibid., p. 129.

73   ibid., p. 130: "Was the ṛṣi   the author of the above hymn, given the
      privilege of having a fore-glimpse of the inner Life of God having its
      entire satisfaction in a co-eternal interior generation? Or, is it mere
      speculation of the human mind which seeks to penetrate into the very
      sanctum sanctorum of Divine Life, but, failing to soar high, it falls

into the error of attributing an outer emanation to God? It is a matter of consideration."

74 See Baago, op. cit., pp. 37-39.

75 Brahmabandhab, *The True Doctrine of Māyā*, in *Sophia*, February and March 1899, Baago, op. cit., *Selections*, pp. 146-147.

76 M. M. Thomas, *Acknowledged*, p. 104: "Probably Brahmabandhab did not commit himself to any of these systems but only used their categories, with a consciousness of the inadequacy of all of them."

77 English translation with slight alterations as printed in the *Prayer Book* Hymn No. 2, *and Hymnal*, 38th International Eucharistic Congress, Bombay, 1964, as cited by Boyd, op. cit., p. 70. Sanskrit text of the hymn is not available to us.

78 ibid., p. 71.

79 Brahmabandhab, *The Incarnate Logos*, in *The Twentieth Century*, 1901, Baago, op. cit., *Selections*, pp. 140-141. The Sanskrit text and English translation is given.

80 ibid., pp. 139-140: "According to the vedanta, human nature is composed of five sheaths or divisions *(kośa)*. They are: (1) physical *(annamaya)* which grows by assimilation; (2) vital *(prāṇamaya)*; (3) mental *(manomaya)*, through which are perceived relations of things; (4) intellectual *(vijñānamaya)*, through which is apprehended the origin of being; and (5) spiritual *(ānandamaya)*, through which is felt the delight of the Supreme Reality. These five sheaths are presided over

by a personality *(ahampratyaya)* which knows itself. This self-knowing individual *(jīva-caitanya)* is but a reflected spark of the Supreme Reason *(kutastha - caitanya),* Who abides in every man as the prime source of life and light. The time-incarnate Divinity is also composed of five sheaths; but it is presided by the Person of the Logos Himself and not by any created personality *(aham).* The five sheaths and the individual agent, enlivened and illumined by Divine reason, Who resides in a special manner in the temple of humanity, make up man. But in the God-man the five sheaths are acted upon direct by the Logos—God and not through the medium of any individuality. The Incarnation was thus accomplished by uniting humanity with Divinity in the person of the Logos."

81 We do not give a short exposition of his teaching on Trinity and Incarnation owing to the following reasons: Brahmabandhab closely follows Catholic doctrine and Thomism. An explanation of his interpretation of the Trinity and Incarnation may be found in Boyd, op. cit., pp. 69-74; pp. 77-82; Baago, op. cit , pp. 40-46. M. M. Thomas, *Acknowledged*, pp. 101-107. Our purpose being an examination of his thoughts on Indian theology does not necessarily require an explanation of them.

82 See Boyd, op. cit., pp. 80-82.

83 ibid.
In the same context is to be understood the permission he gave to the worship of Sarasvathi as a symbol of wisdom in his school in Calcutta. See, Baago, op. cit., p. 46.

84 Brahmabandhab, *The True Doctrine of Māyā*, in *Sophia*, February and March 1899, Baago, op. cit., *Selections*, p. 147.

85 ibid.

85a   ibid., p. 148.

86   ibid.

87   ibid., p. 149.

88   ibid., p. 146.

89   Brahmabandhab, *Christ's Claim to Attention,* in *The Twentieth Century,*
      1901, ibid., pp. 141-146.

90   ibid., p. 142: "His religion does not consist in eclecticism. He did
      not form it by stringing together truths common to current religious
      systems and eliminating their differences, nor by harmonising contradictory
      tenets, nor by gathering scattered rays of wisdom into one focus. He
      revealed a complete system .containing *all* truths necessary for man to
      believe and practise in order to attain salvation. Nothing can be added
      to it or subtracted from it. Addition corrupts it; subtraction destroys
      it. It repudiates progress through acquisition of new truths. But it is
      self-evolving. The relations which bind together its parts are gradually
      unfolded to meet the growing demands of the human intellect; the harmonies
      which impart to it a thorough-going consistency shine forth more and more
      to adequately illumine the expanding area of metaphysics and science; its
      implicit realities are made explicit with the march of time. But in the
      process of evolution it does not admit any novelty or accident. It grows
      not by accomodating contradictions to suit prejudice and ignorance, but
      by widening the vision of man."

91   Brahmabandhab, *The True Doctrine of Māyā,* ibid., p. 146:   "Catholicity is,
      as its name implies, the universal religion, in which all the religious
      truths found elsewhere in scattered, fragmentary and distorted *form* are

united into one perfect sphere of universal truth. A beautiful
illustration of this is found in the relation of the Thomistic
philosophy, which is pre-eminently Catholic, to the philosophies of
Aryo Varta. It is their reconciliation and synthesis - explaining
and harmonising all various *dvaita* (dualism), *viśiṣṭādvaita* (qualified
monism), and *advaita* (monism) schools, while itself far more unitary, so
to speak, in its world-view, than the pure Vedanta school itself."

92   See Brahmabandhab, *The Nature of Parabrahman*, in *Sophia*, January 1898,
     ibid., p. 133; *The True Doctrine of Māyā*, cit.

93   Brahmabandhab, *The Origin of Man*, in *Sophia*, January 1894, ibid., p. 129.

94   The principles and attitudes which were at the origin of these unhappy
     conflicts are present even today. A solution has to be found. That is
     why we are posing this problem again. Ref. 1.1.1.3 no. 5.

95   Baago, op. cit., p. 29. See Ref. 31 & 32.

96   Brahmabandhab, *Conversion of India - An Appeal*, in *Sophia*, October 1894,
     Baago, op. cit., *Selections*, pp. 119-120.

97   Brahmabandhab, *Are We Hindus?* in *Sophia*, July 1897, ibid., pp. 124-125.

98   About the establishment of the sannyāsi order, see Heiler, op. cit., pp.
     54-44; Baago, op. cit., pp. 46-47; Boyd, op. cit., p. 65.
     Here we cannot help making an observation. A bold missionary initiative
     in perfect accordance with Indian tradition and Christian orthodoxy,
     sanctioned by a local bishop, which would have powerfully contributed to
     the evangelization of India, is nipped in the bud by higher ecclesiastical

authorities. Brahmabandhab humbly obeyed.

99   Heiler, op. cit., p. 57.

100   For what follows, see Baago, op. cit., pp. 47-49.

101   Heiler, op. cit., pp. 77-78: "Die römische Hierarchie hat sein Lebenswerk
      zerbrochen, seine Missionskraft gelähmt, seinen Evangelistenmund ver-
      schlossen."

102   Quoted by B. Animānanda, *The Blade: Life and Work of Brahmabandhab
      Upādhyāya* p. 200 as cited by Boyd, op. cit., pp. 68-69. *Sadhan dharma*
      refers to religious life.

103   Boyd, op. cit., p. 69.

104   He did not build up a system of thought, but a system is not the unique
      standard of judging the value of a man or his theology. The impact of the
      thought and initiatives of one on the posterity is more important than the
      construction of a system. His life appears to be a tragedy but it is not
      unlike the tragedy of the cross.

105   Our principal sources for his life and teachings are the following:
      Balwant A. M. Paradkar, *The Theology of Nehemiah Goreh*, Madras, 1969;
      Boyd, op. cit., pp. 40-47; M. M. Thomas, *Acknowledged*, pp. 38-54.

106   See Paradkar, op. cit., pp. 12-21.

107   Nehemiah Goreh, *A Rational Refutation of Hindu Philosophical Systems*,
      Tr. F. Hall, *Selections* in Paradkar, op. cit., pp. 38-39: "In only
      applying names to real things, and to unreal, there is no fault. The

extraordinary error of the vedantins is of quite another character. I
have already said, that they would prove both world and ignorance to be
ignorance – imagined and altogether false. But earnestly as they desire
to have them so, their inner consciousness refuses to rate them as altogether nothing: for the mind of man will not give willing entrance to an
absurdity. The world, the vedantins allege, is veritably nothing, but
because of ignorance, appears to exist; after the manner of macrine
silver. Now, can the mind assent to the notion, that even that ignorance
is nothing whatever? Never: and he who tries to reconcile with it his
own views generally, and the common experience of mankind, will encounter
obstacles at every step. Moreover to call such ignorance nothing, is,
evidently, most venturesome...."

108   Paradkar, op. cit., p. 16.

109   ibid., pp. 17-18.

110   ibid., p. 14.

111   N. Goreh, *Christianity not of Man but of God*, p. 59, as cited by Boyd,
      op. cit., p. 55.

Chapter II

Footnotes & References: Twentieth Century Approach to Indian Theology

1   The factors we recall here are well-known. So special reference is not given.
    The purpose of stating them is only to situate the evolution of Indian
    theology in its context.

2   *Living Faiths and the Ecumenical Movement*, Ed., S. J. Samartha, Geneva, 1971,
    pp. 47-54.

3   The following are the scholars we have chosen for a brief study and the
    motives behind the choice. Pierre Johanns may be considered the link between
    Brahmabandhab and the more recent scholars, and strove to create a Christian
    Vedanta. Jules Monchanin created an awareness of the cultural heritage of
    India and of the need for the Christian to assimilate it. Abhishiktānanda
    gave witness to Christian advaitic experience. Raymond Panikkar is original
    in his approach. Amalorpavadass has done much in the line of adaptation and
    indigenization. Ishanand Vempeny has tried to prove an analogical inspiration
    of non-biblical Scriptures. Joseph Mattam wrote about the contribution of
    some European scholars to a Christian approach to Hinduism. From among the
    Carmelites of Mary Immaculate we have chosen three for a brief study and the
    reasons for this are given in the respective place.

3a For a sketch of the life of P. Johanns, see Joseph Mattam, *Land of the Trinity*,
    A Study of Modern Christian Approaches to Hinduism, (cited as *Land*) Bangalore,
    1975, pp. 19-20.

    The study of his approach made by Mattam, *Land*, pp. 17-43, render a similar
    study unnecessary and our task easier.

5   Olivier Lacombe in his *Preface* to: Pierre Johanns, *La pensée religieuse de l'Inde*, Namur, (1952?) p. ii.   Translation author's own.

6   Mattam, *Land*, pp. 20-37.

7   Pierre Johanns, *A Synopsis of "To Christ Through the Vedanta,"* Parts I-III, Ranchi 1930-1932, Part IV, (n.d.).

8   Johanns, *La pensée religieuse de l'Inde*, pp. 33-35;   61-63 etc.

9   For this biographical note, see, Jules Monchanin, *Ecrits spirituels présentation d'Edouard Duperray*, Paris, 1965, pp. 6-7.

10   Henri de Lubac, *Images de l'abbé Monchanin*, Aubier, 1967, pp. 119-151.

11   Jules Monchanin, *Mystique de l'Inde, mystère chrétien*, (cited as *mystique*) presenté par Suzanne Siauve, Fayard, 1974, p. 154: "Aussi ai-je envers lui un sentiment filial comme si lointainement il était un peu mon guru."

12   Mattam, *Land*, pp. 144-179.

13   Monchanin, *Mystique*, p. 172, *correspondance*, 5 août 1947: "Pendant plusieur sémaines je me suis demandé sérieusement si je n'allais pas sombrer dans la névrose. J'étais incapable de réagir, et j'avais perdu mon centre de gravité ..."

14   ibid., p. 146, *correspondance*, 26th March, 1939: "je ne sais où je suis ni qui je suis, tant douleur et joie se disputent ..."

15   Monchanin, *Ecrits spirituels*, p. 106: "L'Ashram sera sans doute un échec:

d'autres, plus dignes, reprendront l'effort. Prions pour la venue de moines indiens devant lesquels nous pourrons nous effacer et qui réaliseront ce dont nous rêvons seulement. Et attendons dans l'espérance et patience indéfectible (l'espérance, la vertu la plus difficile que donne l'Esprit).

16 Monchanin, *Mystique*, pp. 143-144, correspondance, 28th November, 1938. Translation author's own.

17 ibid., p. 27. Translation author's own.

18 ibid., p. 35: "La pensée indienne identifie vérité et spiritualité: *sat*. Hostile au choix exclusif, elle incline au syncrétisme. Elle doute de la réalité *(māyā)*.

Toute vérité est dans le *sat* de la sainteté, qui peut seule dépasser le syncrétisme, car elle est épreuve directe du Mystère chrétien qui n' exclut - mais impitoyablement - que l'exclusion et recueille toutes les vérités, qui est celle du Plérôme." Translation author's own.

19 ibid., pp. 211-212.

20 J. Monchanin, *The Quest of the Absolute*, in *Indian Culture and the Fullness of Christ*, All India Study Week, 6th-13th December, 1956, Madras, 1957, p. 50.

21 Monchanin, *Mystique*, p. 211, *correspondance*, 17th May, 1955.

22 Monchanin, ibid., pp. 58-61.

23 ibid., pp. 178, 191, 198, Monchanin; *Ecrits spirituels*, pp. 31, 43, 76.

24 Monchanin felt that he came too early or too late. See Monchanin, *Ecrits spirituels*, p. 92.

25 For a short sketch of Abhishiktananda's life, see James Stuart, *Swami Abhishiktananda*, in *The Clergy Monthly*, (CM), 38, 1974, pp. 80–82; For some of his experiences in India see Abhishiktananda, (Henri Le Saux) *Guru and Disciple*, (cited as *Guru*), Tr. Heather Sandeman, London, 1974; For some of his traits, see Sara Grant, *Swamiji - The Man*,in CM, 38, 1974, pp. 487–495; Vandana, *A Messenger of Light, Swami Abhishiktananda as known in Shivanda Ashram, Rishikesh*, in CM, 38, 1974, pp. 495–500.

25a Śankaracārya, a Brahmin, born around 750 A.D. in Kerala,India,made a synthesis of doctrines found in Hindu scriptures and aphorisms *(Sūtras)* and established firmly the advaita system which claims the identity of the individual self with the Absolute. The experience of this identity is called advaitic experience or non-dual experience in which subject - object distinction disappears.

26 Swami Abhishiktananda, *Hindu - Christian Meeting Point within the Cave of the Heart* (cited as *Cave*), Bombay, 1969, p. 109.

27 ibid., p. 110.

28 Abhishiktananda, *Saccidananda, A Christian Approach to Advaitic Experience* (cited as *Sac.*), Delhi, 1974, p. 103.

29 ibid., p. 104.

30 ibid., p. 109.

31 ibid., pp. 43-44.

32 ibid., p. 94.

33 ibid., p. 95.

34   ibid., pp. 63-64. See also p. 45.

35   ibid., p. 85.

36   ibid., p. 115: "But what really needs faith - and a faith that is
      particularly difficult for those who have been touched by the consuming fire
      of Being - is to believe in one's own existence in the presence of the Lord
      God, poor and feeble creature that one is by contrast with what is real and
      abiding."

37   ibid., pp. 195-200. Sara Grant, *Swamiji - The Man*, in CM, cit, p.490:"It is certain,
      however, that the most searching suffering of all came from within his own
      spirit, faced by the terrible challenge of the radical interiority and
      transcendence of the advaitin tradition which can, and perhaps necessarily
      must, in the life of any man who is to experience in his own being the
      relationship of the Hindu revelation to Christ, appear to threaten the very
      foundations of the traditional interpretation of this Christian mystery,
      the reality, the uniqueness and permanent significance of the incarnation
      and the very being of Christ, so totally does it seem to relativize not only
      the Hebraeo - Christian cultural and spiritual traditions, but the whole
      created order in which the incarnation is necessarily rooted. Swamiji himself
      firmly held that no Christian should enter into deep contact with the advaitin
      tradition in its purity unless he has deeply anchored not in mere notional
      knowledge of his faith, but in the experiential wisdom of contemplative
      prayer. He used to say that any one who had this experiential knowledge
      of God would immediately understand by inner affinity the meaning of
      advaita: without it, there was the possibly fatal risk of intellectual
      pride: "Spiritual shipwreck." That he came through this dark night of the
      spirit with his Christian faith not weakened, but immeasurably deepened and
      purified, is proof not only of his level-headedness, but even more of his
      fidelity to the indwelling spirit and his trust in the presence of the same

Spirit at the heart of the Hindu tradition."

38   Abhishiktānanda, *Cave*, pp. 28-30.

39   Abhishiktānanda, *Sac.*, p. 95.

40   ibid., p. 69.

41   Abhishiktānanda, *Guru*, p. 55, 62.

42   Abhishiktānanda, *Sac.*, pp. 62-66;   Abhishiktānanda, *Prayer*, Delhi, 1967,
     pp. 23-29;   Revised edition, *Delhi*, 1975, pp. 21-28.

43   Abhishiktānanda, *Sac.*, p. 196.

44   ibid., p. 71;   See also p. 189;   Abhishiktānanda, *Towards the Renewal of
     the Indian Church*, Bangalore, 1970, pp. 6-7.

45   Abhishiktānanda, *Sac.*, p. 71

46   Abhishiktānanda, *The Further Shore*, Delhi, 1975, pp. 3-4.

47   ibid., p. 4.

48   ibid., pp. 25-31.

49   ibid., p. 37.

50   ibid., p. 34.   Though Abhishiktānanda stressed the aspect of renunciation
     he was alive to the value of various dimensions of human life.   See

ibid., p. 5; *Sac.*, pp. 151-153.

51 Abhishiktananda, *The Further Shore*, p. 55. Proposing a rite of initiation
    for the aspirant to Sannyasa, Abhishiktananda suggests that the Guru "...
    reminds him /the aspirant/ of the uniqueness of the *atman*, and so of his
    total freedom towards all beings, of his lack of obligation to anyone apart
    from the unique Spirit, and of his sole duty which is to remain fixed in
    the vision of his self, the inner mystery which is the non-dual *brahman*,
    while his mind remains totally absorbed in repeating endlessly the sacred
    OM with every breath he takes and every beat of his heart."

52 ibid., pp. 4-5.

53 ibid., p. 43.

54 ibid., p. 27.

55 Abhishiktananda, *Sac.*, Introduction, pp. xi-xii: "Not only is it necessary
    to grant the actual existence of religious pluralism here and now, but it
    is impossible to forsee a time in the historical future when Christianity
    might become for mankind as a whole even the predominant - let alone the
    only-way of realizing their transcendent vocation. It is no longer possible
    to accept the affirmation of 'crisis theology' that outside the biblical
    revelation all is darkness and sin; even the theology of 'fulfilment' is
    unable to do justice to all the facts of religious pluralism. On the other
    hand, a theology of 'cross-fertilization' scarsely leaves room for the claims
    of the Gospel; and the same has to be said of current attempts to discover
    the mystery of Christ in every kind of myth or religious affirmation, despite
    their having little or no relation with the historical mission among men of
    Jesus of Nazareth, even less with the Church which continues his work."

56 ibid., pp. 51-52.

57 Abhishiktānanda, *Cave*, p. 89.

58 ibid., p. 92.

59 ibid., pp. 40-41.

60 ibid., p. 85.

61 Abhishiktānanda, *Sac.*, pp. 11-13; See also p. 86.

62 Abhishiktānanda, *The Further Shore*, p. 25.

63 Abhishiktānanda, *Cave*, p. 105.

64 Abhishiktānanda, *The Further Shore*, p. 38.

65 Abhishiktānanda, *Sac.*, pp. 92; 118-120; 194 and so forth.

66 Abhishiktānanda, *Guru*, p. 8.

67 ibid., p. 104.

68 Abhishiktānanda, *Sac.*, *Introduction*, p. xv.

69 Bede Griffiths, *Christian Ashram, Essays towards a Hindu - Christian Dialogue*, London, 1966, p. 55, 86, 89, 94 etc.

70 Bede Griffiths, *Hinduism and Christianity*, in *The Examiner*,

120, 50, 1969.

71   Bede Griffiths, *Christian Ashram*, pp. 63-65.

72   ibid., pp. 75, 92.

73   Bede Griffiths, *Return to the Centre*, London, 1976. As this book is his latest work and gives his latest theological positions we are following it in our exposition of his approach.

74   ibid., p. 106.

75   ibid., p. 71.

76   ibid., pp. 86-87. This should not give the impression that the author is not aware of the differences between Kṛṣṇa, Christ and Buddha. In fact he brings out the differences too. See, ibid., pp. 82-87.

77   ibid., p. 87.

78   ibid., p. 112.

79   ibid., p. 70.

80   ibid., pp. 24-25.

81   ibid., p. 74.

82   ibid., pp. 25, 112.

83   ibid., p. 68: "The way to the Truth is not that of progress but that of

return. There can be no constant progress in the knowledge of the Truth. There is only a constant movement of return, of *metanoia*, of turning back. There can only be a constant striving to return to the Source, to the Origin, to what the Chinese call the 'uncarved block'." The author lays much stress on 'return to the Centre'. See p. 98, 104: About the depth of the soul he writes on p. 98: "It was from this Centre that man fell and it is to this Centre that he must return."

84   ibid., p. 118.

85   ibid., p. 119.

86   ibid., p. 120.

87   ibid., p. 126.

88   ibid., pp. 129-131.

89   ibid., p. 131.

90   ibid., p. 134.

91   ibid., pp. 136-139.

92   ibid., pp. 140-143.

93   ibid., p. 143.

94   ibid., pp. 145-146.

95   It is very difficult to present the rich, original theology of Panikkar
     as a unified whole on any topic owing to various reasons. He has written
     much and in many languages. It is difficult to have access to them all.
     Thoughts and ideas are expressed in a highly technical language. Con-
     sequently an effort to condense his thoughts runs the risk of watering them
     down and oversimplifying them. Our presentation of his theological thinking
     is in no way complete and is expressed in a simpler form within the limited
     perspective of our work. If some references may seem to be taken out of
     their proper context, it is on account of our concern for presenting what
     interests us as a whole.

96   The typology given in this paragraph is summarized from Raimundo Panikkar,
     The Emerging Myth in *Seed-Thoughts in Cross-Cultural Studies*, (cited as
     Seed-Thoughts) *Percées dans la problématique pluriculturelle* in *Monchanin*,
     numero - spécial, 8, 1975, pp. 8-11. *The Emerging Myth*
     is an English translation of Panikkar's *Preface* to Jacques Langlais' book
     Le Bouddha et les bouddhismes, Montreal, 1975.

97   ibid., p. 10.

98   ibid., pp. 10-11.

99   R. Panikkar, *The Category of Growth in Comparative Religion, A Critical Self-
     Examination* (cited as *Growth*), in *The Harvard Theological Review*, (HTR) Reprint, 66,
     1973, p. 114. The context is Panikkar's defence of his method of approach.
     What he says seem to be relevant to our context: "It seems to me that the
     deepest divergency with some of my critics is not so much in method as in
     the understanding of the fundamental Christian fact. Ultimately I would
     not accept an absolutization of Christianity so as to consider its truth
     an exclusive claim monopolizing salvation."

215

100   Raymond Panikkar, *Kerygma und Indien zur heilsgeschichtlichen Begegnung mit Indien* (cited as *Kerygma*), Hamburg - Bergstedt, 1967, p. 31: "Ein Christ besitzt nicht das Monopol sittlicher Qualität , weder auf der sogenannten natürlichen, noch auf der übernatürlichen Ebene."
p. 32: "Der Christ hat kein *Monopol der Wahrheit*: weder der menschlichen Wahrheit; denn menschliche Vernunft ist überall ein legitimes Mittel zu wahrer Erkenntnis; noch einer religiösen oder übernatürlichen Wahrheit. Die meisten der sogenannten christlichen Wahrheiten finden sich auch in anderen Religionen."
p. 33: "Der Christ hat endlich kein *Monopol des Heils*." See also, R. Panikkar, *Relation of Christians to their non-Christian Surroundings* in *Indian Ecclesiastical Studies*, (IES), 4, 1965, pp. 306-308.

101   Raymond Panikkar, *The Trinity and World Religions, Icon - Person - Mystery,* (cited as *Trinity*), Madras, 1970, pp. 3-4; Panikkar, *Kerygma*, pp. 102-103.

102   Panikkar, *Trinity*, p. 3.

103   Panikkar, *Growth*, in HTR, p. 120: "It is highly probable that parallel effor to those made from the christian side to liberate the christian kernel from i contingent forms may have to be made by all other religions of the world, though we should refrain from judging how far a particular religion has to go in this disentanglement, which some might like to call demythologizati and dekerygmatization."

104   ibid., pp. 123-124.
Raimundo Panikkar, *Le mythe comme histoire sacrée,* estratto, archivio di filosofia, diretto da Enrico Castelli, Roma, 1974, p. 313: "Nous retrouvons ici une invariante humaine qui, sous différents noms et aspects, se trouve dans toute culture humaine: *mokṣa,* ou textuellement,

libération, suivant toute la tradition indienne. *Soteria, salus*, liberté, émancipation, délivrance, indépendance sont autant de termes dans d'autres cultures et d'autres latitudes."

105 Panikkar, *Growth*, in HTR, pp. 130-132.

106 ibid., p. 132: "In order to know what a religion says, one has to under-
     stand what it says, but for this, one has somehow to believe in what it
     says. Religions are not purely objectifiable data; they are also
     essentially personal and thus subjective. In other words, the particular
     belief of the believer belongs essentially to religion. Without that
     belief no theology of religions is possible."

107 ibid., p. 133. P. 134: "The main reason, however, in favour of the
     possibility of such an enterprise is not the psychological capacity of the
     individual to experience sincerely more than one religious tradition, but
     the fact that there exists something like a fundamental religiousness, a
     constitutive religious dimension in man, an inbuilt religious or basic -
     human factor, or whatever we may care to call it. No religious tradition,
     surely, catches hold of the whole human being so as to leave no room for
     intercommunication and dialogue. Man, in fact, transcends his historical
     and cultural boundaries."

108 Raimundo Panikkar, *Have 'Religions' the Monopoly on Religion? Editorial*
     in *Journal of Ecumenical Studies*, 11, 1974, p. 517.

109 ibid., See also Panikkar, *Seed Thoughts*, in *Monchanin*, p. 49.

110 For this topic, see Raymondo Panikkar, *Kultmysterium in Hinduismus und
     Christentum, Ein Beitrag zur vergleichenden Religionstheologie* (cited as

Kult). Freiburg/München, 1964, pp. 39-44. No special references are given
since the ideas are condensed from the pages cited above. For differences
concerning time, the following article may be referred to: *Le temps
circulaire: temporisation et temporalité,* in *Temporalité et aliénation,*
Ed. Enrico Castelli, Aubier, 1975, pp. 207-246.

111 Panikkar, *Kerygma,* p. 21: "Das hingegen, was Indien hauptsächlich gesehen,
     erlebt und erlitten hat, sind im allgemeinen leider Verzerrungen, wenn
     nicht Karikaturen der *Einheit,* der *Apostolizität,* der *Heiligkeit* und
     der *Katholizität* der Kirche."
     p. 24: "Man halte hier nicht das Beispiel der Kirchen von Malabar entgegen
     als Beweis dafür, dass die Kirche in Indien nicht fremd ist. Es ist eine
     Tatsache, dass einerseits diese Kirchen die Grenzen Keralas nicht über-
     schritten haben, und dass andererseits die Situation im Innern selbst so
     komplex ist, dass sie hier kaum als Beispiel dienen kann. Doch nun steht
     es so, dass die Kirche nach zweitausendjähriger Existenz in Indien sich
     hier noch immer wie ein Importgut ausnimmt."

112 ibid., p. 17, 22.

113 ibid., p. 17: "Das Christentum ist einerseits wesentlich unabhängig von
     jeder Kultur und jeder Kultur überlegen, zweitens aber braucht das Christentum
     immer *eine* Kultur als Ausdrucksmittel, als notwendige Gestalt. Hierin
     liegt die ungeheure geschichtliche Spannung und die innere Dialektik des
     Christentums."

114 ibid., p. 47.

115 ibid., pp. 48-49: "Das Christentum ist, soziologisch gesprochen sicher
     eine Religion, es ist das antike Heidentum, oder, um es genauer zu sagen,

die komplexe hebräisch-hellenistisch-griechisch-lateinisch-keltisch-gotisch-
moderne Religion, *bekehrt* zu Christus mit mehr oder weniger Erfolg. Das
Christentum in Indien, um ein Beispiel zu geben, sollte nicht jene im-
portierte, voll entfaltete und hochentwickelte Religion sein, sondern der
Hinduismus selbst, der *bekehrt* ist - oder Islam, Buddhismus oder was es
sonst sein mag. Man muss sofort hinzufügen, dass dieser bekehrte Hinduismus
seiner Substanz nach das gleiche ist wie der alte und doch davon unter-
schieden, nämlich eine neue Kreatur."

116 ibid., p. 49: "Mit einem Wort, die Kirche bringt jede wahre und echte
Religion durch einen Prozess von Sterben und Auferstehen zu ihrer
Erfüllung. Das ist die tiefe Bedeutung der Bekehrung: Wahres Christentum
ist die Erfüllung jeder Religion durch Bekehrung." Translation author's own.

117 ibid.

118 ibid., p. 48: "Wir können hier nur soviel sagen: Christus kam nicht, um
eine Religion zu gründen, und noch weniger eine neue Religion, sondern um
alle Gerechtigkeit zu erfüllen und um jede Religion der Welt zu ihrer
Fülle zu bringen."
    This should not give the impression that Panikkar conceives ful-
filment as a one way traffic. He sees a mutual fulfilment, he proposes
also a cross-fertilization or mutual fecundation of religions: Panikkar,
Kult, p. 11: Indian idea of cult can help the West to overcome the split
between theory and practice; ibid., p. 175: India can contribute something
positive to the idea of contemplation; Panikkar, *Trinity*, p. 61: Advaita
can help to solve intratrinitarian problem and so forth. Panikkar, *Kerygma*,
p. 82: Hinduism and Christianity say that there was the Word in the beginning;
Panikkar, *Trinity*, p. 3: Christianity has to free itself for a fecundation
that will affect all religions. See also, ibid., p. 43; R. Panikkar,

The *Mutual Fecundation, Forward,* in *The Emerging Culture in India, Father Zacharias Lectures,* Ed. Thomas Paul, Alwaye, 1974, pp. 9-11.

119   R. Panikkar, *The Unknown Christ of Hinduism,* London, 1968, p. 11.

120   ibid., pp. 124-125.

121   ibid., pp. 125-126.

122   A defense of this method of christological interpretation of Hindu texts may be read in Panikkar, *Growth,* in HTR, pp. 121-123.

123   Panikkar, *The Unknown Christ of Hinduism,* pp. 126-131; An evaluation of Panikkar's approach is given by, J. Dupuis *The Unknown Christ of Hinduism,* in *The Clergy Monthly* (CMS) 7, 1965, pp. 278-283.

124   The sources available to us on the problem of the identity of Jesus is: R. Panikkar, *The Meaning of Christ's Name in the Universal Economy of Salvation,* in *Service and Salvation* (cited as *Meaning in Salvation*), *Nagpur Theological Conference on Evangelization,* Ed. Joseph Pathrapankal, Bangalore 1973, pp. 235-263: The same article is found in Estratto da *Evangelisation Dialogue and Development, Documenta Missionalia,* 5, Roma, 1972, pp. 195-218. R. Panikkar, *Action and Contemplation as Categories of Religious Understandi* in *Main Currents in Modern Thought,* 30, 1973, pp. 78-79; See also Panikkar, *Growth,* in HTR, pp. 113-140. Special references except for quotations are not given as the sources are indicated.

125   Panikkar, *Meaning in Salvation,* p. 242.

126   ibid., pp. 246-247.

127   There is no singularity without plurality; individuality is that which

220

distinguishes one from others. Uniqueness leaves no room for comparison.

128 Panikkar, *Meaning* in *Salvation*, p. 250.

129 ibid.

130 ibid., p. 255.

131 ibid., p. 257.

132 This paragraph is derived from Panikkar, *Growth*, in HTR, pp. 126-130.

133 ibid., p. 128.

134 Panikkar, *Kerygma*, p. 44.

135 ibid., p. 35: "Ein wirklicher Kontakt mit der Gottheit ist immer, bewusst oder unbewusst, trinitarisch, so dass ein totes oder monistisches Absolutes nur eine Illusion ist."

136 *Karma mārga* is way of ritual action, *bhakti mārga*, way of loving devotion and *jñāna mārga*, way of knowledge. Panikkar describes these three ways. Panikkar, *Trinity*, pp. 11-39. See also Panikkar, *Kerygma*, pp. 102-120.

137 Panikkar, *Trinity*, pp. 41-42.

138 ibid., p. 44. For Panikkar's interpretation of the mystery of the Trinity, reference may be made also to Panikkar, *Kerygma*, pp. 120-133.

139 Panikkar, *Trinity*, ibid.

140   Panikkar, *Trinity*, pp. 44-45.

141   ibid., p. 46.

142   ibid., p. 50.

143   ibid., p. 59.

144   ibid., p. 67.

145   See also ibid., pp. 11-39.

146   ibid., p. 46.

147   ibid.

148   ibid., pp. 50-53.

149   ibid., pp. 62-64.

150   ibid., p. 69.

151   ibid., pp. 69-70; For this and for what follows on theandrism see also
       Panikkar, *Kerygma*, pp. 133-138.

152   Panikkar, *Trinity*, pp. 70-72.

153   ibid., p. 72.

154   ibid., p. 73.

155   ibid., pp. 75-80.

156   ibid., p. 80. For theandrism as a spirituality, see also, Raimundo Panikkar, *The Theandric Vocation*, in *The Living Word*, 81, 1975, pp. 67-75.

157   For Panikkar's use of the word dimension see Panikkar, *Le mythe comme histoire sacrée*, op. cit., p. 299, 301; Panikkar, *Kerygma*, p. 76, 100, 118, 120; Panikkar, *Kult*, p. 23, 107, 189, 204; Pannikkar, *Trinity*, p. 35, 42 etc.

158   It is not possible for us to study Panikkar's idea of truth. Reference is given to certain aspects interesting from our point of view.

159   Panikkar, *The Unknown Christ of Hinduism*, p. 67.

160   Panikkar, *Kerygma*, p. 87.

161   Panikkar, *Seed-Thoughts*, in *Monchanin*, p. 57, 59.

162   The Source is Raimundo Panikkar, *Some Notes on Syncretism and Eclecticism Related to the Growth of Human Consciousness* in *Religious Syncretism in Antiquity, Essays in Conversation with Geo Widengren*, Ed. Birger A. Pearson, Santa Barbara, 1975, pp. 47-62.

163   ibid., pp. 48-49.

164   ibid., p. 54.

165   ibid., p. 55.

166   ibid., p. 50.

167   ibid., p. 53.

168   ibid., p. 55.

169   ibid., pp. 51-55.

170   ibid., pp. 55-59.

171   Panikkar, *Growth*, in HTR, p. 137.

172   Panikkar, *Some Notes on Syncretism and Eclecticism*, in *Religious Syncretism in Antiquity*, p. 61.

173   D. S. Amalorpavadass, *Destinée de l'Eglise dans l'Inde d'aujourd'hui. Conditionnements de l'évangélisation* (cited as *Destinée*), Fayard-Name, 1967, pp. 42-64.

174   ibid., p. 44.

175   ibid., pp. 45-46.

176   ibid., p. 46.

177   ibid., pp. 47-49.

178   ibid., pp. 50-57.

179   ibid., p. 57. For a detailed explanation of these reactions, see pp. 57-64

180   ibid., pp. 65-66; p. 66: "L'Inde est peut-être aujourd'hui dans le creuse (melting pot), mais elle doit harmoniser de façon organique l'élément durab

et transcendant de sa tradition spirituelle avec tout ce qui est profitable
et nécessaire dans la civilisation mondiale. L'âme de l'Inde ne peut vivre
sans le spirituel; son corps a besoin du matériel pour subsister. Quand
l'Inde vivra corps et âme - l'âme au-dessus du corps, mais pour l'animer -
alors elle présentera la synthèse vivante et originale que le monde entier
attend d'elle."

181   Amalorpavadass, *Destinée*, pp. 73-78.

182   ibid., pp. 78-81.

183   ibid., pp. 81-85.

184   ibid., pp. 85-86: "Reste à l'Inde un autre Sauveur: le Christ. Nous
       savons qu'il n'est pas comme d'autres un 'imposteur' (Mat. 27, 62), mais
       le vrai Rédempteur, le Sauveur unique de l'univers, de toute l'humanité.
       Son message de salut, l'Evangile, son instrument de salut, l'Eglise, peuvent
       apporter à l'Inde le remède parfait à ses maux. Le vide creusé dans les
       esprits par la destruction des dieux anciens, la vanité qu'ils découvrent
       dans les nouvelles idoles, les inclinent précisément non pas au communisme
       athée, mais au christianisme sauveur. La lutte de l'âme indienne pour
       implanter une spiritualité aux racines profondes dans les structures profanes
       imposées par la civilisation technico-matérielle est un appel évident à une
       religion qui est par sa nature même, une véritable incarnation du spirituel
       dans le matériel, un appel au Dieu incarné et à l'Eglise son corps."
       Translation author's own.

185   For this paragraph see Amalorpavadass, *Destinée*, pp. 95-102. No special
       reference is given unless quoted.

186   ibid., p. 102:   "La conclusion s'impose naturellement: puisque toutes

les religions sont également bonnes et nécessaires, également impuissantes
et inadéquates, toutes méritent une tolérance égale."

187   ibid., pp. 102-103.

188   ibid., pp. 103-106.

189   ibid., pp. 111-124.

189a   ibid., p. 117. A church in Vardhaman Nagar, a village in the State of
       Bihar was profaned by the members of the Hindu Maha Sabha during mass in Octo
       1955. For some other incidents see ibid., pp. 115-119.

190   For such favourable and unfavourable factors arising from Hinduism see ibid.,
       pp. 140-144.

191   For the whole paragraph refer ibid., pp. 151-152.

192   For more details see D. S. Amalorpavadass, *Preaching the Gospel Today.
       Main Problems in Mission Lands*. Bangalore, 1973, pp. 25-26; Amalorpavadass,
       Destinée, pp. 210-211.

193   For details, refer D. S. Amalorpavadass, *L'Inde à la rencontre du Seigneur*,
       (cited as *L'Inde*), Paris, 1964, pp. 238-322; Amalorpavadass,*Preaching the
       Gospel Today*, pp. 12-24; Amalorpavadass, *Destinée*, pp. 152-210. No special
       reference is given unless quoted since we give only a very general view.

194   Amalorpavadass, *L'Inde*, pp. 318-319: "Aujourd'hui nous attendons tout de Ro
       dans notre fidelité à la tradition. Même si Rome nous demande de nous servi
       notre intelligence, de notre cerveau comme il faut, nous préférons recevoir
       tout de Rome, jusqu'aux derniers détails. Nous avons simplement identifié l

tradition avec un musée éternel des idées et des règles dont le plus grand
est à Rome.

... Elle voudrait se montrer plus romaine que Rome, plus papiste que
le Pape et plus italienne que l'Italie. Elle est tellement obéissante à
Rome qu'elle va même jusqu' à désobéir à Rome, si paradoxal qu'il soit.
Autrement dit, l'Eglise de l'Inde ne veut pas changer si Rome ne donne
pas l'ordre formel, tous les détails tout cuits." Translation author's
own.

195   D. S. Amalorpavadass, *Theology of Evangelization in the Indian Context*,
Bangalore, 1973, p. 10.

196   ibid., pp. 10-11.

197   ibid., pp. 11-12.

198   For this paragraph refer D. S. Amalorpavadass, *Approach Meaning and Horizon
of Evangelization*, (cited as *Approach*), Bangalore, 1973, pp. 15-23. No
special reference is given unless quoted.

199   ibid., p. 17.

200   The following is Resolution No. 2 of the World Congress of Theology on the
Future of the Church, Brussels 12th - 17th September, 1970, quoted by
Amalorpavadass, ibid., p. 17: "Theology is 'a reflection of Christians upon
their faith and their Christian experience in a particular time and culture.
Hence only Christian communities, involved in the life of the contemporary
world, and taking active responsibility within their society can fashion
the theology of the future'."

201   Amalorpavadass, *Approach*, p. 17.

202   Amalorpavadass relies much on the teaching of the Nagpur Theological
      Conference and on that of the Bombay Seminar. The reference to the same
      is found in the book of Amalorpavadass to which we are giving reference.
      Hence special reference to the above mentioned events is not given.

203   Amalorpavadass, *Approach*, p. 55.

204   ibid., p. 54.

205   ibid., pp. 56-57.

206   ibid., p. 57.

207   See *Research Seminar on Non-Biblical Scriptures* (cited as
      Research Seminar), Ed. D. S. Amalorpavadass, Bangalore, 1975. Later
      special reference will be made to this Seminar.

208   Amalorpavadass, *Approach*, pp. 57-58.

209   ibid., p. 58.

210   D. S. Amalorpavadass, *Approaches in our Apostolate Among Non-Christians*,
      Bangalore, 1970, p. 5.

211   ibid., pp. 27-28.

212   ibid., p. 28.

213   The principal ideas of this topic may be found in Amalorpavadass, *Theolog*
      of Evangelization, pp. 19-23:, Amalorpavadass, *Approach*, pp. 89-93. No

special reference is given unless quoted.

214   Amalorpavadass, *Approach*, p. 89.

215   ibid., p. 49.

216   For Local Church see ibid., pp. 48-51; Amalorpavadass, *Theology of Evangelization*, pp. 17-19; D. S. Amalorpavadass, *Towards Indigenisation in the Liturgy, Reflection, Policy, Programme and Texts* (cited as *Liturgy*), Bangalore, (1972?), pp. 14-18. A summary of the thought of Amalorpavadass on the Universal Church is found in *Approach*, pp. 37-48; it is beyond our scope to deal with it. For a comprehensive view of his ecclesiology, his major works *L'Inde* and *Destinée*, are to be referred to. No special reference is given unless quoted.

217   Amalorpavadass, *Approach*, pp. 48-49.

218   Amalorpavadass, *Liturgy*, p. 14.

219   ibid., p. 17.

220   Amalorpavadass, *Destinée*, pp. 258-259: "En prenant notre nature, en se faisant l'un de nous, en venant sauver le genre humain, le Christ a assumé, sauvé et intégré tout ce qui est humain, non seulement les individus, mais les ensembles collectifs, toutes les réalités matérielles, toutes les civilisations et cultures, toutes les formes de pensée, toutes les religions, tout ce qui fait l'homme et tout ce que l'homme fait, toute l'existence humaine et toute l'activité humaine, toute la création de l'homme aussi bien que toute la création de Dieu, particulièrement toute l'attente et la recherche de Dieu et du salut. Le Christ a tout récapitulé, a tout sauvé, a tout marqué du signe de croix, a tout amené à son achèvement en intégrant tout

dans la marche de l'humanité sauvée, vers le Père, par le Fils et dans l'Espr
dans le courant de la charité trinitaire. Ainsi, dans le mystère de
l'Incarnation et de la Rédemption universelle, nous trouvons le fondement
de toute l'adaptation, et, dans le Christ, nous avons le modèle parfait de
l'adaptation missionnaire." Translation author's own.

221 ibid., p. 259: "L'Eglise, le Corps mystique du Christ, en participant
intimenent à ce mystère du Christ - l'Incarnation et la Rédemption -
continue le Christ à travers l'espace et le temps, et continue l'adaptation
du Christ lui-même."

222 ibid.,

223 For a more comprehensive view of the problem of adaptation, what has
already been achieved and remains to be done in India, Refer Amalorpavadass,
L'Inde; *Destinée*, pp. 147-324 etc.

224 Amalorpavadass, *Liturgy*, p. 21.

225 ibid., p. 22.

226 ibid., pp. 23-24.

227 ibid., pp. 56-57.

228 ibid., pp. 33-150. Among the suggestions, an important one is the use of
Hindu and other scriptures in Liturgy. See ibid., p. 51.

229 ibid., pp. 78-83; 87-94.

230   ibid., p. 48: "In the II All-India Liturgical Meeting held in Bangalore
      28th November - 4th December 1971 it was studied in depth, approved and
      unanimously hailed as a very enriching addition to the prayer of the
      Indian people. The delegates requested the Chairman of the Commission to
      get the approval of the CBCI for use in India. It was submitted to the
      bishops at the Ordinary General Meeting of the CBCI held in Madras 6th -
      14th April 1972, for their approval. Though it obtained 60 votes out of
      80, it has not been declared passed due to a dispute on the majority
      required." CBCI abbreviation of Catholic Bishops Conference of India.

231   *Letter of James Cardinal Knox, Prefect, Sacred Congregation for Divine
      Worship to Joseph Cardinal Parecattil, Chairman of the Indian Episcopal
      Conference.* Prot.n. 789/75 Vatican City dated 14th June 1975. *A
      Communication from the Standing Committee of the Catholic Bishops'
      Conference of India to (I) All Local Ordinaries, and (2) Major Superiors
      of Religious (Men and Women),* dated 20th October 1975. A copy of these
      documents have been received by us in an unoffical communication from the
      CBCI Secretariate, New Delhi, Ref. No. DSG/MIS/141/77 dated 15th February
      1977. The same documents have been published by *The Laity,* a monthly, well-
      known for its attachment to tradition. See *The Laity, Journal of Christian
      Thought and Action,* 4, 1976, pp. 12-15.

232   Amalorpavadass, *Destinée*, p. 296.

233   ibid., pp. 296-298.

234   ibid., p. 300; Amalorpavadass, *Approach*, p. 61: "It /dialogue/ gradually leads
      the partners towards that ultimate vision and perfect unification of all men
      which can be discerned in the convergent aspects of the various religious
      traditions."

235   Amalorpavadass, *Destinée*, p. 301.

236   ibid., pp. 301-308.

237   ibid., p. 310.

238   ibid., p. 315, 322.

239   ibid., p. 322. See also Amalorpavadass, *Approaches in our Apostolate among Non-Christians,* p. 29.

240   Amalorpavadass, *Approach* , p. 61.

241   ibid., pp. 62-63.

242   ibid., pp. 63-65. P. 65: "This salvation of the whole man and of all men and the re-creation of a new earth consists in the humanization of man in the whole gamut of his relationships within family, social, economic, political and cultural spheres, in liberating him from all forms of alienation, psychological, existential, social, ideological and cosmic and in the redemption of all the realities of the temporal order." See also D. S. Amalorpavadass, *Theology of Development*, Bangalore, 1972, p. 7.

243   Amalorpavadass, *Theology of Development*, p. 10.

244   Amalorpavadass, *Approach,* pp. 65-68. *Theology of Development*, pp. 11-12.

245   Amalorpavadass, *Theology of Development*, p. 9.

245a   See Ref. 231.

246   At present Vempeny is preparing a doctoral thesis on the Doctrine of Divine
Incarnation in the *Gītā* and the New Testament in the Gujarat university,
Ahmedbad.

246a Ishanand Vempeny, *An Approach to the Problem of Inspiration in the Non-
Biblical Scriptures,* in *Research Seminar.,* op. cit., (Ref. 207) pp. 160-164.
According to the author the a priori pluralistic approach tries to enter into
non-Christian religious experience from the point of view of non-Christians
themselves bracketing for a while their own faith. While this gives due
consideration to the personalistic dimension of religion and favours
tolerance, it adopts an artificial renunciation of one's own faith and
leads to unhealthy pluralism.

247   ibid., pp. 164-167. In the opinion of Vempeny this method tries to acquire
doctrinal knowledge of non-Christian religions starting from Christian
doctrines found in the Bible and as interpreted by the Church; it
preserves the commitment dimension of Christianity but misses the experiential and commitment dimensions of non-Christian religions.

248   ibid., pp. 167-170.

249   Ishanand Vempeny, *Inspiration in the Non-Biblical Scriptures,* Bangalore
1973, p. 23.

250   For some such passages refer ibid., pp. 25-29. The author cites these
passages and speaks of their inspiring nature but not as a proof of the
inspiration of non-biblical Scriptures. See ibid., p. 22.

251   One of the references for a parallel passage cited by Vempeny is the
following. *Mahābhārata,* XIII, 5571, quoted by Panikkar in

Relation of Christians to their Non-Christian Surroundings in *Christian Revelation and World Religions*, Ed. Neuner J. & Roos H., London 1967, p. 178 as cited by Vempeny, *Inspiration in the Non-Biblical Scriptures*, op. cit., p. 30: "This is the summit of all virtues: deal with others as you wish that others deal with you. When you please or displease them you do good or have to hurt... you will follow the just norm if you consider your neighbour as yourself." Vempeny does not give any reference to NT texts. The texts quoted are similar to Mt 7.12; 22.39. For other texts, ibid., pp. 29-31.

252   The following texts are quoted by the author to show that OT texts are influenced by them. *Ancient and Near Eastern Texts*, Ed. James B. Pritchard, Princeton 1950, pp. 423 and 426 as cited by Vempeny, *Inspiration in the Non-Biblical Scriptures*, p. 33: "One thing are the words which men say, Another is that which the God does.

Unto your opponent do not evil; Your evil-doer recompense with good; Unto your enemy let justice (be done)." No specification is given by Vempeny except that they are writings of the Near East. Compare these texts with Pr 19.21; 16.9;   25. 21-22; Dt. 32.4. For other texts from the writings of the Near East, see Vempeny, ibid., pp. 31-34.

253   Vempeny, *Inspiration in the Non-Biblical Scriptures*, pp. 33-34.

254   ibid., pp. 34-37.

255   ibid., p. 42.

256   ibid.

257   ibid., pp. 44-46.

258   ibid., pp. 46-47.

259   ibid., p. 47.

260   ibid., To substantiate his statement the author gives the example of Vedic
       literature which expresses the life of the vedic man.   See also pp. 48-59.

261   ibid., p. 58.

262   ibid., p. 59.   The author refers to K. Rahner, *Inspiration in the Bible*,
       Tr. Charles H. Henkey, New York, 1963.

263   K. Rahner, *Inspiration in the Bible*, op. cit., p. 50 as cited by Vempeny,
       Inspiration in Non-Biblical Scriptures, p. 43.

264   The author gives various texts from the NT in support of his statement.
       See Vempeny, *Inspiration in Non-Biblical Scriptures*, pp. 72-73
       and on p. 73 remarks: "The OT and the NT together constitute one reality,
       and the one is unintelligible without the other."

265   ibid., p. 74: "Another reason... which makes us posit this vital
       connection between the two Testaments is the result of God's positive
       intervention in history, in space and time."   Vempeny refers to Hb. 1.12;
       Gal. 4.4; 2 Cor. 1.20, etc., and continues: "The point we want to make
       is that the preparation for the arrival of Christ in Israel was not
       something just by way of God's transcendental causality but by HIS
       positive interventions in history...   Indeed the central elements for the
       jewish creed such as the promise (Gen. 12.1-3) and the election (Dt. 7.6;
       Ex. 19.6) were the expressions of Yahweh's interventions in history."

266   ibid., pp. 76-77: "The Church, down the centuries, has firmly held the
       truth that the experience of God described in the Bible is an experience

due to his interventions in history, in contrast with the experience of
God one may have by contact with the natural realities. This historical
nature of the Biblical revelation is almost clearly taught by Vat. II.
According to the Council, revelation in the Bible is one through his
'words and deeds having an inner unity.' (D.V. 2). The Dogmatic
Constitution first speaks of God's revelation 'through the created realities'
(no. 3) and then goes on to explain God's various salvific deeds from
Adam to Christ.

Then when we speak of the ontological connection between the two
Testaments we mean primarily the two points we have just made above,
viz., that the OT religion was caused by God and it was oriented towards
the NT religion. Now, as in the case of any socio-religious phenomenon
the OT is the constitutive element of the OT religion. Hence, God's
causality with regard to the OT religion itself. Here we are positing
inspiration in the OT transposing Fr. Rahner's thesis on inspiration in
the NT."

267   ibid., p. 77.

268   ibid., pp. 117-119. This hostility arose from political hostility and
       turned into religious hostility since at that time no distinction was made
       between religion and politics and each tribe invoked its God against the
       other. The NT may not always be sympathetic to the gentiles but the
       condemnations pronounced against the Jewish leaders should not be for-
       gotten. What is condemned is sinfulness and corruption.

269   ibid., pp. 119-121. The author quotes 1 Tim. 2.4; Rom. 3.21-31;
       Jn. 10.16, and other texts in support of his arguments and refers to the
       Fathers of the Church and some theologians.

270   ibid., pp. 90-93.

271   ibid., p. 95.

272   ibid., pp. 96-116. The author gives various institutional expressions
      of Hindu faith experience such as temples, festivals, pilgrimages, sources
      of Hindu agape such as family and hospitality.

273   ibid., p. 124.

274   ibid., pp. 125-134. The election of Israel was an election for others
      (pp. 126-127); the role of Abraham for the whole mankind, the blessing
      to Abraham in which all nations participate already beginning to operate
      through his grandson Joseph to whom people from all over the world came to
      buy corn in time of famine show election and non-election fall into the
      economy of salvation (pp. 127-128). The same universalism is seen in
      Deutero-Isiah, in the theology of the Book of Jonah and in the approbation
      of the pagan relgions in the Bible and in the NT attitude to pagans (pp.
      128-134).

275   ibid., p. 134.

276   ibid., pp. 137-138.

277   ibid., pp. 139-144. Vempeny gives a short explanation of this interior
      revelation in p. 142: "We hold this as true revelation because here God
      communicates Himself as He is, inviting man to salvific commitment. It is
      historical in the sense that it occurs in space and time, in the secret
      recesses of each individual person."

278   ibid., p. 147.

279   ibid., p. 148.

280   ibid., p. 167.

281   ibid., pp. 177-178. Vempeny puts the whole conclusion in capital letters.
       While quoting we do not find it necessary to put them in capital letters.

282   Mattam, *Land*, (Ref. 3a).

283   Since our purpose is not to make a detailed critical study of Mattam's
       approach we give general reference to his summary and evaluation and special
       reference in case of quotations.

284   Olivier Lacombe was born at Liège, Belgium in 1904. He is considered to
       be an authority on Hinduism in the French speaking world. He was Professor
       and held a number of responsible posts such as Professor of Humanities at
       the University of Lille and Professor of Comparative Philosophy at the
       Sorbonne. For more details refer to Mattam, *Land*, pp. 44-45. For a
       summary and evaluation of Lacombe's approach see ibid., pp.
       62-68.

285   ibid., pp. 62-63.

286   If we understand correctly, Mattam's description of the division of élan
       may be reduced to the following:
       élan at the ontic level = the experienced unexpressed level = advaitic
       experience. Elan at the conscious level = the expressed level corresponds
       to *bhakti*. See Mattam, *Land* pp. 64-67.

287   ibid., p. 68.

288   Jacques Albert Cuttat was born in Delémont in Switzerland in 1909. He
       became a professor and diplomat. He was Swiss Ambassador to India.

For more details refer to Mattam, *Land*, pp.74-75. For a summary and evaluation of his approach refer ibid., pp. 101-104.

289   ibid., p. 103:"...the 'distance' he speaks of between man and God which is necessary according to the Western system of thinking needs to be overcome." Mattam remarks that the distinction between the two spiritualities /b̄hakti and advaita/ may be justified on the conceptual level.

290   ibid., p. 104.

291   Robert Charles Zaehner was born in 1913 in England and was converted to Catholicism in 1946. He was Spalding Professor of Eastern Religions and Ethics at the University of Oxford till his death in 1974. For more details refer to Mattam, *Land.*, pp. 111-112. For a summary and evaluation of his approach refer ibid., pp. 135-139.

292   ibid., p. 136.

293   ibid., p. 138.

294   ibid., pp. 180-188. Except for quotations no special reference is given since we are depending only on the few above mentioned pages.

295   ibid., p. 187.

296   ibid., 186.

297   We have not so far been able to verfiy whether the work of T. M. Manickam, *Dharma according to Manu and Moses* at present in print deals directly with Indian theology.

297a   The establishment of a Centre for the Study of World Religions, the
publication of the *Journal of Dharma, An International Quarterly of
World Religions*, Bangalore, and that of *Jeevadhāra, A Journal of Christian
Interpretation*, in two editions, English and Malayalam, Aleppey, are to be
considered contributions to the formation of an Indian theology.

298   Some of their publications are John B. Chethimattam and Antonio T. de
Nicolas, *A Philosophy in Song - Poems, Selected Song - Poems of the
Ṛgveda*, Bangalore, 1971; Kurian T. Kadankavil, *The Philosophy of the
Absolute, A Critical Study of Krishnachandra Bhattācharya's Writings*,
Bangalore, 1972; Kurian T. Kadankavil, *The Quest of the Real, A Study
of the Philosophical Methodology of Muṇḍakopaniṣad*, Bangalore, 1975;
Augustine G. Aranjaniyil, *The Absolute of the Upaniṣads, Personal or
Impersonal?* Bangalore, 1975.

298a   Chethimattam seems to be the first among them to give a certain orientation
and suggest various possible approaches; Nambiaparampil is engaged in
dialogue with religions on an all-India level and Manickam proposes to
build an Indian Christology on experience *(anubhava)* as criterion
(pramāṇa). These are the reasons which motivated our
choice.

299   John B. Chethimattam, *Consciousness and Reality, An Indian Approach to Metaphysics*, New York, 1971, p. 91. Writing on the capacity to integrate the
various levels of thought in the Indian approach, Chethimattam remarks: "Th
both proceed from knowledge to the study of reality, consciousness takes
the thing in all its aspects, while rational analysis takes a particular
aspect of the phenomenon apart and studies it in isolation."

300   ibid., p. 207. An example of divergent approach: "For the Greeks, God,

the Supreme Being is the climax of the cosmic order. Hence, He is
conceived as the One, the unifying point of everything, the absolute
Good and Beauty from which everything else gets its share... Approach
to God from consciousness interiorizes God. God, who is called *brahman*,
the one who is really big, the all, is also the *ātman*, the real self of
every being. An exteriorized God is no God but a mere phenomenon –
at best, a symbol of the divine, with only a pschological and pedagogical
value." For the divergence and complementary character of the western
and Indian approaches refer ibid., pp. 122, 147-148, 202-209.

301   ibid., p. 209.

302   John B. Chethimattam, *Patterns of Indian Thought, A Students Introduction,*
      London, 1971, p. 150.

303   John B. Chethimattam,   *Theology as Human Interiority: Search for the One
      Teacher* in *Unique and Universal, Fundamental Problems of an Indian Theology*,
      (cited as *Unique*), Ed. J. B. Chethimattam, Bangalore, 1972, p. 183.

304   ibid., pp. 183-184. He does not classify the methods. "Another method for
      Hindu-Christian encounter was to go behind the particular structures of
      religious expression and see the problems involved in an experience and to
      see also the solution actually proposed." For us what he refers to does not
      seem to be quite clear. He continues: "Here one managed to break through
      the barriers of Christianity and Hinduism and strove to understand the
      common religious problems of both. This method also is defective since it
      fails to understand what is unique either to Christianity or to Hinduism.
      ... A third method proposed has been for the Hindu to express his faith
      using the idioms and expressions of Christianity and for the Christian
      to meditate on Christian revelation in and through Hindu interiority. Here
      again there is a certain comparison involved and there is no clear meeting
      point between two faiths."

305   ibid., pp. 184-187.

306   ibid., p. 186. Refer our own ch. 1.2.3.2.f.

307   ibid., p. 187.

308   ibid., p. 188.

309   ibid., pp. 188-189.

310   ibid., p. 189.

311   ibid., p. 189. The Buddhist and Jains stressed the importance of community and the *Ṛgveda* that of priestly community, which shows a certain ecclesial aspect of religion in Indian tradition. For these communities the Buddha, the Tīrthankara and the Guru are models. The author does not give any reference for these statements.

312   ibid., p. 190.

313   ibid., pp. 190-195.

314   Albert Nambiaparampil, *Linguistic Philosophy and Indian Theology* in *Unique*, pp. 44-47.

315   Albert Nambiaparampil, *Religious Language in a Dialogic Context - A Linguistic Approach* in *Research Seminar*, p. 570.

316   ibid., pp. 570-572.

317   ibid., pp. 572-573.

318   ibid., pp. 573-574.

319   ibid., p. 575

320   ibid., p. 576. The author gives only the following reference to his state-
       ment. *Summa Theologica* II/II q 45, a.2. No reference to Maritain is given.

321   ibid.

322   Nambiaparampil, *Linguistic Philosophy and Indian Theology*, in *Unique*, p. 50.

323   ibid.

324   Albert Nambiaparampil, *Dialogue in India, An Analysis of the Situation, a
       reflection on experience* in *Journal of Dharma*, 1, 1976, pp. 267-283.

325   Nambiaparampil, *Linguistic Philosophy and Indian Theology*, in *Unique*, p. 51.

325a   Thomas Marshal Manickyakuzhy usually employs a shorter form of his name:
       T. M. Manickam. We use this shorter form throughout.

325b   As our work is going to the press, we have received information that
       Manickam's thesis is published. Refer Supplementary Bibliography.

326   T. M. Manickam, *Anubhava as Pramāṇa of an Indian Christology*
       (cited as *Anubhava*) in JD, 1, 1971, pp. 234-238.
       Confrontation with the powers of nature caused an experience
       of wonder *(sambhramānubhava)* and awakened them to the perception of a
       Mysterious Power encircling them which commanded respect and veneration;
       this in turn led to *sādarānubhūti*, an experience of reverence for a
       Mysterium Tremendum, an awe-inspiring and terrible hidden Being, to worship
       and religion; imagination and personifications of natural powers led to
       polytheistic experience though attempts to go deeper to the realm of the
       Mysterious Power itself are not wanting. These experiences are characterized
       as *prakṛtyanubhava*. Oral transmission of this experience is termed

243

śrutyanubhava about which more details are given in the text itself. *Bhaktyanubhava* is an experience of devotion arising from man's perception of a Supreme Power as personal God; it leads to commitment and communion with God, which is the ultimate point of realization.

327   ibid., pp. 235-236. *Śruti* stands for scriptures in the Indian tradition. Manickam remarks that gradually the experiential aspect of *śruti* was neglected and the liturgical role of *śruti* began to dominate; this in turn necessitated the development of a pedagogical role to interpret vedic *anubhava*; the pedagogical role exercised by Gurus around whom disciples sat led to the formation of *Upaniṣads*.

328   T. M. Manickam, *'Insight' as Inspiration and 'Anubhava' as Revelation in the Hindu Scriptures* (cited as *Insight*) in *Research Seminar*, pp. 325-326; 332.

329   ibid., p. 326, 329.

330   ibid., pp. 327-329.

331   ibid., pp. 329-330.

332   ibid., p. 325.

333   ibid., p. 333

334   T. M. Manickam,*Theology as Experience of Revelation,* in *Unique*, pp. 198-199.

335   ibid., pp. 198-199.

336   ibid., p. 199

337   ibid., p. 199.

338   Manickam, *Insight* in *Research Seminar*, p. 335.

339   ibid.

340   Manickam, *Anubhava*, in JD, p. 228.

341   ibid.

342   ibid., pp. 228-229.

343   ibid., p. 229.

344   ibid.

345   ibid., pp. 230-231.

346   ibid., pp. 239-240.

347   ibid., p. 239.

348   ibid., pp. 230-232.

349   ibid., p. 239; The following on pp. 241-242 gives a concise sketch of
       the Christ - experience of some Indian devotees: "Christ as *Divine Cit*
       (God's Consciousness) working in us was the content of Brahmabandhab
       Upādhyāya's Christ - experience. Sadhu Sunder Singh had the *anubhava*
       of the *Living Christ* who is the *antaryāmin* (Indweller in us). For Ram
       Mohan Roy, Christ was the great *dharmādhyāpaka* (Moral Teacher) to whom
       he could commit himself. Keśub Cunder Sen had a meditative awareness

of Christ's *Divine humanity*. P. C. Mazoomdar's experience of Christ
as 'the *Divine Spirit in human form*' may yet to be clarified. Swami
Vivekananda's acceptance of Christ as *Jīvanmukta* has a deeper meaning
in our religious tradition. Dr. Radhakrishnan's *anubhava* of the 'Mystic
Christ,' and Mahatma Gandh's ideal of Christ as the *Supreme satyāgrahi,*
are also indicators of the deepest levels of the mystery of Christ who
is 'the Light which enlightens every man.'"

350   ibid., p. 241.

351   ibid., p. 242.

352   ibid., pp. 243-244.

353   For details the following books may be consulted: 1. *All-India Seminar
       on the Church in India Today*, May 15th - 25th, 1969, *Preparatory
       Seminars, An Assessment,* New-Delhi, (1969?)   2. *All-India Seminar on
       the Church in India Today*, Bangalore, May 15th - 25th, 1969, *Orientation
       Papers*, New-Delhi, 1969; 3. *All India Seminar Church in India
       Today*, Bangalore 1969, New-Delhi, 1969. We quote only from the book
       mentioned last and is referred simply as *Church in India*.

354   *Church in India*, p. 29: "The Seminar..., was an event that called for
       intense preparation; and one, moreover, that involved all sections
       of the People of God from every part of the country... Bishops and
       priests, men and women, religious and laity, young and old, met and
       discussed the Seminar topics at length in 14 Regional Seminars, 51
       Diocesan Seminars, 9 National Consultations, 19 Seminary Seminars
       and a large number of seminars organized by special groups. Participants
       at all these gatherings numbered over 10,000."

355 *Declaration of the All India Seminar on the Church in India Today* in
     Church in India, p. 241:

> "Within the Christian fellowship we have not always placed the
> accent on the essentials of our faith; and in our relations with others
> we have tended in many ways to lack understanding and to stand aloof from
> the mainstream of India's thought patterns and traditions as well as of
> her contemporary development, by confining ourselves to the fostering of
> our narrow, domestic interests."

356 *Seminar Resolutions* in *Church in India*, pp. 249-50: "... since each
     nation and culture reflects a particular aspect of the infinite mystery
     of Christ, and India, for all her profusion of popular religion, has
     always been drawn more strongly perhaps than any other people to the
     contemplative way of silence, solitude and total detachment, anticipating
     by many hundred years with the *'neti, neti,'* (not this, not this) of her
     ṛṣis the total renunciation of the early Christian monks and hermits, the
     vocation of the Church in India must surely be to show forth to the world
     in an especially striking way this facet of the mystery of Christ, who
     after days of intense and crowded labour 'went into the mountains alone'
     and spent 'the whole night in the prayer of God.'" See also p. 253.

357 ibid., p. 254.

358 *Declaration of the All India Seminar on the Church in India Today* in
     Church in India, p. 242: "We urgently need a theology that is truly
     Indian in its categories of thought and in the situations that it
     envisages, a theology that springs from a Christian faith that is lived
     and pondered in the vital context of the Indian spiritual tradition and
     its heritage of sacred literature as well as of the conditions and the
     mentality that prevail in our country today."

359   *Seminar Resolution* in *Church in India*, p. 262.

360   For details refer *Salvation*, (Ref. 124).

361   *Declaration of the International Theological Conference on Evangelization and Dialogue in India* in *Salvation*, pp. 4-5.

362   ibid., p. 5.

363   ibid., pp. 3-4, No. 8-11.

364   ibid., pp. 5-7, No. 18-22.

365   ibid., pp. 7-9, No. 23-29.
      No. 26: "By its very nature dialogue... tends towards that ultimate vision of a perfect unification of all men which can be discerned in the convergent aspirations of the various religious traditions. Dialogue like other works of service and charity, like education, concern for justice and reform, is good in itself, because it fosters mutual communion and edification."

366   ibid., pp. 9-11, No. 30-37.

367   ibid., pp. 12-13, No. 38-47.

368   For details refer *Research Seminar*, (Ref. 207).

369   *Statement of Research Seminar on Non-Biblical Scriptures* in *Research Seminar*, p. 663, No. 1-2.

370 *Research Seminar*, pp. 14-15; 39-44.

371 *Statement of Research Seminar on Non-Biblical Scriptures* in *Research Seminar*, pp. 671-672, No. 17-20.

372 ibid., p. 689, No. 61, iii.

373 ibid., p. 695, No. 78.

374 ibid., p. 680, No. 42; p. 689, No. 61, iii-vi; p. 692, No. 68-69.

375 ibid., p. 678, No. 34: "The christocentric approach is not shared by all theologians. As Christians some are convinced that Christ is certainly of central significance to the whole of mankind, yet they feel uneasy about the way in which christology is applied to other religions and other religious Scriptures." To have an idea of certain tensions reference may be made to *Reports of Discipline-Wise Workshop* in *Research Seminar*, pp. 616-643.

376 Such a study has to be a volume in itself and has to take into consideration various documents of the Second Vatican Council like *Ad Gentes, Nostra Aetate,* relevant parts of *Lumen Gentium, Gaudium et Spes* and so forth, various papal pronouncements and that of the hierarchy which is beyond our scope. For a commentary on conciliar documents reference may be made to *Lexicon für Theologie und Kirche, Das Zweite Vatikanische Konzil*, Band I-III, Herder, 1967-1968; *Commentary on the Documents of Vatican II*, Ed. Herbert Vorgrimler, Vol. I-V, Herder, 1967-1969.

377 Paul VI, The letter *Cum jam*, 21st September, 1966, *AAS*, 58, 1966, p. 878. Tr. CM, 31, 1967, p. 59.

378   *AAS*, ibid., p. 879; Tr. ibid., pp. 59-60.

379   *AAS*, ibid., pp. 879-890; Condensed Tr. ibid., p. 60.

380   Paul VI, *Africae Terrarum*, 31st July, 1969, *AAS*, 61, 1969, p. 577.
      Pope Paul restated the same idea to the Asian Bishops' Symposium, 28th
      November, 1970; *AAS*, 63, 1971, p. 26: "Just as Jesus Christ shared
      the condition of those who were his own, so the man of Asia can be a
      Catholic and remain fully Asian. As we declared a year ago in Africa,
      if the Church must above all be Catholic, a pluralism is legitimate and
      even desirable in the manner of professing one common faith in the one
      same Jesus Christ."

381   Paul VI, *Allocution*, 26th October, 1974, *AAS*, 66, 1974, pp. 636-637;
      Tr. *Holy Fathers Concluding Address*, in *Evangelization of the Modern
      World, (Synod of Bishops Rome, 1974)* Special Number of *Word and Worship*, (W
      Ed., D. S. Amalorpavadass, 8, 1975, p. 107.

382   D. S. Amalorpavadass, *Pastoral Recommendations for Evangelization* in
      Evangelization of the Modern World, op. cit., p. 37.

383   D. S. Amalorpavadass, *A Reflection and Summary of the Part Devoted to
      Theological Questions*, ibid., p. 27.

384   ibid., pp. 27-28. Refer also ibid., p. 28.c.

385   If there was no confusion the Synod would have been able to offer a
      clear statement. Amalorpavadass exercised a great influence on the same
      Synod. See René Laurentin, *L'évangélisation après le quatrième synode*,
      Paris, 1975.

386   As reported in *The Examiner*, 127, 10, 1976, p. 114.

387   *Evangelization A. The Communication from the CBCI to the Synod of Bishops in Rome* in *Report* of *the General Meeting* of *the Catholic Bishops' Conference of India*, Calcutta, January 6th – 14th, 1974, p. 128. No. 12.

388   ibid., p. 140. No. 53.

389   ibid., p. 142. No. 61. P. 134. No. 34 speaks about Indian spirituality and on p. 141. No. 57 about contemplation. What the CBCI has to say about pluralism is interesting: p. 133. No. 31: "On the other hand, the fact of religious pluralism in India will demand from the Church a greater appreciation of pluralism within herself. The understanding of each other of the three individual Churches and their collaboration in the evangelisation of the country should reveal the integrating power of the Spirit of Jesus Christ."

390   B. M. Aguiar, *Behind the Closed Doors, (editorial), The Examiner*, 127, 4, 1976, p. 37 gives a vivid picture of these sessions: "For five general sessions the doors and windows of the main hall, where the discussions took place, were closed, the microphones switched off, and an official of the CBCI secretariat even went round to see if any words could be heard from outside and whether the press and members of the CRI /Conference of Religious India/ were eaves-dropping. The secrecy was obsessive. Bishops were hesitant after the closed sessions even to mention the topics that had been discussed. It was a perfect picture of pre-Vatican siege mentality: the bishops locked in the hall, talking to each other in hushed tones, afraid that secrets would leak out to the world outside, represented by three religious and three members of the Catholic Press!"

391   The CBCI sessions in January 1976 were held in St. John's Seminary, Hyderabad and the majority of the Bishops were staying there. During the last two days of the CBCI sessions we were staying in St. John's Seminary, Hyderabad. Our purpose was to interview as many bishops as possible to make an enquiry and to study the position of the Indian hierarchy on the problem of an Indian theology. We will refer to the enquiry itself later. Much could not be done because of the tension which existed on the very subject we wanted to discuss. A few bishops advised us to be extremely cautious in meeting the bishops to discuss the problem because of tension caused by the letter of Cardinal Knox of the Sacred Congregation for Divine Worship, already referred to, (Ref. 231) forbidding liturgical experiments and the use of the Indian anaphora. They counselled us against meeting some bishops. Two or three bishops frankly told us that they could not devote much time to theology, engrossed as they are in administrative affairs. One bishop complained about the prevailing confusion of terminologies. Another Bishop whom we were meeting for the first time frankly and openly spoke about North-South polarization in the CBCI, the tension between the conservative South and progressive North caused by the letter of Cardinal Knox; the Bishops in the South who desire to follow the directives of the Second Vatican Council were isolated by the disinterested majority. The impression that we could gather from our two days stay was that there is confusion and a concealed disagreement among members of the CBCI on vital issues. See also, B. M. Aguiar, *Behind the Closed Doors*, cit.

392   Joseph Parecattil, *Vision of the Church and the Role of the CBCI*, Ernakulam, 1976, pp. 17-18: "Since the CBCI works through Commissions and Committees, their mutual relationship and responsibilities are to be clearly studied and defined. For example, how far the CBCI as such is

252

responsible for a directive emanating from a commission, or rather can the CBCI wash its hands of all responsibility for the action of a commission? This question was put to me apropos of the Indian Anaphora for which the CBCI apparently disclaimed all responsibility in the recent statement of the Standing Committee. This Anaphora was officially prepared by the CBCI Commission for Liturgy, if I am not mistaken, and certified by the Chairman of the Commission as permitted for experimental use in Experimentation Centres."

393   About the number of votes obtained by the Indian anaphora refer Amalorpavadass, *Liturgy*, p. 48.

394   We prefer to use the term *Protestant* rather than *Separated Brethren* on account of the following reasons. The term Protestant is commonly accepted. If it evokes some past unpleasant historical situation, the term separated brethren no less evokes separation. The term Christian is common to both Catholic and Protestant. Our use of the term Protestant includes also the Anglican confession, since the Church of South India is a union of more than one Protestant confession and includes also the Anglican Church.

395   From among the Protestant authors and scholars we have chosen Sādhu Sundar Singh, A. J. Appasamy, V. Chakkarai, P. Chenchiah, P. D. Devanandan, M. M. Thomas and S. J. Samartha for a short study. The reasons which motivated our choice are the following. Sādhu Sundar Singh had a mystical approach and was concerned mostly with the spiritual. A. J. Appasamy is a Bishop and made use of a Hindu religious tradition to interpret Christian faith. V. Chakkarai and P. Chenchiah tried to rethink Christianity in India and concerned themselves with christological problems. P. D. Devanandan, M. M. Thomas and S. J. Samartha, though each has his own

traits, mark a new approach and may be termed the dialogue group.

396   For more details about the life and activity of Sundar Singh, see Boyd,
       op. cit., pp. 92-94; A. J. Appasamy, *A Biographical Introduction* in the
       English edition of: Sādhu Sundar Singh, *The Real Life*, Madras, 1966,
       pp. XIV.

397   Boyd, op. cit., p. 92.

398   Sundar Singh, *The Search After Reality*, Madras, 1971, p.1.

399   ibid., pp. 2-3.

400   Sundar Singh, *Reality and Religion*, Madras, 1971, pp. 25-26: "Truth has
       many aspects. Everyone, according to his God-given capacity, reveals or
       gives expression to different aspects of Truth. A tree may appeal to one
       man because of its fruits; to another because of its pretty flowers.
       Man appreciates and explains those aspects of the tree which appeal to
       them. So the philosopher, the scientist, the poet, the painter, and the
       mystic, each according to his capacity and temperament, will define and
       describe the different aspects of Reality by which they have been influence
       It is not possible for one man to have an all-embracing view of Reality
       and to describe all its different phases."

401   ibid., p. 15.

402   ibid.

403   ibid., p. 23.

404   ibid.: "Just so the eyes of the heart gaze on the deep things of God, and

254

this insight urges man to worship Him, in whom only he has the needs of his heart satisfied perfectly for ever." See also, Sundar Singh, *The Search After Reality*, pp. 39-41.

405   Sundar Singh, *The Search After Reality*, p. 39: "For God has created man that they may continue in fellowship together, therefore He has also endowed him with a sense of the Reality and with the capacity to enjoy Him. The fact of His having given these spiritual feelings is the proof that Reality means man to enjoy His fellowship,..."

406   ibid., p. 41. Sundar Singh affirms that Reality is separate from man. He rejects advaita. See ibid., pp. 13-17.

407   Sundar Singh, *At the Master's Feet*, Madras, 1974, p. 9.

408   ibid., p. 14.

409   Sundar Singh, *The Spiritual Life*, Madras, 1970, pp. 13-14.

409a Sundar Singh, *The Search After Reality*, pp. 39-40.

410   Sundar Singh, *Reality and Religion*, p. 13.

411   Sundar Singh, *At the Master's Feet*, pp. 5-6.

412   ibid., pp. 5-7.

413   Sundar Singh, *The Spiritual World*, Madras, 1974, p. 48.

414   Sundar Singh, *At the Master's Feet*, pp. 7-8.

415   ibid., pp. 11-12.

416   ibid., pp. 13-14.

417   ibid., pp. 49-50. See also Sundar Singh, *The Spiritual World*.

418   Sundar Singh, *At the Master's Feet*, p. 17.

419   ibid., pp. 42-48.

420   ibid., pp. 24-25.

421   For details see A. J. Appasamy, *A Bishop's Story*, Madras, 1969. This
       book is an autobiography.

422   A. J. Appasamy, *The Johannine Doctrine of Life, A Study of Christian
       and Indian Thought* (cited as *Johannine*), London, 1934, p. 9.

422a   A. J. Appasamy, *Christianity as Bhakti Mārga, A Study in the Johannine
       Writings* (cited as *Bhakti*), London, 1927, pp. 20-21.

423   ibid. See also *Johannine*, pp. 48-68. Appasamy emphasizes that Jesus
       is less than the Father and denies his identity with God. P. 59:
       "Jesus then had no experience of identity in His relation with God.
       He did say, 'I and the Father are one,' but in the light of other
       statements in the Gospel, we cannot interpret these words to mean
       identity. They rather indicate a completeness of harmony between
       Him and God in thought and purpose." It is evident that the advaitic
       approach is rejected.

424   A. J. Appasamy, *My Theological Quest*, Bangalore, 1964, pp. 27-28.

P. 27: "The saying of Jesus, 'I and my Father are one,' quoted in the Gospel of St. John and confirmed by the life and teaching of Jesus as set forth in the Synoptic Gospels points to the supreme importance of a life lived in close fellowship with God." See also *Bhakti*, pp. 13-14; *Johannine*, pp. 59-68.

425   Appasamy, *Bhakti*, p. 21.

425a   Rāmānuja was born around the second half of the eleventh century of our era in the region of Madras. He rejected the advaita system of Śankara (Ref. 25a   ) but taught a new system, *viśiṣṭādvaita*, qualified monism. He taught that reality is one, undivided *brahman* with a threefold distinction, the unconscious material universe of nature, the conscious community of souls and the transcendent Lord *brahman*. This distinction offers a place for *bhakti*, loving devotion in the system. For more details see R. De Smet, *Rāmānuja and Mādhava* in *Religious Hinduism, A Presentation and Appraisal*, Ed. R. De Smet & J. Neuner,   Bombay, 1964, pp. 63-69.

426   Appasamy, *A Bishop's Story*, p. 75.

427   Appasamy, *Bhakti*, pp. 36-37.

428   ibid., pp. 34-45.

429   Appasamy, *Bhakti*, pp. 38-39. Appasamy has been criticized for making no clear distinction between indwelling and immanence and for interchangeably using these two terms. See *A Theological Approach to Hinduism* by The Gurukul Theological Research Group, Madras, 1956, pp. 12-13.

430   Appasamy, *My Theological Quest*, p. 31. See also *Johannine*, p. 7.

431 Appasamy, *My Theological Quest*, p. 32.

432 Appasamy, *Bhakti*, pp. 51-55.

433 ibid., p. 22.

434 Appasamy, *My Theological Quest*, p. 28.

435 Appasamy, *Bhakti* , p. 59; *Johannine* P. 117: "The fundamental idea which
     lies at the basis of all *bhakti* religion is that of the separateness of
     man from God. *Bhakti* whether Christian or Hindu, does not resolve God
     and man into one; but maintains that there is always a difference between
     God and man.... *Bhakti* is the path of love, not merely of love to God,
     though that is its supreme passion, but also of love to man."

436 Appasamy, *Bhakti*, pp. 60-61. Appasamy has stressed the role of the ethical
     element, morality, in *Bhakti*. See ibid., p. 13, 16, pp. 222-224.

437 ibid., pp. 61-62.

438 ibid., pp. 62-63.

439 A. J. Appasamy, *The Theology of Hindu Bhakti*, Madras, 1970, p. 103: He
     mentions the tendency of many Hindu thinkers to make light of sin. P. 123:
     He says that there is a real inconsistency between *bhakti* and the doctrine
     of *karma*. See also p. 129.

440 See Appasamy, *Bhakti*, pp. 117-122. The problem of suffering is dealt with.
     The author gives the example of a Tamil king who wished to participate in
     the pain and agony of Rama. It seems to us that the example is rather

258

far-fetched. See also pp. 143-146.

441   ibid., pp. 162-164.

442   ibid., p. 165.

443   ibid., p. 218.

444   A. J. Appasamy, *What Shall We Believe ? A Study of Christian Pramāṇas*,
      Madras, 1971, pp. 12-17. *Pramāṇa* is a criterion for testing and dis-
      covering truth. For more details about *pramāṇa*, reference may be made
      to the second part of the thesis.

445   ibid., For more detailed explanations, refer pp. 18-72.

446   ibid., p. 16.

447   ibid., pp. 79-90.

448   ibid., pp. 85-86.

449   ibid., pp. 86-87.

450   Chetty is the name of the caste to which Chakkarai belonged and is the highest
      after the Brahmin caste. For more details about his life see Boyd, op. cit.,
      pp. 165-166.

451   Our principal sources are: P. T. Thomas, *The Theology of Chakkarai with
      Selections from his Writings*, Bangalore, 1968; *Rethinking Christianity
      in India* (cited as *Rethinking*), Ed. D. M. Devasahayam & A. N. Sudarisanam,

Madras, (m.d. probably 1938); R. H. S. Boyd, op. cit., pp. 165-185;
Herwig Wagner, *Erstgestalten einer einheimischen Theologie in Südindien*,
München, 1963, pp. 198-259; *Indian voices in Today's Theological Debate*,
Ed. Horst Bürkle & Wolfgang M. W. Roth, Lucknow, 1972; *A Christian
Theological Approach to Hinduism*, op. cit., (Ref. 429), pp. 29-48. We
could not get a copy of Vengal Chakkarai, *Jesus The Avator*, Madras,
1927, and Vengal Chakkarai, *The Cross and Indian Thought*, Madras, 1932.

452 Boyd, op. cit., p. 167 explains further the thought of Chakkarai: "Religion
cannot begin with *nirguṇa* or *avykta* (unmanifested) *brahman*. The
Christian *bhakta* must begin with the *vykta Iśvara* God made manifest in
Christ, in whom *Deus absconditus* becomes *Deus revelatus*."

453 ibid., p. 168.

454 V. Chakkarai, *Jesus the Avatar*, 1927, pp. 172-173 as cited by Boyd, op. cit.
p. 167.

455 See *Indian Voices in Today's Theological Debate*, p. 7; P. T. Thomas, op.
cit., p. 17.

456 V. Chakkarai, *The Historical Jesus and the Christ of Experience* in *The
Guardian*, 22, 13-16, 1944, P. T. Thomas, op. cit., *Selection*,
pp. 88-89.

457 ibid., pp. 90-99. P. 94: "His life as a man, or the Man, was supremely
not merely unselfish but egoless." P. 95: "Jesus was the most egoless
person known in history, and therefore the most universal of all."
Chakkarai gives also a description of the dereliction of Jesus on the cross
terming the final phase of Christ's experience as *nirvāṇa* or *śunya* or *kenosī*

See ibid., pp. 97-99. Wagner, op. cit., pp. 206-208 discusses briefly
Chakkarai's views on kenosis.

458   P. T. Thomas, op. cit., pp. 18-21.

459   ibid., pp. 28-29.

460   ibid., p. 29. The First is *dāsa mārga*. master - servant relation or
       literally way, the second is *pita - putra mārga*, father - son relation, or way,
       and the third and the highest is *mitra mārga*, friend to friend relation
       or way of friends.

461   ibid., pp. 28-29.

462   V. Chakkarai, *The Relations between Christianity and Non-Christian Faiths*
       in *Rethinking*, p. 64.

463   ibid., p. 71.

464   ibid.

465   ibid., p. 72.

466   V. Chakkarai, *The Background for an Indian Christian Theology* in *The
       Guardian*, 25, 15-16, 1947,
       P. T. Thomas, op. cit., *Selections*, p. 101: "The first and original
       impression made on my mind regarding God came from my Hindu surroundings
       and instructions. After all, the most vivid and even vital of later
       impressions must build on the early foundation, however new the additional
       material may be."

467 ibid.

468 ibid.

469 For categories used by Chakkarai, see Boyd, op. cit., pp. 167-185. For a critical evaluation of Chakkarai's use of Indian categories reference may be made to *A Christian Theological Approach to Hinduism*, pp. 41-45.

470 For more details about his life and context see D. A. Thangasamy, *The Theology of Chenchiah with Selections from his Writings*, Bangalore, 1966, pp. VII-XIX; Boyd, op. cit., pp. 144-147.

471 The name Rethinking Group was attributed to them from the title of their main publication, *Rethinking Christianity in India*, op. cit., (Ref. 451).

472 Boyd, op. cit., 146: "The aspects of Aurobindo's thought which helped him most were the ideas of a spiritual power which comes *from outside* with a transforming strength, and that of the evolution – empowered by this descent from above – of a new and better type of humanity."

473 The full name of CVV is Kanchupati Venkata Rao Venkatasami Rao. He was the guru of a school of Yoga on the banks of the river Kāveri at Kumbakonam. Boyd, op. cit., p. 146: "Master CVV's teaching is world-affirming. The creation is for him not just *māyā*; rather it is precisely through creation that God reveals himself and demonstrates his power *(śakti)*. For more details about Chenchiah's relation to Master CVV and Aurobindo see Wagner, op. cit., pp. 183-194.

474 P. Chenchiah, *Jesus and Non-Christian Faiths*, in *Rethinking*, p. 50.

475   ibid: "These traditions, doctrines and rituals become a centre of
       influence and begin to energise by themselves, slowly clouding the original
       fact. The traditions and the Churches in spite of their protestations to
       the contrary, become the centres of influence, the source of salvation, the
       objects of loyalty."

476   P. Chenchiah, *The Church and the Indian Christian* in *Rethinking*, p. 97.

477   ibid., p. 98.

478   ibid., p. 93. The Gurukul Theological Research Group in *A Christian
       Theological Approach to Hinduism*, op. cit., p. 65, makes the following
       comments on his criticism of the Church: "There is another glaring
       omission in his theology: there is no Church. Whenever Mr. Chenchiah
       speaks of the Church his voice is hardened and raised. Perhaps the Church
       has in this time no critic more severe than Mr. Chenchiah. She deserves
       and needs criticism. But it should be fair and constructive. Mr.
       Chenchiah's criticism is neither." For a brief exposition, evaluation and
       criticism of various aspects of the theology of Chenchiah see ibid.,
       pp. 50-65.

479   Chenchiah,   *The Christian Message in a Non-Christian World, A Review of
       Dr. Kraemer's Book* in *Rethinking, Appendix,* p. 8.

480   Chenchiah,   *Jesus and Non-Christian Faiths* in *Rethinking*, p. 53.

481   ibid.

482   ibid., p. 60.

483   ibid., p. 58.

484   Thangasamy, op. cit., p. 17.

485   Thangasamy, op. cit., pp. 42-43.

486   ibid., p. 19.

487   ibid., p. 23.

488   P. Chenchiah, *Christianity and Hinduism*, Pamphlet, 1928. *Selections* in Thangasamy, op. cit., p. 217.

489   ibid.

490   ibid., p. 218.

491   P. Chenchiah, *The Christian Message in a Non-Christian World, A Review of Dr. Kraemer's Book* in *Rethinking, Appendix*, pp. 10-11.

492   P. Chenchiah, *The Makings of Indian Christian Theology*, *Editorials* in *The Pilgrim*, March 1949, Thangasamy, op. cit., *Selections*, pp. 84-85.

493   Thangasamy, op. cit., pp. 4-5. Thangasamy is explaining what Chenchiah strove to do and we find it applicable in the context of an Indian Christian theology.

494   Chenchiah, *The Makings of Indian Christian Theology*, cit., Thangasamy, op. cit., *Selections*, p. 84.

495   ibid., p. 83.

496   Thangasamy, op. cit., p. 33.

497   ibid., pp. 40-41.

498   For more details see S. J. Samartha, *Paul David Devanandan (1901-1962), A Biographical Introduction* in *I will Lift up Mine Eyes unto the Hills, Sermons and Bible Studies of P. D. Devanandan*, Ed. S. J. Samartha & Nalini Devanandan, Bangalore, 1963, pp. 1-11; Boyd, op. cit., pp. 186-187.

499   For a detailed study of Devanandan's theology and his contribution, see Joachim Wietzke, *Theologie in modernen Indien - Paul David Devanandan*, Bern, 1975.

500   P. D. Devanandan, *The Dravida Kazhagam, A Revolt against Brahminism*, Bangalore, 1959.

501   Dravida Kazhagam is a socio-political movement organized by non-Brahmins in South India to liberate themselves from Brahmin domination. Hereafter we shall use the shorter form Kazhagam for the movement unless clarity demands the full form.

502   Devanandan, *The Dravida Kazhagam*, p. 2. For what follows and for historical details see ibid., pp. 2-19.

503   The independent Dravidastan was to comprise the states of Tamilnadu, Kerala, Karnataka and Andhra Pradesh, practically the whole of South India. Devanandan traces the history of the movement only up to 1959. To complete the picture we may add the following: Canjeevaram Natarajan Annadurai, commonly known as C. N. Annadurai, led Dravida Munnetra Kazhagam (DMK) and

won a landslide victory in the 1967 General Election in Tamilnadu, nearly two thirds of the total number of seats in the State assembly, and formed the first DMK ministry. Annādurai, a man of culture, a moderate and a realist, did not press his demands for a separate Dravidastan but ruled the state for the welfare of the people with exemplary integrity and honesty. He died of cancer during the night of 2nd/3rd February, 1969. Those who succeeded him were not able to keep to the high standards set by Annādurai.

504 Devanandan, *The Dravida Kazhagam*, p. 1.

505 ibid., p. 24.

506 ibid., pp. 24-25.

507 ibid., p. 25.

508 ibid.

509 ibid., p. 2. See also p. 26.

510 ibid., p. 29.

511 ibid., p. 30.

512 ibid.

513 P. D. Devanandan, *Christian Concern in Hinduism* (cited as *Concern*), Bangalo 1961, pp. 127-129..

514   P. D. Devanandan, *Preparation for Dialogue, A Collection of Essays on Hinduism and Christianity in New India,* (cited as *Preparation*), Ed. Nalini Devanandan & M. M. Thomas, Bangalore, 1964, p. 33.

515   ibid., pp. 80-96.

516   P. D. Devanandan, *Christian Issues in Southern Asia,* (cited as *Issues*), New York, 1963, p. 69; Devanandan, *Preparation*, p. 32.

517   Devanandan, *Preparation*, pp. 21-22: "The religious situation in India today is the outcome of the interaction between the traditional emphases of religious orthodoxy and the changing circumstances of modern life. On the one hand, religious leaders have been pressed to find justification for the claims of traditional religion to be meaningful in its modern context; on the other, the strain of far-reaching changes in social attitudes and traditional moves increasingly demand a restatement of long-accepted beliefs. The consequent resurgence of Hinduism is evidence both of its inner vitality and its capacity to adapt itself to the environment."

518   Devanandan, *Concern*, pp. 10-13.

519   ibid., pp. 13-16. The principal cause of reform movements are mostly extraneous factors working primarily from without for discarding old ideas and practices and for incorporating new ones and the emphasis is on the New. Revival movements are caused by forces acting from within to revitaltise the Old, to give it new resistance and relevance. Renaissant movements are caused by forces acting from within and without, a mutual interaction of the external stimulus and of the religious system leading

to revival and restatement of fundamentals resulting in a new vitality and new meaning for the old faith. Revolt movements are violent reactions of environment to ancestral faith leading to a total rejection of credal affirmations and religious practices of the ancestral religion for the sake of new values and new ideas.

520   ibid., pp. 16-17.

521   Devanandan, *Preparation*, pp. 3-4.

522   ibid., p. 27.

523   Devanandan, *Concern*, p. 59.

524   ibid.

525   Devanandan, *Preparation*, p. 7; Devanandan, *Concern*, pp. 40-41.

526   Devanandan, *Concern*, pp. 18, 43-44.

527   Devanandan, *Preparation*, p. 37.

528   ibid., p. 34.

529   ibid., p. 13.

530   ibid., pp. 13-15.

531   ibid., p. 69.

532   ibid., p. 33.

533   ibid., p. 16.

534   ibid., pp. 61-62. P. 15: "It would not be true to say that throughout the
      long history of Hindu culture the present obligations of life were altogether
      neglected, that Hindu people never did take life seriously. The annals of
      Indian history indicate that this is not so. We have evidence of the far-
      reaching commercial enterprise of the Indian peoples, their widespread
      cultural contacts in South-East Asia, and their substantial contribution
      to the growth of ancient arts and sciences."

535   Devanandan, *Issues*, p. 65. See also Devanandan, *Preparation*, pp. 61-65.

536   Devanandan, *Concern*, p. 63.

537   ibid., p. 64.

538   Devanandan, *Issues*, p. 85.

539   One of the principal concerns of Devanandan seems to have been the
      evangelization of Asia. He uses the term evangelism for evangelization,
      but we are using the latter, except in quotations, as Catholic circles
      are more used to it.

540   Devanandan, *Issues*, pp. 142-148.

541   Devanandan, *Concern*, pp. 118-122.

542   ibid., pp. 91-92.

543   Devanandan, *Preparation*, pp. 37-41. Here, though Devanandan does not
      expressly state it, it seems to us that it is his mind.

544 Devanandan, *Concern*, p. 85.

545 ibid., p. 96.

546 ibid., p. 107.

547 Devanandan, *Preparation*, p. 181. See also pp. 179-193. For a more
comprehensive view of Devanandan's concept of evangelization especially as
witness to the kingdom of God here and now and to its eschatalogical aspect,
it is necessary to refer to Devanandan, *I will lift up Mine Eyes Unto the
Hills*, op. cit. See pp. 85-91; 113-127. For other aspects of evangelizatî
see Devanandan, *Concern*, pp. 114-142.

548 Devanandan, *Preparation*, p. 181.

549 ibid., p. 180.

550 Devanandan, *Issues*, pp. 136-137.

551 ibid., pp. 138-139.

552 Devanandan, *Preparation*, p. 176.

553 ibid.

554 ibid., p. 177.

555 Devanandan, *Issues*, p. 39.

556 ibid., p. 98.

557 ibid., pp. 98-105. Joachim Wietzke, op. cit.,

p. 128 says that the ecumenical enthusiasm of Devanandan in the forties, gave way to sober assessment of ecumenical possibilities owing to his disappointment with the misunderstanding of Christians in the West.

558   Devanandan, *Concern*, p. 88.

559   Devanandan, *Preparation*, p. 178.

560   Devanandan, *Issues*, p. 112.

561   Devanandan, *Preparation*, p. 173.

562   ibid., p. 191.

563   Our thanks are due to the Secretariate of the World Council of Churches for supplying the bio-data on M. M. Thomas. We have kept the initials M. M. throughout the reference for the sake of distinguishing him from others who have the same name Thomas. The surname Madathilparampil is not employed as he is commonly known as M. M. Thomas.

564   M. M. Thomas, *Man and the Universe of Faiths* (cited as *Universe*), Bangalore, 1975, pp. 3-13. The scientific and technological revolution, the revolt of the oppressed classes, races and nations, the disintegration of the traditional bond between religion, society and state, the enormous destructive power of military technology capable of annihilating mankind which compels the Big Powers to peaceful coexistence, struggle against racism, poverty and famine are some aspects of the revolutionary social, political and international situation.

565   ibid., *Introduction*, p. xiii. It is given as one of the reasons for exploring the pattern of relation between the fundamental vision of God and modern self-understanding of man.

566   ibid., pp. xi-xii.

271

567   ibid., p. xi. This statement of M. M. Thomas may be compared with the
       approach of Abhishiktananda. Refer 2.1.3.

568   M. M. Thomas, *Universe*, p. 33.

569   ibid., p. 34.

570   ibid: "The characteristic of the messianic faith is that it sees God
       in terms of His 'mighty acts' in human history through the prophets and
       the Messiah, and the messianic people of His election, to bring mankind
       and all the world to the fulfilment of the ultimate purpose for which
       they have been created by Him."

571   ibid., pp. 35-37.

572   ibid., p. 38.

573   ibid., p. 34.

574   ibid., p. 42.

575   ibid., p. 45. We may give the following explanation based on Thomas'
       exposition, ibid., pp. 45-46 in order to clarify the meaning of the
       quotation given in the text. There is a profound change taking place in
       the unitive faiths of Asia and Africa on account of the interaction of
       modern culture based on technology and social progress. The religions of
       Asia and Africa cannot ignore the need of social change and progress;
       they are bound to find a basis for such social developments in their
       theology and relate theology to such social changes and economic developmen
       In fact, religious renaissances which integrate such values are taking
       place in these religions. As a consequence, the unitive faiths are moving

towards some form of dynamic messianism and anthropology.

576   ibid., pp. 45-46.

577   ibid., pp. 49-61. We may add the following observation. At present,
       it may be too much to speak of an African humanism or of an African
       contribution because Africa is not a unified whole. It is a
       continent. There are numerous tribes, many languages and dialects.
       The socio-political situation in South Africa is far different from
       the North. All these render it difficult to speak of Africa as a unified
       whole.

578   ibid., p. 62.

579   This subtitle should not give the impression that there is only one
       Buddhism. In fact there are Buddhisms, for example, the Mahāyāna and
       Hīnayāna. Thomas is concerned with the resurgence of Buddhism and
       messianism in Buddhism in a general way. Hence he does not go into details.

579a   M. M. Thomas, *Universe*, p. 95: "Largely in reaction against a theocratic
       messianism Christianity which has expressed itself in association with foreign
       imperialism, political communalism or cultural religious aggression,
       Buddhist messianism often emerged with the militance of the theocratic
       spirit, in association with narrow expression of will - to - power of
       Buddhist nations, races or communities."

580   ibid., p. 94. *Bodhisattva* literally means an Enlightenment - being.
       According to Buddhists, a *bodhisattva* is a being who is full of wisdom
       and compassion and knowingly delays his own entry into *nirvāṇa* to save
       others. For more details, refer, Christmas Humphreys, *Buddhism*, Penguin,
       1969, pp. 158-165. Only Mahāyāna Buddhism hold the doctrine of *bodhisattva*.

273

581   ibid., p. 94: The *bodhisattvas* are said to identify themselves with
       human existence. But they are productions of the mind without any
       historical basis. This ideal symbolized in the figure of the bodhisattva
       was actualized in Jesus Christ within historical existence. Thus the
       common ground for dialogue is the identification with human existence
       to save humanity.

582   ibid. We may add that while certain advantages may justify such a step,
       care has to be taken that such advantages are not sought after at the cost
       of sacrificing essentials.

583   ibid., pp. 96-109. M. M. Thomas is speaking of Islam in a general way. We m
       remark that there are various types of Islam, for example, the Arab,
       Pakistani and Indonesian types. Such differences are also to be taken
       into consideration when dialogue comes to grip with concrete problems.
       The reinterpretation of Islamic tenets also varies according to countries.
       The following is an example of reinterpretation. P. 109: "... many
       Muslim theologians have sought to reinterpret *jihad* /holy war/ in terms
       of its essential intention as activity in pursuance of the true mission
       of Islam."

584   ibid., pp. 107-111.

585   ibid., p. 63, 151.

586   For a detailed study of Hindu Renaissance, See M. M. Thomas,
       Acknowledged, (Ch. 1, Ref. 41).   A brief survey of Hindu Renaissance
       may be found in M. M. Thomas, *Universe*, pp. 63-80.

587   M. M. Thomas, *Acknowledged*, p. 111; M. M. Thomas, *Salvation and Humanisation*

Some Crucial Issues of the theology of Mission in Contemporary India, (cited as *Humanisation*) Bangalore, 1971, p. 20.

588   M. M. Thomas, *Acknowledged*, p. 111.

589   M. M. Thomas, *Humanisation*, pp. 27-28.

590   M. M. Thomas, *Acknowledged*, pp. 117-118.

591   ibid., p. 121.

592   ibid., p. 154.

593   ibid., p. 294.

594   M. M. Thomas, *Humanisation*, p. 29.

595   ibid.

596   ibid., pp. 29-30.

597   ibid., p. 30. Thomas explains further the second component. He refers to 1 Cor. 15 where the risen Christ is seen as the first fruits of a harvest and as the beginning of a historical movement towards Christ's victory over sin and death to be consummated in the kingdom of God.

597a ibid., pp. 30-31.

598   ibid., p. 31.

599   ibid.

600   ibid.

601   ibid., pp. 31-32.

602   Sarvodaya is a movement which follows Gandhian ideals and strives to
       establish a welfare society through various non-violent social means, the
       principal one of which is a free gift of land to the landless through
       persuasion.

603   M. M. Thomas, *Humanisation*, p. 44.

604   M. M. Thomas, *Universe*, p. 74.

605   M. M. Thomas, *Humanisation*, p. 50.

606   M. M. Thomas, *Acknowledged*, p. 287.

607   ibid., p. 32.

608   M. M. Thomas, *Universe*, p. 137.

609   ibid., pp. 150-151.

610   M. M. Thomas, *The Secular Ideologies of India and the Secular Meaning of
       Christ*, (cited as *Secular*), Bangalore, 1976.   In this book, Thomas studies
       Indian secularism.   In his *Preface* to the same book he says that his purpose
       is to evaluate them "in the light of the humanism and the gospel of Jesus
       Christ."   This book is a companion volume to his earlier work *The
       Acknowledged Christ of the Indian Renaissance*, op. cit.

611   M. M. Thomas, *Secular* , pp. 1-16. Rationalism, nationalism, economic nationalism
      and concern for social reform are some of the characteristics of Indian
      liberalism.

612   ibid., pp. 18-21. Some of the Indian liberal leaders are M. G. Ranande
      (1842-1901), Tej Bahadur Sapru (1875-1949), Dhadabhai Naoroji (1825-1917).

613   ibid., p. 26.

614   ibid., p. 32.

615   ibid., pp. 29-33.

616   ibid., p. 33.

617   ibid., p. 34.

618   ibid., pp. 35-84. M. M. Thomas, in his description of the spiritual framework of
      Socialist Humanism brings out well Nehru's concern for morality and his
      search for something spiritual. P. 54: Nehru is aware that science alone
      is not enough. P. 55: Nehru speaks about the necessity of recognizing
      the supremacy of the moral law in national and international relations.
      See also pp. 60-64. P. 64: He believes that Indian spirituality can offer
      a basis for tolerance in national and international life. Equally interesting
      are Thomas' views on Jayaprakash Narayan, Asok Mehta and other Indian leaders.
      Refer pp. 51-75.

619   ibid., pp. 85-123. M. M. Thomas speaks of the contribution Marxism-Leninism to
      India and the one-sidedness of it, p. 122: " It has brought to Indian politics
      an understanding of man as a bodily, social and historical being, with a

277

responsibility for his earthly destiny. This is indeed a great spiritual
gain. But taken by itself, its objectivism is as one-sided as the
traditional subjectivism, its materialist monism is as incapable of
comprehending the total dimension of the historical being of man." P. 123:
"Thus Marxism-Leninism is not dialectical enough to comprehend the total
human reality."

620 ibid., pp. 124-156. For Christian influence on those whose opposed Brahmin
domination, see pp. 151-155. P. 152: "Considering the fact that the
Christian Missions were the first in many parts of India to treat the
Untouchables as human beings, and to bring them the gospel of their
dignity in Christ as well as education, Christianity has played a part
in arousing and strengthening Anti-Brahminism."

621 For the ideologies of the three leaders, Subhas Chandra Bose, M. N. Roy and
M. R. Masani, see ibid., pp. 156-166, 166-184, and 1ß5-192 respectively.
Thomas sees in the ideology of national socialism (samyavāda) as developed
by Subhas Chandra Bose, an Indian national leader and freedom-fighter, a
synthesis between communism and fascism. PP. 159-160: What Bose aims at
is not communism or fasicm but a synthesis of nationalism and socialism.
M. N. Roy abandoned his communist allegiance and taught radical humanism.
P. 172: "For Roy... the new messiah is not the proletariat facing a pre-
determined historical inevitability, but the people who can appreciate that
'ethical values are greater than economic interests' and will dare to create
world anew." P. 176: Roy gives a secular, rational sanction to morality.
P. 184: Roy's criticism of religions including Christianity has validity
in so far as traditional doctrines like Creation, Providence and
Teleology were interpreted in a static manner for the preservation of existin
order. The religions were too much concerned with the origins of man. The
radical humanism of Roy runs the same risk and its "absolutely secularised

eschatology runs the risks of dehumanisation as in the case of Marxian communism." P. 185: The political ideology of M. R. Masani, a leader of the Swatantra party may be termed liberal secular conservatism. PP. 186-188: The two of the ideas which appeal much to Masani are a minimum of government control, and government as a helper in industry and trade and not as a participant.

622   ibid., p. 193.

623   ibid., p. 194.

624   ibid., pp. 194-195.

625   ibid., p. 195.

626   ibid., pp. 195-196.

627   ibid., p. 196: From such a sense of the mystery of man's personhood has arisen the modern demand that societies and states should recognise the fundamental rights of the human person for freedom, for self-determination and for the pursuit of truth, goodness and beauty, and the right to follow the path of service to God as dictated by his own reason and conscience, in this freedom."

628   ibid.

629   ibid.

630   ibid., pp. 196-197.

631   ibid., p. 197.

632   ibid., p. 198.

633 ibid.

634 ibid.

635 ibid.

636 ibid., pp. 198-199. P. 199: "Centrality of the Divine Forgiveness releases
     men and women from the idolatry of communalism of religion, race, nation,
     class, sex and caste or even ideology which, in alienated conditions,
     provided spiritual and social security. For in 'the new humanity of
     Christ which is being renewed in knowledge after the image of its maker,'
     the distinctions of nature, history, culture and religion are not
     absolutised but transcended in the awareness of solidarity with all mankind
     and common participation in the new humanity in Christ."

637 ibid., pp. 199-200.

638 ibid., p. 202.

639 ibid.

640 ibid.

641 ibid., pp. 202-203: "The historical process is affirmed through its
     transformation which is as radical as the one which happened quietly in the
     inhuminisation of God in Jesus in the history of the world, or as what
     happened with greater trauma in the resurrection through death of the
     historical humanity of Jesus."

642 ibid., p. 203.

643 See for example 2.2.6.2.

644   M. M. Thomas, *Humanisation*, p. 26.

645   ibid., p. 35; M. M. Thomas, *Secular*, p. 194: "The God of the Bible is the God of
       history. He is the 'God of Abraham, Issac and Jacob, not the God of the
       philosophers' as Pascal has said. Therefore, in the Biblical approach
       to the saving knowledge of God, the central emphasis is on doing the will
       of God or responding to the purpose of God in the historical realm, and
       not on philosophical vision or mystic union."

646   M. M. Thomas, *Universe*, p. 79.

647   M. M. Thomas, *Acknowledged*, pp. 290-301.

648   ibid., p. 291: "And when theology speaks of the unchanging core of Dogma,
       it is thinking of the givenness of the fact of Jesus interpreted as the
       deed of God for man among men. It is the datum of all theological
       formulations."

649   ibid., p. 298.

650   ibid., pp. 301-302.

651   ibid., p. 302.

652   ibid., p. 303.

653   ibid., pp. 303-304.

654   ibid., p. 305.

655   ibid., pp. 306-316.

656   ibid., p. 308.

657 Our gratitude is due to the Secretariate of the World Council of Churches for furnishing the bio-data on Samartha.

658 S. J. Samartha, *The Hindu Response to the Unbound Christ*, (cited as *Response*), Bangalore, 1974, p. 2.

659 ibid.

660 ibid., pp. 2-3.

661 ibid., pp. 3-5.

662 ibid., p. 5.

663 ibid., pp. 116-117: "Christology in the sense of trying to understand the meaning and mystery of Christ is the task of the Church in all countries and at all times, although the method and approach might vary according to particular needs... The 'conceptualisation of faith' is not just an intellectual exercise but is part of our total response to Christ as providing answers to the ultimate questions of life."

664 ibid., p. 117.

665 For Rammohan Roy, see ibid., pp. 19-41 and for Mahatma Gandhi, ibid., pp. 73-97. Samartha gives the general characteristics of this kind of response to Christ. Some of them are the acceptance of experience as the authority in religion and not scriptures or institution, selective use of scriptures Hindu or Christian to interpret Christ, the Church considered as unnecessary to understand the scriptures, no importance attached to the historicity of Christ, esteem for the ethical teaching of Christ,

and an attempt to separate Christ from Christianity. For details, see ibid., pp. 118-121.

666   ibid., p. 117.

667   Subba Rao stays in the cultural context of Hinduism, is committed to Christ, preaches Christ and exercises a healing ministry in the name of Christ. He rejects baptism and every form of religion. For him Christ is a guru to be followed. For details see ibid., pp. 121-128.

668   ibid., p. 117.

669   See above 2.2.3 and 2.2.4.

670   Samartha, *Response*, pp. 117-118.

671   ibid.

672   ibid., pp. 162-165. P. 165: "... in modern India a good deal of effort is being made to re-interpret the basic categories of *advaita* in such a way as to bring it in relation to modern thought and life so that what may be described as *neo-advaita* is shaping itself in modern Indian thought. *Brahman* as the ground of all being, *māyā* as a doctrine of the world, *karma* as a law of justice, *mokṣa* as the final destiny of man and *brahma-loka* as the final consummation of the cosmos – all these are being reshaped although their roots in the scriptural tradition are recognised and nourished."

673   ibid., p. 166.

674   ibid., p. 167.

675   ibid., p. 151.

676   ibid.

677   ibid.

678   ibid.

679   ibid., p. 154.

680   ibid., p. 157: "It is of course recognised that without the historical
      figure of Jesus Christ there can be no authentic Christianity. But one
      should not forget that Gautama the Buddha and the Prophet Muhammad were
      also historical figures. Mere historicity is not a matter of final
      significance."

681   ibid.

682   ibid.

683   ibid., pp. 158-159.

684   ibid., p. 159.

685   ibid., p. 160.

686   ibid.

687   ibid., p. 161.

688   ibid.

689   ibid.

690   ibid., pp. 161-162.

691   ibid., p. 162: "What may be attempted justifiably is to recognise the ontological status of Christ as well as his relation to the mystic consciousness, while holding fast to the historic anchorage of the fact of Christ. Without this, any Christology in India is likely to be a leaky boat without moorings in the swirling waters of Indian philosophy and religion."

692   ibid., p. 170.

693   ibid.

694   ibid., p. 171.

695   ibid.

696   ibid.

697   ibid., pp. 173-177.

698   ibid., p. 177.

699   ibid., p. 178. Samartha refers to R.V. De Smet, *Categories of Indian Philosophy and Communication of the Gospel* in *Religion and Society* (RS), 10, 1963, pp. 20 ff to point out that the classical Greek understanding of person as subsistent, distinct, complete and intelligent could be applied to *brahman*. See Samartha, *Response*, pp. 178-179. P. 179:" "De Smet is right in pointing out, that to call *nirguṇa brahman*, 'the impersonal Absolute' is quite misleading because, in the sense described above '*nirguṇa brahman* ' is 'the most personal Being.'"

700   ibid., pp. 180-182.

701   ibid., p. 182.

702   ibid., p. 183.

703   ibid., p. 184.

704   ibid.

705   ibid., p. 187: "Both the existential understanding of the self as 'a
       Being - next - to God' as Heidegger remarks and the mystical description
       of ātman as being identical with brahman himself do not seem to give
       sufficient importance to man as a historical personality, where his ego
       is a permanent centre of responsible freedom and where personality should
       be considered as the product of the moral ego, exercising its freedom in
       relation to concrete historical situations and therefore moving in a state
       of continuous relationships."

706   ibid., pp. 189-190.

707   ibid., pp. 190-191.

708   ibid., p. 192.

709   ibid., pp. 192-193: "... it is necessary, however to point out that in
       this scheme,as it is and as it influences the life and thought of many
       people, the following categories do not receive sufficent attention:
       the freedom and responsibility of the individual personality; the social
       and historical dimensions of human life; the possibilities for the
       emergence of the new both in nature and in history; the fact of tragedy
       and evil within human spirituality sometimes masquerading as goodness;

the persistence of sin, guilt and death in human existence, particularly
at a time when with new weapons of total destruction at the disposal of
man, which may wilfully be used or accidentally released, there is the
possibility of human existence coming to an abrupt *finis* without ever
having an opportunity of reaching its *telos*."

710   ibid., p. 193.

711   ibid.

712   ibid., p. 196.

713   ibid., p. 197.

714   ibid., pp. 198-199.

715   ibid., p. 199.

716   S. J. Samartha, *The Progress and Promise of Inter-Religious Dialogues*,
      Reprint from *The Consultation on Inter-Religious Dialogue*, Kyoto, October,
      1970, pp. 469-471 gives reasons for the concern for dialogue. There is
      cultural diversity among the nations of Africa and Asia; national
      independence from colonialism has brought this diversity into greater
      lights; culture is bound up with religion; so there is hope of bringing
      people together through inter-faith dialogues. Nation building is a major
      problem; it needs the cooperation of men of different faiths and not
      competition. There is a certain dissatisfaction with secularization and
      technology and many have a thirst for the authentic sacred, the mysterious.
      Finally dialogue can create living relationships between people of different
      faiths. All these are common factors which have caused great interest in
      inter-faith dialogues.

717   S. J. Samartha, *Introduction* in *Living Faiths and the Ecumenical Movement*
      (cited as *Living*), Ed. S. J. Samartha, Geneva, 1971, p. 11.

718   S. J. Samartha, *Dialogue as a Continuing Christian Concern* in *Living*,
      p. 143.

719   ibid., p. 154.

720   ibid., pp. 153-154.

721   S. J. Samartha, *Dialogue: Significant Issues in the Continuing Debate*
      in *The Ecumenical Review*, (TER), 24, 1972, p. 334.

722   ibid. Our main theological concern is the crucial problem of truth,
      satyam in Sanskrit, *emet* in Hebrew and *alētheia* in Greek.

723   Samartha, *Introduction* in *Living*, p. 8.

724   Samartha, *The Progress and Promise of Inter-Religious Dialogue*, Reprint,
      op. cit., p. 472.

725   S. J. Samartha, *Reflections on a Multilateral Dialogue, An Interpretation
      of a Meeting held at Colombo*, Sri Lanka, 17th - 26th April, 1974 in
      TER, 26, 1974, p. 643.

726   ibid.

727   Samartha, *Dialogue as a Continuing Christian Concern* in *Living*, p. 151.

728   ibid., p. 152.

729   Samartha, *Reflections on a Multilateral Dialogue*, cit., in TER,   p. 640.

730   ibid., p. 645.

731   Samartha, *The Progress and Promise of Inter-Religious Dialogues*, Reprint, op. cit., p. 472. This problem is given by Samartha as an example of an essential demand of particular faiths which should not be hidden.

Chapter III

Footnotes & References: Types of Indian Theology

1   For example compare the theology of Amalorpavadass, Devanandan and M. M.
     Thomas.   See above 2.1.6;   2.2.5;   2.2.6, pp. 81-94, 131-138, 139-154.

2   A strict and compartmentalized classification leaves no room for the less
     pronounced tendencies and could give a false impression of being assigned
     a very specific category.

3   See above 1.1.1, pp. 22-23.

4   2.1.6. We feel that much of the attack directed against Amalorpavadass
     directly or indirectly is based more on sentiment or hearsay than on reason.
     An example of indirect attack is found in *The Loyal Members of the Catholic
     Church in India, An Appeal to the Hierarchy of India from the People of God*
     in *The Laity, Journal of Christian Thought and Action*, 4, 1976, pp. 5-11
     in which the activities of the National Biblical Catechetical and Liturgical
     Centre (NBCLC) of which Amalorpavadass is the Director are called in question.
     An example of judging by hearsay seems to be found in P. K. George,
     Experimentation in Liturgy in *The Laity*, 4, 1976, p. 101: "Those who
     need experimentation in order to choose between *Kalaśam*/pinnacle especially
     on the top of a temple/ and the Cross or between the image of Natarāja
     /image of dancing Śiva/ and of Christ is experimenting not with liturgy but
     with religion." As far as we can understand, the reference to the image
     of Natarāja is probably to the image of a pilgrim, a man, going round the
     world depicted on a window of the chapel of the NBCLC which has some remote
     resemblance to the image of Natarāja. It has been interpreted as Natarāja

either unknowingly or uncharitably. During our stay in Bangalore early in
1976, we ourselves sent a well-meaning and serious person who came to us
with the same complaint. We encouraged him to visit the chapel and he
returned fully satisfied that it is not Nataraja. An example of direct
attack is found in the forum, Veritas, *Food for Thought*, in *The
Laity*, 4,1976, pp. 103-104. There could be differences about the extension
or modes of liturgical experimentation and there should be healthy discussions.
But misrepresentation of facts, however good the motive may be, is unjusti-
fiable.

5   See above 2.1.6.1 and 2.1.6.2, pp. 81-86, 86-90.

6   2.2.5.2.e, p. 136.

7   2.2.6.3, p. 147.

8   2.2.7, pp. 155-165.

9   2.2.5.1, pp. 132-133.

10   2.1.5,1.f, p. 69.

11   2.1.2, pp. 50-52.

12   2.1.3, pp. 53-60.

13   2.1.4, pp. 60-65.

14   2.1.6, pp. 81-94.

15   2.1.7, pp. 94-99.

16   See above 2.1.9, pp. 102-104.

17   2.1.10, pp. 104-106.

18   2.1.11, pp. 106-110.

19   2.1.5, pp. 65-81.

20   2.2.6, pp. 139-154.

21   2.2.7, pp. 155-165.

22   1.2.2.1.c, p. 32.

23   1.2.3.2.a, p. 35.

24   1.2.2.2, p. 33.

25   2.1.2.1.a, p. 50.

26   For example, See above 2.1.5.2 c,d. Panikkar points out elements of
     mutual fulfilment, but does not stop there, pp. 70-71.

27   See above 2.1.4.1.b. This is only one aspect of his theology, p. 61.

28   2.1.9.1.a, p. 103.

29   2.1.3.1.h, p. 58.

30   2.1.5.1.b and Ref. 118, p. 67.

31 Mattam, *Land*, p. 17 uses this term and we find it quite suitable.

32 See above 1.2.3.2.b, p. 36.

33 2.1.1.1, pp. 48-49.

34 1.2.3.2.c, pp. 37-38; and Ref. 81.

35 2.1.2.1, pp. 50-52.

36 2.1.3, pp. 53-60.

37 2.1.4, pp. 60-65.

38 2.1.5, pp. 65-81.

39 2.2.7, pp. 157-165.

40 2.2.1, pp. 118-121.

41 2.2.2, pp. 121-124.

42 2.2.3, pp. 125-127.

43 2.2.4, pp. 128-131.

44 2.2.4.1.c, pp. 129-130.

45 2.2.5.2.f, p. 137.

46 2.1.7, pp. 94-99.

47 2.1.12.3, pp. 112-113.

48 1.1.2.2, pp. 27-28.

49 1.2.3.2.f, p. 40.

50 2.1.9.1.c, p. 103.

51 2.1.11, pp. 106-110.

52 2.1.8, pp. 99-102.

53 It is too early to judge the theological options of authors like Vempeny, Mattam, Nambiaparampil and Manickam as they are still at the beginning of their theological work. Chethimattam is more concerned with philosophy than theology and unless some major theological work comes forth, it is difficult to judge his preference.

Chapter IV

Footnotes & References: Fundamental Problems in Indian Theology

1   Abhishiktānanda, Griffiths and Panikkar are among those who stress these
    aspects; Panikkar pays less attention to sannyāsa and monasticism.

2   We are not saying that theologians like Abhishiktānanda, Griffiths or Panikkar
    are not interested in social or human problems. See above Ch. 2, Reference 50.
    The fact is that the theocentric emphasis is so great that other social and
    secular aspects do not receive much attention.

3   Panikkar has universalized Christ to such an extent that Christ almost disappea
    in the Father. See Panikkar, *The Meaning of Christ's Name* in *Salvation*, pp.
    235-263. See also *Trinity*, pp. 50-57. P. 56: "If we remain attached
    exclusively to the 'Saviour', to his humanity and his historicity, we block,
    in a manner of speaking, the coming of the Spirit and thus revert to a stage
    of exclusive iconolatry." Exclusive attachment to the humanity of the
    Saviour and his historicity is certainly to be avoided. But that is no reason
    to water them down either.

4   Amalorpavadass, M. M. Thomas and Samartha, for example, are among those who
    follow a christocentric approach.

5   See above 2.2.6.2, pp. 143-147.

6   Monchanin has insisted on the need of reshaping Christian concepts. See above
    2.1.2.1.d; p. 51. Abhishiktānanda speaks about the social and culture-conditi
    formulations of Hindu and Christian concepts. See above, 2.1.3.1.i, p. 59.
    Griffiths tries to go behind concepts and categories to discover the original
    Mystery. See above 2.1.4.1, pp. 60-65. See above Panikkar's views on the

same, 2.1.5.1, pp. 66-69; Chenchiah relativizes the Church totally. See above 2.2.4.1.a, pp. 128-129.

7   We have drawn attention to this problem several times. See above, for example 1.1.2.1; 1.2.3.3; 2.1.6.3.c, pp. 27, 41-42, 92.

8   See above 2.1.5.2.b; 2.1.6.1.f; 2.1.6.2.f; 2.1.6.3, pp. 70, 90-94.

9   2.1.6.1.g, pp. 85-86.

10   See *Declaration of the International Theological Conference on Evangelization and Dialogue in India*, No. 18-22, in *Salvation*, pp. 5-7.

11   If such an integration was achieved, there would not have been so much discussion on the problem. See above 2.1.6.1.g; 2.1.6.3; 2.2.5.2.e, pp. 85-86, 90-94, 136-137.

12   See above 2.1.6.3, pp. 90-94.

13   2.2.5.2; 2.2.6.2; 2.2.6.3, pp. 133-139, 143-147, 147-152.

14   2.2.7.3.e, p. 165.

15   See above 2.1.7, pp. 95-99. Griffiths accepts the complementary character of revelation. See above 2.1.4.1.b, p. 61.

16   See above 2.1.6.1.c; 2.2.5.2.b, pp. 83-84, 134.

17   Panikkar, *The Unknown Christ of Hinduism*, pp. 46-57.

18   See above 2.1.3.1.g, pp. 57-58.

19   See above 2.2.6.4.a, p. 152.

20   2.1.3; 2.2.1; 2.1.11, pp. 53-60, 119-121, 106-110.

21   2.2.1; 2.2.2, pp. 119-121, 121-124.

22   2.1.3.1; 2.1.5.4.c, pp. 53-60, 77-78. See also Panikkar, *Trinity*,
      pp. 24-39.

23   See above 2.1.3.1, pp. 53-60.

24   2.2.6.4.a; 2.2.7.2, pp. 152, 159-162.

25   2.1.3.1.i, pp. 59-60.

26   2.1.5; 2.1.4; 2.2.5, pp. 65-81, 60-65, 131-139.

27   1.2.3.2, pp. 35-40.

28   2.1.4; 2.1.11, pp. 60-65, 106-110.

29   2.1.2.1.d, pp. 51-52.

30   2.2.6.4.c, pp. 153-154.

31   The term *dharma* for example could mean religion, duty, law, righteousness
      and so forth.

32   See above 1.2.2.1.c, p. 32.

33   1.2.3.2.f, p. 40.

34   1.2.4.1, p. 44.

35   2.1.4.1, pp. 60-65.

36   2.2.7.3, pp. 162-165.

37   2.1.5.1.e, pp. 68-69.

38   2.1.2.1.c, p. 51.

39   2.1.8.1, pp. 99-101.

40   2.1.8.2; 2.1.3.1.h, pp. 101-102, 58-59, and Ref. 55.

41   See above Ref. 16.

BIBLIOGRAPHY

Aids

Baago, K.,   *Library of Indian Christian Theology, A Bibliography*,
                             Madras, 1969.

Anderson, G. H.,   *Bibliography of the Theology of the Missions in the Twen-
                             tieth Century*, 3rd ed., revised and enlarged, New York,
                             1966.

Baumgartner, J.,   *Missionswissenschaft im Dienste der Weltkirche 25 Jahre
                             Neue Zeitschrift für Missionswissenschaft, Schriftenreihe
                             der Neuen Zeitschrift für Missionswissenschaft* XXII,
                             Schöneck/Beckenried (Schweiz), 1970.

Gispert, S. G.,   *Indology Library Bulletin*, in IES, 10, 1971, pp. 217-225;
                             11, 1972, pp. 132-144.

Rommerskirchen G., conti-   *Bibliografia Missionaria*, Vol. XXVIII-XLI,   Roma, 1964-
Willi Henkel & others,   1978.

1.1.1   The Theology of the Early Indian Church

Hambye, E. R.,

Madey, J.,   *1900 Jahre Thomas-Christen in Indien*, Freiburg, (Schweiz),
                             1972.

Mansi J. D., (Ed.),   *Diamperitana Synodus in Malabria*. Qua Christiani S. Thomae,
                             Vulgo dicti, "fidem catholicam amplexi sunt", et disciplina
                             in tota Malabria instituta, Anno 1599 habita, in Mansi,
                             Amplissima Coll. Concil, 35 B., Ann. 1414-1724. Paris,
                             1902, Col. 1161-1368. /A very important document which gives
                             an insight into the practices of the early Indian Church/.

297

Moraes, G. M.,	*A History of Christianity in India. From early times to St. Francis Xavier*: AD 52-1542, Bombay, 1964.
Mundadan, M. A.,	*Sixteenth Century Traditions of St. Thomas Christians*, Bangalore, 1970.
Perumalil, A. C.,	*The Apostles of India*, Patna, 1971.
Podipara, P. J.,	*Die Thomas-Christen*, Würzburg, 1966.
"	*The Malabar Christians*, Alleppey, 1972.
Thaliath, J.,	*The Synod of Diamper*, Roma, 1958.

1.1.2   Robert De Nobili

De Nobili, R.,	*Première apologie, 1610, texte inédit latin.* Tr. et annoté, Pierre Dahmen /under the title/ *Robert De Nobili l'apôtre des brahmes*, Paris, 1931.
"	*Informatio de quibusdam Moribus Nationis Indicae ad Patrem nostrum Generalem* (a work considered to be lost and lately discovered), Ed. & Tr. Rajamanickam /under the title/ *Robert De Nobili on Indian Customs*, Palayamkottai, 1972.
Bachmann, P. R.,	*Roberto Nobili 1577-1656. Ein missionsgeschichtlicher Beitrag zum christlichen Dialog mit dem Hinduismus*, Roma, 19
Camps, A.,	*Jerome Xavier S. J. and the Muslims of the Mogul Empire. Controversial Works and Missionary Activity*, Fribourg (Switzerland), 1957.
Cronin, V.,	*A Pearl to India. The Life of Roberto De Nobili*, New York 1959.
Dahmen, P.,	*Robert De Nobili, Ein Beitrag zur Geschichte der Missionsmethode und der Indologie*, Münster in Westfalen, 1924.

Hambye, E. R.,   *Robert De Nobili and Hinduism,* in *God's Word Among Men.*
                                Papers in honour of Fr. Joseph Putz S. J. & others, Ed. G.
                                Gispert-Sauch, Delhi, 1973.

Jeyaraj, D.,   *The Contribution of the Catholic Church in Tamilnadu in the*
                                17th-19th Centuries to an Understanding of Christ, in
                                IJT, 23, 1974, pp. 181-190.

1.2.1   Raja Rammohan Roy

Roy, R. R.,   *The Precepts of Jesus: the Guide to Peace and Happiness,*
                                Calcutta, 1820.
"   *An appeal to the Christian Public in Defence of the Precepts*
                                of Jesus, Calcutta, 1820.
"   *Second Appeal,* Calcutta, 1821.
"   *Final Appeal,* Calcutta, 1824.

Boyd, R. H. S.,   *Rammohan Roy (1772-1833),* in R. H. S. Boyd, *An Introduction*
                                to Indian Christian Theology, Madras, 1975, pp. 19-26.

Farquhar, J. N.,   *Modern Religious Movements in India,* London, 1929.

Ganguly, N. G.,   *Raja Ram Mohun Roy,* Calcutta, 1934.

Thomas, M. M.,   *Rammohan Roy: the Christ of 'The Precepts',* in M. M. Thomas,
                                The Acknowledged Christ of the Indian Renaissance, London,
                                1969.

Max Müller, F.,   *Rammohan to Ramakrishna,* Calcutta, 1952.

Singh, I.,   *Rammohan Roy. A Biographical Inquiry into the making of*
                                Modern India, Vol. I, *The First Phase,* Bombay, 1958.

Tagore, S.,   *Raja Rammohun Roy,* New Delhi, 1966.

Kolencherry, A.,   *Universalitätsanspruch des neuzeitlichen Hinduismus. Reform-*
                                bewegung des Brahma Samāj, seine Entwicklung und Stellung
                                zum Christentum, /Unpublished Doctoral Dissertation/,
                                Katholisch-Theologische Fakultät der Universität, Wien, 1976.

1.2.2   Keshab Chandra Sen*

Sen, K. C.,   *Keshub Chunder Sen's Lectures in India*, Vol. I - II, London, 1901, 1904.

"   *The New Dispensation*, Vol. I - II, Calcutta, 1915-1916.

Boyd, R. H. S.,   *Keshab Chandra Sen (1838-1884)*, in R. H. S. Boyd, *An Introduction to Indian Christian Theology*, Madras, 1975, pp.26-

Thomas, M. M.,   *Keshub Chunder Sen: The Doctrine of Divine Humanity*, in M. M. Thomas, *The Acknowledged Christ of the Indian Renaissance*, London, 1969, pp. 56-81.

1.2.3   Brahmabandhab Upādhyāya

Baago, K.,   *Brahmabandhab Upādhyāya*, in *Pioneers of Indigenous Christianity*, Madras, 1969, pp. 26-49; selections pp. 118-150.

Boyd, R. H. S.,   *Brahmabandhab Upādhyāya (1861-1907)*, in R. H. S. Boyd, *An Introduction to Indian Christian Theology*, Madras, 1975, pp. 63-85.

Heiler, F.,   *Christlicher Glaube und indisches Geistesleben*, München, 1926.

Thomas, M. M,,   *Brahmabandhab Upādhyāya: Christ as 'Cit'*, in M. M. Thomas, *The Acknowledged Christ of the Indian Renaissance*, London, 1969, pp. 99-110.

Väth, A.,   *Im Kampfe mit der Zauberwelt des Hinduismus*, Berlin, 1928.

Gispert, S. G.,   *The Sanskrit Hymns of Brahmabandhab Upādhyāya*, in RS, 19, 1972, pp. 60-79.

1.2.4   Nehemiah Goreh

Paradkar, A. B.,   *The Theology of Nehemiah Goreh*, Madras, 1969.

Boyd, R. H. S.,   *Nehemiah Goreh (1825-95)*, in R. H. S. Boyd, *An Introduction to Indian Christian Theology*, Madras, 1975. pp. 40-57

*The asterisk after the names refers to the Supplementary Bibliography.

Thomas, M. M., *Some Indian Christian Defences against Brahmosim*: *Lal Behari Day and Nehemiah Goreh*, in M. M. Thomas, *The Acknowledged Christ of the Indian Renaissance*, London, 1969, pp. 38-55.

2.1.1   Pierre Johanns

Johanns, P., *A Synopsis - To Christ Through the Vedanta*, Ranchi, Part, I, *Śankara*, 1930; II, *Rāmānuja*, 1931; III, *Vallabha*, 1932; IV, *Caitanya* (n.d.).

" *La pensée religieuse de l'Inde*, Tr. Louis Marcel Gauthier, Namur, 1952.

2.1.2   Jules Monchanin

Monchanin, J., *Ecrits spirituels*, (Présentation d'Edouard Duperray), Paris, 1965.

Monchanin, J., (Swāmi Paramārubyānandam) *Mystique de l'Inde, mystère chrétien. Ecrits et inédits*, Ed. Suzanne Siavue, Fayard, 1974.

" *De l'esthétique à la mystique*, Casterman, 1967.

" *The Christian Approach to Hindus*, in *India Missionary Bulletin*, I, 1952, pp. 46-50.

" *The Quest of the Absolute*, in *Indian Culture and the Fullness of Christ*, Madras, 1957, pp. 46-51.

" *Yoga et hésychasme*, in *Axes*, I, 1969, pp. 13-21.

Apophatisme et apavada, in *Axes*, I, 1970, pp. 18-30.

De Lubac, H., *Images de l'abbé Monchanin*, Aubier, 1967.

" *Monchanin informations*, 1, 1-9, 1968.

2.1.3   Abhishiktānanda *

Le Saux (Dom), (Abhishiktānanda), *Sagesse hindoue-mystique chrétienne. Du vedanta à la trinité*, Paris, 1965.

" *Indische Weisheit - Christliche Mystik, von der Vedanta zur Dreifaltigkeit*, München, 1968.

301

Abhishiktānanda	*Hindu- Christian Meeting Point within the Cave of the Heart* Bangalore, 1969.
"	*The Church in India, An Essay in Christian Self-Criticism,* Madras, 1969.
"	*Towards the Renewal of the Indian Church,* Cochin, 1970.
"	*Guru and Disciple,* Tr. Heather Sandeman, London, 1974.
"	*Saccidānanda. A Christian Approach to Advaitic Experience,* Delhi, 1974.
"	*The Further Shore. Two Essays, Sannyāsa, and the Upaniṣads An Introduction,* Delhi, 1975.
"	*Prayer,* Delhi, 1975.
"	*Christians Meditate on the Upaniṣads,* in *Logos,* 6, 1965, pp. 1-16.
Le Saux Henry – Rogers, M.,	*Lettera aperta ai Cristiani d'Occidente che sperano di venire in India,* in *Le Missioni Cattoliche,* 96, 1967, pp. 177-178.
Abhishiktānanda	*Indianizing Worship. A Study of Hindu Symbolism,* in WW, I, 1968, pp. 298-307.
"	*An approach to Hindu Spirituality,* in *The Clergy Review,* 54, 1969, pp. 163-174.
"	*Hindu Scriptures and Christian Worship,* in WW, 6, 1973, pp. 187-195; 243, 253.
"	*The Upaniṣads and the Advaitic Experience,* in CM, 38, 1974, pp. 474-487.
"	*Yoga and Christian Prayer,* in CM, 35, 1975, pp. 472-477.
Grant, S.,	*Swamiji – The Man,* in CM, 38, 1974, pp. 487-495.
Irudayaraj, X.,	*Sannyāsa- Swami Abhishiktānanda,* in CM, 38, 1974, pp. 501-508.

Stuart, J.,   *Swami Abhishiktānanda*, in CM, 38, 1974, pp. 80-82.

Vandana (Sr.)   *A Messenger of Light. Swami Abhishiktānada as known in*
                            Shivanda Aśram, Rishikesh, in CM, 38, 1974, pp. 496-500.

2.1.4   Bede Griffiths*

Griffiths, B.,   *Christian Ashram, Essays Towards a Hindu-Christian Dialogue*,
                            London, 1966.
"   *Christ in India*, New York, 1967.
"   *Return to the Centre*, London, 1976.
"   *The Ecumenical Approach in the Missions*, in *India*, 15, 1964,
                            pp. 144-149.
"   *The Dialogue with Hinduism*, in CMS, 7, 1964,
                            pp. 144-149.
"   *Further Towards a Hindu-Christian Dialogue*, in CM, 32, 1968,
                            pp. 213-220.
"   *Man and God in India*, in *The Tablet*, 25, 1971, pp. 5-6.
"   *Indian Christian Contemplation*, in CM, 35, 1971, pp. 277-281.

2.1.5   Raymond Panikkar*

Panikkar, R.,   *Die vielen Götter und der eine Herr. Beiträge zum Ökumenischen*
                            Gespräch der Weltreligionen, Weilheim/Oberbayern, 1963.
"   *Kultmysterium in Hinduismus und Christentum. Ein Beitrag zur*
                            vergleichenden Religionstheologie, München, 1964.
"   *Christus der Unbekannte im Hinduismus*, Luzern, 1965.
"   *Religionen und die Religion*, München, 1965.
"   *Māyā e Apocalisse: L'Incontro dell'Induismo e del*
                            Cristianesimo, Roma, 1966.
"   *Kerygma und Indien. Zur heilsgeschichtlichen Problematik der*
                            christlichen Begegnung mit Indien, (Theologische Forschung.
                            Wissenschaftliche Beiträge zur kirchlich-evangelischen Lehre),
                            Hamburg, 1967.

303

Panikkar, R.,   *Offenbarung und Verkündigung. Indische Briefe*, Freiburg, 196

"   *The Unknown Christ of Hinduism*, London, 1968.

"   *L'homme qui devient Dieu. La foi dimension constitutive de l'homme*, Aubier, 1969.

"   *The Trinity and World Religions. Icon - Person - Mystery*, Madras, 1970.

"   *Le Christ de l'hindouisme: une présence cachée*, Paris, 197

"   *Worship and Secular Man. An Essay on the Liturgical Nature of Man, considering Secularization as a Major Phenomenon of our time and Worship as an apparent fact of all times. A Study towards an integral Anthropology*, London, 1973.

"   *The Trinity and the Religious Experience of Man. Icon - Person - Mystery*, London, 1973.

"   *Relation of Christians to their Non-Christian Surroundings*, in IES, 4, 1965, pp. 303-348.

"   *Confrontation Between Hinduism and Christ*, in Logos, 10, 1969, pp. 43-51; New Blackfriars, 50, 1968/69, pp. 197-204 *St. Teresa and St. John of the Cross. Some Aspects of the Spiritulaity of Saint John of the Cross and Saint Teresa*, in LW, 76, 1970, pp. 258-267.

"   *Advaita and Bhakti, Love and Identity in a Hindu-Christian Dialogue,*, in JES, 7, 1970, pp. 299-309.

"   *Faith and Belief. A Multireligious Experience. An Objectified Autobiographical Fragment*, in Anglican Theological Review, 53, 1971, pp. 219-237.

"   *Christ, Abel and Melchizedek, (The Church and the Non-Abrahamic Religions)*, in JD, I, 1971, pp. 391-403.

"   *The Ultimate Experience, The Ways of the West and the East*, in IES, 10, 1971, pp. 18-39.

Panikkar, R.,   *Some Aspects of Suffering and Sorrow in the Vedas*, in JD. 2, 1972, pp. 387-398.

"   *The Meaning of Christ's Name in the Universal Economy of Salvation*, in *Service and Salvation*, *Nagpur Theological Conference on Evangelization*, Ed. Joseph Pathrapankal, Bangalore, 1973, pp. 235-263.

"   *The Category of Growth in Comparative Religion: A Critical Self-Examination*, in HTR, 66, 1973, pp. 113-140.

"   *Action and Contemplation as Categories of Religious Understanding*, in *Main Currents in Modern Thought*, 30, 1973, pp. 75-81.

"   *Have "Religions" the Monopoly on Religion?* (editorial) in JES, 11, 1974, pp. 515-517.

"   *Forward: The Mutual Fecundation*, in *The Emerging Culture in India*, *Father Zacharias Lectures 1974* Ed. Thomas Paul, Alwaye,1974, pp.9-11.

"   *Le mythe comme histoire sacrée: Sunakṣepa, un mythe de la condition humaine* (Estratto Archivio di Filosofia diretto da Enrico Castelli), Roma, 1974.

"   *Towards a Typology of Time and Temporality in Ancient Tradition*, in JES, 24, 1974, pp. 161-164.

"   *Philosophy and Revolution: The Text, The Context, and the Texture*, in LW, 81, 1975, pp. 387-399.

"   *Seed-Thoughts in Cross-Cultural Studies. Percées dans la problématique pluriculturelle*, Numéro spécial, *Monchanin*, 8, 1975.

"   *The Theandric Vocation*, in LW, 81, 1975, pp. 67-75.

"   *Le temps circulaire: temporisation et temporalité*, from *Temporalité et aliénation*, actes du colloque organisé par le Centre International d'Etudes Humanistes et par l'Institut d'Etudes Philosophiques de Rome, Rome, 3-8 janiver, 1975, aux soins de Enrico Castelli, Aubier, 1975, pp. 207-246.

Panikkar, R.,   *Some Notes on Syncretism and Eclecticism Related to the Growth of Human Consciousness* in *Religious Syncretism in Antiquity*. Essays in Conversation with Geo Widengren, Ed. Birger A. Pearson, University of California, 1975, pp. 47-62.

Chethimattam, J. B.,   *R. Panikkar's Approach to Christology* in IJT, 23, 1974, pp. 219-222.

2.1.6 Duraisamy Simon
 Amalorpavadass*

Amalorpavadass, D. S.,   *L'Inde à la rencontre du Seigneur*, Paris, 1964.
"   *Destinée de l'Eglise dans l'Inde d'aujourd'hui*, Paris, 196
"   *Post-Vatican Liturgical Renewal in India*, Bangalore, 1968.
"   *Adult Catechumenate and Church Renewal*, Bangalore, 1970.
"   *Approaches in our Apostolate Among Non-Christians*, Bangalore, 1970.
"   *Theology of Evangelization in the Indian Context.* (Inaugural Key-note address delivered at the International Theological Conference on Evangelization & Dialogue in Asia, Nagpur, 6-12 October, 1971), Bangalore, 1973.
"   *Towards Indigenization in the Liturgy. (Theological Reflection, Policy, Programme and Texts)*, Bangalore, 1971
"   *Theology of Cathechesis.* (Key-note address delivered at the World Congress of Catechetics, Rome, September, 1971) Bangalore, 1971.
"   *Theology of Development,* (A lecture delivered at the Second Missionary Zonal Consultation held in Bombay from the 20th - 23rd September, 1969), Bangalore, 1972.
"   *Preaching the Gospel Today. Main Problems in Mission Lands,* (A Speech delivered at the International Missionar Conference, Lyon, 9th - 12th November, 1972), Bangalore, 1973.

Amalorpavadass, D. S.,   *Main Problems in Preaching the Gospel Today*, (A Speech
delivered at the International Missionary Conference,
Lyon, 9th - 12th November, 1972), Bangalore, 1973.

"   *Approach, Meaning and Horizon of Evangelization*, (The
theological orientation speech delivered at the All-India
Consultation on Evangelization at Patna, 3-8 October, 1973),
Bangalore, 1973

"   *Evangelization of the Modern World, (Synod of Bishops*, Rome,
1974, Special Number of WW, Jan-Feb, 1975), Ed. D. S.
Amalorpavadass, Bangalore, 1975.

"   *Characteristics of Catechetical Pedagogy*, in WW, 5,
1972, pp. 1-7.

"   *Liturgy Relevant to Life*, in WW, 6, 1973,
pp. 233-242.

"   *Conclusions of the World Congress of Catechetics*, in
WW, 6, 1973, pp. 67-76.

"   *Indigenization and the Liturgy of the Church* in
International Review of Mission, 65, 1976, pp. 164-181.

"   (Ed.) *Nairobi Assembly of the World Council of Churches* (A
special Number of WW, Jan-Feb, 1976), Bangalore,
1976.

2.1.7   Ishanand Vempeny

Vempeny, I.,   *Inspiration in the Non-Biblical Scriptures*, Bangalore,
1973.

"   *Inspiration in the Non-Biblical Scriptures* in WW,
Bangalore, 1973, pp. 163-173.

"   *Dialogical Standpoint Illustrated by the Caste-System*,
in JD, 3, 1973, pp. 428-444.

"   *An Approach to the Problem of Inspiration in Non-Biblical
Scriptures*, in *Research Seminar on Non-Biblical Scriptures*,
Ed. D. S. Amalorpavadass, Bangalore, 1975, pp. 153-178.

2.1.8   Joseph Mattam *

Mattam, J.,   *Land of the Trinity. A Study of Modern Christian Approaches*
                           to Hinduism, Bangalore, 1975.

"   *Modern Catholic Attempts at Presenting Christ to India*, in
                           IJT, 23, 1974, pp. 206-218.

"   *Interpreting Christ to India Today: The Calcutta School*, in
                           IJT, 23, 1974, pp. 191-205.

2.1.9   John B. Chethimattam*

Chethimattam, J. B.,   *Consciousness and Reality. An Indian Approach to Meta-*
                           physics, London, 1971.

"   *Patterns of Indian Thought*, London, 1971.

"   (Ed.) *Unique and Universal. An Introduction to Indian Theology*,
                           Bangalore, 1972.

"   *Psychology and Personality in the Indian Tradition*, in IES,
                           7, 1967, pp. 101-117.

"   *The Spirit and Orientation of an Indian Theology*, in JD,
                           1, 1971, pp. 452-262.

"   *Towards a Theology of Liberation*, in JD, 2, 1972, pp. 25-34.

"   *Indian Approaches to Christology: Contribution of the*
                           Syro-Malabar Church, in IJT, 23, 1974,
                           pp. 176-180.

"   *Man's Dialogical Nature and the Dialogue of Religions*, in
                           Journal of Dharma, 1, 1975, pp. 10-29.

2.1.10   Albert Nambiaparampil

Nambiamparampil, A.,   *Religious Language in a Dialogical Context: A Linguistic*
                           Approach, in *Research Seminar on Non-Biblical Scriptures*,
                           Ed. D. S. Amalorpavadass, Bangalore, 1975, pp. 569-579.

"   *Linguistic Philosophy and Indian Theology*, in *Unique and*
                           Universal, An Introduction to Indian Theology, Ed. J. B.
                           Chethimattam, Bangalore, 1972, pp. 44-52.

308

Nambiamparampil, A.,   *Witnessing to Interior Life in the Context of Indian*
                       Spirituality, in LW, 77, 1971, pp. 74-83.

"   *Comment l'hindouisme se comprend lui-même,* in *Bulletin*
                       Secretariatus pro Non-Christianis, 7, 1972, pp. 26-46;
                       English edition, 3, pp. 25-44.

"   *Dialogue in India:* An Analysis of the situation, a
                       reflection experience, in Journal of Dharma, 1, 1976,
                       pp. 267-283.

2.1.11 Thomas Marshal
  Manickyakuzhy *

Manickam, T. M.,   *Anubhava as Pramāṇa of an Indian Christology,* in JD, 1,
                       1971, pp. 228-244.

"   *Manu's Vision of the Hindu Dharma,* in *Journal of Dharma,*
                       1, 1975, pp. 101-117.

"   *'Insight' as Inspiration and 'Anubhava' as Revelation in*
                       the Hindu Scriptures, in *Research Seminar on Non-Biblical*
                       Scriptures, Ed. D. S. Amalorpavadass, Bangalore, 1975,
                       pp. 325-339.

"   *Theology as Experience of Revelation,* in *Unique and Universal,*
                       Ed. J. B. Chethimattam, Bangalore, 1972, pp. 197-208.

2.1.12   Theological Events

                       All India Seminar on the Church in India Today, Bangalore,
                       May 15-25, 1969.

                       All-India Seminar on the Church in India Today, Bangalore,
                       May 15-25, 1969. *Preparatory Seminars,* An Assessment, New
                       Delhi, 1969.

                       All India Seminar, Church in India Today, Bangalore, 1969,
                       Orientation Papers, New Delhi, 1969.

                       Service and Salvation, Nagpur Theological Conference on
                       Evangelization, Ed. Joseph Pathrapankal, Bangalore, 1973.

Research Seminar on Non-Biblical Scriptures, Ed. D. S.
Amalorpavadass, Bangalore, 1975.

2.1.13   Pronouncements of the Hierarchy of the Church

Vatican Council II, *The Concilliar and Post Concilliar
Documents*, Gen. Ed. Austin Flannery, Tenbury Wells,
Worcs; 1975.
*Lexikon für Theologie und Kirche. Das Zweite Vatikanische
Konzil*, Band I-III, Herder, 1967-1968.
Commentary on the Documents of Vatican II, Ed. Herbert
Vorgrimler, Vol. I-V, Herder, 1967-1969.

Paul VI   *The Letter, Cum Jam*, 21st September, 1966, Ad E.mum P. D.
Josephum S.R.E. Cardinalem Pizzardo, Praefectum S.
Congregationis Seminariis Studiorumque Universitatibus
praepositae, cum Romae congressus Internationalis de
Theologia Concilii Vaticani Secundi haberetur, AAS, 58,
1966, pp. 877-881.   Condensed, Tr. in CM, 31, 1967,
pp. 59-63.

"   *Allocution*, 1st October, 1966, Exc.mis Praesulibus
ceterisque S. Theologiae cultoribus, qui Conventui ex
omnibus nationibus Romae habito de Theologia Concilii
Vaticani Secundi, AAS, 58, 1966, pp. 889-896.

"   *Allocution, Africae Terrarum*, 31st July, 1969, E.mis
Patribus Cardinalibus et Exc.mis Praesulibus, qui
"Episcoporum Symposio" ex universa Africa in urbe Kampala
habito interfuerunt, AAS, 61, 1969, pp. 573-578.

"   *Allocution*, 28th November, 1970, In aede Studiorum
Universitatis S.Thomae dicatae, ad juvenes Athenaea
frequentantes, /Manila7, AAS, 63, 1971, pp. 19-21.

"   *Allocution*, 28th November, 1970, E.mis Patribus Cardinalibus et Exc.mis Praesulibus, qui "Episcoporum Symposio" e
universa Asia orientali in urbe Manila habito interfuerun
AAS, 63, 1971, pp. 21-27.

| Paul VI | *Allocution*, 26th October, 1974, E.mis Patribus Cardinalibus et Exc.mis Praesulibus e Synodo Episcoporum, cum tertius generalis Coetus exitum haberet, AAS, 66, 1974. |

The Hierarchy of India *Reports of the General Meetings of the Catholic Bishops Conference of India*, 1966-1974, New Delhi, *Reports of the Standing Committee of the Catholic Bishops Conference of India*, 1966-1974.

"   *Some Interventions of Synodal Fathers from India on behalf of the CBCI in Evangelization of the Modern World* (Synod of Bishops, Rome, 1974), Special Number of WW, Ed. D. S. Amalorpavadass, Bangalore, Jan-Feb, 1975, pp. 124-138.

Fernandes, A.,   *A Bishop in the Church of Christ*, (cyclostyled), Hy. 6/4176, Hyderabad, 1976, p. 10.   *A Note on the Nature of the Directory on the Pastoral Ministry of Bishops*, (cyclostyled), Hy. 9/4176, Hyderabad, 1976, p. 2.

Parecattil, J.,(Card), *The Vision of the Church and the Role of the CBCI*, Cochin, 1976.

2.2.1   Sādhu Sunder Singh

Singh, S. S.,   *The Real Life*, Madras, 1966.

"   *The Real Pearl*, Tr. M. R. Robinson, Madras, 1966.

"   *The Spiritual Life*, (Originally published under the fuller title: *Meditations on Various Aspects of the Spiritual Life*), Madras, 1970.

"   *The Search After Reality*, Madras, 1971.

"   *Reality and Religion, Meditations on God, Man and Nature*, Madras, 1971.

"   *At the Master's Feet*, Tr. Arthur & Rebecca Parker, Madras, 1974

"   *The Spiritual World*, (Originally published under the fuller title: *Visions of the Spiritual World*), Madras, 1974.

311

Appasamy, A. J.,   *The Sadhu*, (jointly with Canon B. H. Streeter), London, 1921.

"   *Cross in Heaven, Life and Writings of Sadhu Sunder Singh*, London, 1957.

"   *Sundar Singh*, London, 1958.

2.2.2   Aiyadurai Jesudasan Appasamy

Appasamy, A. J.,   *Christianity as Bhakti Mārga, A Study in the Mysticism of the Johannine Writings*, London, 1927.

"   *Church Union. An Indian View*, Madras, 1930.

"   *Temple Bells. Readings from Hindu Religious Literature*, Calcutta, 1930.

"   *What is 'Mokṣa'? A Study in the Johannine Doctrine of Life*, Madras, 1931.

"   *The Johannine Doctrine of Life. A Study of Christian and Indian Thought*, London, 1934.

"   *'Christ' in the Indian Church. A Primer of Christian Faith and Practice*, Madras, 1935.

"   *Christ answers Youth's Problems*, Calcutta, 1939.

"   *The Christian Task in Independent India*, London, 1951.

"   *My Theological Quest*, Bangalore, 1964.

"   *Tamil Christian Poet, The Life and Writings of H. A. Krishna .Pillai*, London, 1966.

"   *A Bishop's Story*, Madras, 1969.

"   . *The Theology of Hindu Bhakti*, Madras, 1970.

"   *What shall we Believe? A Study of the Christian Pramāṇas*, Madras, 1971.

2.2.3   Vengal Chakkarai

Chakkarai, V.,	*Jesus the 'Avatar'*, Madras, 1927.
"	*The Cross and Indian Thought*, Madras, 1932.
"	*Rethinking Christianity in India*, (Co-author), Madras (1938), 1939[2].
"	*'Ašramas' Past and Present*, (Co-author), Madras, 1941.
Boyd, R. H. S.,	*V. Chakkarai (1880-1958)* in R. H. S. Boyd, *An Introduction to Indian Christian Theology*, Madras, 1975, pp. 165-185.
Bürkle H. & Roth M. W., (Eds.)	*Indian Voices in Todays Theological Debate*, Lucknow, 1972.
Thomas, P. T.,	*The Theology of Chakkarai with Selections from his Writings*, Bangalore, 1968.
Wagner, H.,	*Die Erfahrungstheologie V. Chakkarais* in Herwig Wagner, *Erstgestalten einer einheimischen Theologie in Südindien*, München, 1963, pp. 198-259.

2.2.4   Pandipeddi Chenchiah

Chenchiah, P.,	*Rethinking Christianity in India* (Co-author), Madras, (1938), 1939[2].
	'Ašramas', Past and Present (Co-author), Madras, 1941.
Boyd, R. H. S.,	*P.Chenchiah (1886-1959)* in R. H. S. Boyd, *An Introduction to Indian Christian Theology*, Madras, 1975, pp. 144-164.
Bürkle H. & Roth M. W., (Eds.)	*Indian Voices in Todays Theological Debate*, Lucknow, 1972.
Wagner, H.,	*Die spekulative Theologie P. Chenchiah's* in Herwig Wagner, *Erstgestalten einer einheimischen Theologie in Sudindien*, München, 1963, pp. 107-197.

2.2.5   Paul David Devanandan

Devanandan, P. D.,   *The Dravida Kazhagam. A Revolt Against Brahminism,*
Bangalore, 1959.

"   *Christian Concern in Hinduism,* Bangalore, 1961.

"   *Christian Issues in Southern Asia,* New York, 1963.

"   *Preparation for Dialogue. A Collection of Essays on
Hinduism and Christianity in New India,* Ed. Nalini
Devanandan & M. M. Thomas, Bangalore, 1964.

"   *Our responsibility to Non-Christian Members.
The YMCA Today and Tomorrow,* Calcutta, 1953.

"   *The Concept of Māyā. An Essay in Historical Survey of
the Hindu Theory of the World with Special Reference to
the Vedanta,* London, 1950; Calcutta, 1954.

"   *Living Hinduism,* CISRS Pamphlets, Bangalore, 1958.

"   *The Gospel and the Hindu Intellectual,* CISRS Pamphlets,
Bangalore, 1958.

"   *Our Task Today. Revision of Evangelistic Concern,* CISRS
Pamphlets, Bangalore, 1958.

"   *Resurgent Hinduism. Review of Modern Movements,* CISRS
Pamphlets, Bangalore, 1958.

"   *The Gospel and Renascent Hinduism,* I.M.C. Research Pamphl
London, 1959.

Samartha, S. J. &   *I Will Lift up Mine Eyes Unto the Hills.*
Devanandan, N., (Eds.)   *Sermons and Bible Studies of P. D. Devanandan,* Bangalore,
1963.

Wietzke, J.,   *Theologie im modernen Indien – Paul David Devanandan,*
Bern, 1975.

2.2.6 Mamen Thomas Madathilparampil*

Thomas M. M., *The Acknowledged Christ of the Indian Renaissance,*[1] London, 1969.

" *Salvation and Humanization. Some Crucial Issues of the Theology of Mission in Contemporary India*, Madras, 1971.

" *Man and the Universe of Faiths*, Madras, 1975.

" *The Secular Ideologies of India and the Secular Meaning of Christ*, Bangalore, 1976.

" *Issues Concerning the Life and Work of the Church in a Revolutionary World*, in TER, 20, 1968, pp. 410-419.

" *Report of the Executive Committee by the Chairman*, in TER, 23, 1971, pp. 89-104.

" *Report of the Chairman of the Executive Committee*, in TER, 24, 1972, pp. 395-410.

" *Christian Action in the Asian Struggle*, in *National Christian Council Review*, 93, 1973, pp. 399-404.

" *Two Kinds of Messianisms, Report of the Chairman of the Executive Committee*, in TER, 26, 1974, pp. 546-562.

" *Significance of Marxist and Barthian Insights for a Theology of Religion*, in RS, 21, 1974, pp. 58-66.

2.2.7 Stanley J. Samartha*

Samartha, S. J., *Hindus vor dem universalen Christus. Beiträge zu einer Christologie in Indien*, Stuttgart, 1970.

" *The Hindu Response to the Unbound Christ*, Bangalore, 1974.

" *The Progress and Promise of Inter-Religious Dialogues*, in JES, 9, 1972, pp. 463-476.

[1]For the lives of the National Leaders of India, see *Dictionary of National Biography*, Ed. S. P. Sen, Vol. I-IV, Calcutta, 1972-1974.

Samartha (Ed).,   *Dialogue Between Men of Living Faiths*, Papers Presented a
a Consultation held at Ajaltown, March, 1970, Geneva, 197

"   *Living Faiths and the Ecumenical Movement*, Geneva, 1971.

"   *The Progress and Promise of Inter-Religious Dialogues*,
reprinted from *The Consultation on Inter-Religious Dialog*
Kyoto, Japan, October, 1970, pp. 463-474.

"   *Introduction*, in *Living Faiths and the Ecumenical Movemen*
Ed. S. J. Samartha, Geneva, 1971, pp. 5-11.

"   *The World Council of Churches and Men of Other Faiths and*
Ideologies, in *Living Faiths and the Ecumenical Movement*,
Ed. S. J. Samartha, Geneva, 1971, pp. 73-82.

"   *Dialogue as a Continuing Christian Concern*, in *Living*
Faiths and the Ecumenical Movement, Geneva, 1971, pp. 143
157.

"   *Dialogue as a Continuing Concern* in TER, Addis Ababa Issu
23, 1971, pp. 129-142.

"   *The Progress and Promise of Inter-Religious Dialogues*, in
The Japan Missionary Bulletin, 25, 1971, pp. 503-507.

"   *Dialogue, Significant Issues in The Continuing Debate*, in
TER, 24, 1972, pp. 327-340.

"   *.... And Ideologies*, in TER, 24, 1972, pp. 479-486.

"   *The Holy Spirit and People of Various Faiths, Cultures an*
Ideologies, in *The Holy Spirit*, Ed. Dow Kirkpatrick,
Tennessee, 1974, pp. 20-39.

"   *Reflections on a Mulitilateral Dialogue, An Interpretatio*
of a Meeting held at Colombo, Sri Lanka, 11, 1974,
in TER, 26, 1974, pp. 637-646.

SUPPLEMENTARY BIBLIOGRAPHY

1.2.2   Keshab Chandra Sen

Pape, W. R.,   *Keshub Chunder Sen's Doctrine of Christ and the*
                               Trinity : *a Rehabilitation* in IJT, 25, 1976,
                               pp. 55-71.

2.1.3   Abhishiktananda

Rogers, M. C.,   *Swamiji, the Friend,* in RS, 23, 1976, pp. 76-87.

2.1.4   Bede Griffiths

Griffiths, B.,   *The Indian Spiritual Tradition and the Church in*
                               India in *The Outlook,* 15, 1976, pp. 98-104.

  "   *The Mystical Dimension in Theology,* in *Indian*
                               Theological Studies, (ITS), 14, 1977, pp. 229-246.

  "   *Om as the Word of God,* in WW, 10, 1977, pp. 334-335.

  "   *Christian Monastic Life in India,* in *Journal of*
                               Dharma, 3, 1978, pp. 122-135.

  "   *The Advaitic Experience and the Personal God in the*
                               Upaniṣads and Bhagavadgītā, in ITS, 15, 1978, pp. 71-86.

2.1.5   Raymond Panikkar

Panikkar, R.,   *Action and Contemplation as Categories of Religious*
                               Understanding, in IJT, 25, 1976, pp. 17-29.

  "   *Samdhya the Vedic Prayer,* in ITS, 14, 1977, pp. 22-38.

2.1.6   Duraisamy Simon Amalorpavadass

Amalorpavadass, D. S.,   (Ed.) *Ministries in the Church in India. Research Seminar*
                               and Pastoral Consultation, New Delhi, 1976.

  "   *Biblical Meditation,* in WW, 9, 1976, pp. 356-358.

  "   *A Survey of Catholic Hospital System in India,* in WW,
                               9, 1976, pp. 366-367.

  "   *Relation between Catholic Church (RCC) and the World*
                               Council of Churches (WCC), in WW, 9, 1976, pp. 379-
                               386.

  "   *Synodal Theme* (Editorial), in WW, 9, 1976, pp. 406-
                               407.

  "   *Catholic Pedagogy for Youth,* in WW, 9, 1976,
                               pp. 422-428.

Amalorpavadass, D. S.,	*Trends of Catechetical Movements in India and its New Orientations,* in WW, 10, 1977, pp. 3-8.
"	*Charismatic Renewal,* in WW, 10, 1977, pp. 54-56.
"	*Meaning and Role of Charismatic Renewal in India Today-Its Challenges,* in WW, 10, 1977, pp. 100-108.
"	*"Penance" an Ongoing Process and a Regular Articulation,* in WW, 10, 1977, pp. 129-130.
"	*The Form of Celebrating Reconciliation,* in WW, 10, 1977, pp. 131-141.
"	*A Quality Document of the CBCI* (Extraordinary Meeting of the CBCI, Jan.1977), in WW, 10, 1977, pp. 152-154.
"	*Penance Needs the Word,* in WW, 10, 1977, p. 166.
"	*The Leadership of the Indian Hierarchy through the Biennial Plenary of the CBCI,* in WW, 11, 1978, pp. 42-49.
"	*A Fresh Start in Liturgical Renewal and Inculturation (At the CBCI General Meeting, Mangalore),* in WW, 11, 1978, pp. 50-82.
"	*Evangelization and Culture,* in WW, 1978, pp. 104-108.
"	*Review of Life: on the Exercise of Authority Based on Mark 10:35-45,* in WW, 11, 1978, pp. 135-137.
"	*Basis of Authentic Inculturation,* in WW,11,1978,pp.148-15|
"	*Inculturation and 'Hinduisation'* in WW, 11, 1978, pp. 180-187.
"	*Gospel and Culture. Some Practical Implication and Conclusions,* in WW, 11, 1978, pp. 262-266.

2.1.8 Joseph Mattam

Mattam, J.,	*The Mystery of the Trinity in Christian Life,* in *Vidyajoyti,* 40, 1976, pp. 338-348.
"	*The Sacrament of our Redemption: The Eucharist,* in *Vidyajyoti,* 41, 1977, pp. 161-169.
	The Sacrament of "Fore-given" Love: Confession, in *Vidyajyoti,* 42, 1978, pp. 275-279.

318

1.9   John B. Chethimattam

ethimattam, J. B.,   *Meditation*: *A Discriminating Realization* in *Journal of Dharma*, 2, 1977, pp. 164-172.

1.11   Thomas Marshal Manickyakuzhy

mickam, T. M.,   *Dharma According to Manu and Moses*, Bangalore, 1977.

"   *The "Myths of Origins", Aryan, Hebrew* : *A Comparative Interpretation*, in *Journal of Dharma*, 2, 1977, pp. 397-408.

"   *The Ethical Motives of Manu and Moses*, in LW, 83, 1977, pp. 335-353.

2.6   Mamen Thomas Madathilparampil

omas, M. M., &   *Christian Participation in Nation-Building*, Bangalore,
Devanandan, P. D., (Eds). 1976.

omas, M. M.,   *The Christian Response to the Asian Revolution*, London, 1966.

"   *Towards an Evangelical Social Gospel*, Madras, 1977.

"   (Ed.) *Some Theological Dialogues.* /Ā collection of correspondence between M. M. Thomas and some theologians from other parts of the world on subjects pertaining to the theology of the Christian Mission/, Bangalore, 1977.

"   *Search for a New Humanism as Foundation for the Struggle for a Just Society* in *Political Prospects in India*, Ed. S. K. Chatterji, Madras, 1971, pp. 181-192.

"   *Some Issues of Christian Ethics in Asia*,in RS, 23, 1976, pp. 63-73.

"   *Some Trends in Contemporary Indian Christian Theology*, in RS, 24, 1977, pp. 52-59.

2.7   Stanley J. Samartha

martha, S. J.,   *Courage for Dialogue* : *An Interpretation of the Nairobi Debate*, in RS, 23, 1976, pp. 22-35.

"   *Dialogue in Community* : *A Step Forward, an Interpretation of the Chiang Mai Consultation*, in RS, 24, 1977, pp. 52-59.